Advanced API Security

Securing APIs with OAuth 2.0, OpenID Connect, JWS, and JWE

Prabath Siriwardena

Advanced API Security: Securing APIs with OAuth 2.0, OpenID Connect, JWS, and JWE

ISBN-13 (pbk): 978-1-4302-6818-5

ISBN-13 (electronic): 978-1-4302-6817-8

Publisher: Heinz Weinheimer
Lead Editor: Robert Hutchinson
Developmental Editor: Gary Schwartz
Technical Reviewer: Michael Peacock
Editorial Board: Steve Anglin, Mark Beckner, Ewan Buckingham, Gary Cornell, Louise Corrigan, James DeWolf, Jonathan Gennick, Robert Hutchinson, Michelle Lowman, James Markham, Matthew Moodie, Jeff Olson, Jeffrey Pepper, Douglas Pundick, Ben Renow-Clarke, Dominic Shakeshaft, Gwenan Spearing, Matt Wade, Steve Weiss
Coordinating Editor: Rita Fernando
Copy Editor: Tiffany Taylor
Compositor: SPi Global
Indexer: SPi Global
Cover Designer: Anna Ishchenko

Distributed to the book trade worldwide by Springer Science+Business Media New York, 233 Spring Street, 6th Floor, New York, NY 10013. Phone 1-800-SPRINGER, fax (201) 348-4505, e-mail orders-ny@springer-sbm.com, or visit www.springeronline.com. Apress Media, LLC is a California LLC and the sole member (owner) is Springer Science + Business Media Finance Inc (SSBM Finance Inc). SSBM Finance Inc is a Delaware corporation.

For information on translations, please e-mail rights@apress.com, or visit www.apress.com.

Apress and friends of ED books may be purchased in bulk for academic, corporate, or promotional use. eBook versions and licenses are also available for most titles. For more information, reference our Special Bulk Sales–eBook Licensing web page at www.apress.com/bulk-sales.

Any source code or other supplementary materials referenced by the author in this text is available to readers at www.apress.com. For detailed information about how to locate your book's source code, go to www.apress.com/source-code/.

This book is dedicated to two great ladies: my mother and my wife.

Contents at a Glance

Contents

About the Author

Prabath Siriwardena is the Director of Security Architecture at WSO2 Inc.,
a company that produces a wide variety of open source software from data to screen.
He is a member of the OASIS Identity Metasystem Interoperability (IMI) TC, OASIS
eXtensible Access Control Markup Language (XACML) TC, OASIS Security Services
(SAML) TC, OASIS Identity in the Cloud TC, and OASIS Cloud Authorization
(CloudAuthZ) TC. Prabath is also a member of Apache Axis PMC and has spoken at
numerous international conferences including OSCON, ApacheCon, WSO2Con, the
European Identity Conference (EIC), IDentity Next, the API Strategy Conference,
and OSDC. He has more than ten years of industry experience and has worked with
many Fortune 100 companies. Advanced API Security is his second book. His first
book was *Enterprise Integration with WSO2 ESB* (Packt Publishing, 2013).

About the Technical Reviewer

Michael Peacock is an experienced software developer and team lead from Newcastle, UK. Michael holds a degree in software engineering from the University of Durham.

After spending a number of years running his own web agency and subsequently working directly for a number of software startups, Michael now serves as a technical consultant for a range of companies, helping with application development, software processes, and technical direction.

He is the author of *Creating Development Environments with Vagrant, PHP 5 Social Networking, PHP 5 E-Commerce Development, Drupal 7 Social Networking, Selling online with Drupal e-Commerce*, and *Building Websites with TYPO3*. Michael has been involved with other publications including *Mobile Web Development, Jenkins Continuous Integration Cookbook*, and *Drupal for Education and E-Learning*, on which he served as a technical reviewer.

Michael has presented at a number of user groups and technical conferences including the PHP UK Conference, the Dutch PHP Conference, ConFoo, PHPNE, PHPNW, and Could Connect Santa Clara.

You can follow Michael on Twitter (@michaelpeacock) or find out more about him through his web site (www.michaelpeacock.co.uk).

Acknowledgments

I would first like to thank Jonathan Hassel, senior editor at Apress, for evaluating and accepting my proposal for this book. Then, of course, I must thank Rita Fernando, coordinating editor at Apress, who was extremely patient and tolerant of me throughout the publishing process. Thank you very much Rita for your excellent support—I really appreciate it. Also, Gary Schwartz and Tiffany Taylor did an amazing job reviewing the manuscript—many thanks, Gary and Tiffany! Michael Peacock served as technical reviewer—thanks, Michael, for your quality review comments, which were extremely useful. Thilina Buddhika from Colorado State University also helped in reviewing the first two chapters of the book—many thanks, again, Thilina!

Dr. Sanjiva Weerawarana, the CEO of WSO2, and Paul Fremantle, the CTO of WSO2, are two constant mentors for me. I am truly grateful to both Dr. Sanjiva and Paul for everything they have done for me. I also must express my gratitude to Asanka Abeysinghe, the Vice President of Solutions Architecture at WSO2 and a good friend of mine—we have done designs for many Fortune 500 companies together, and those were extremely useful in writing this book. Thanks, Asanka!

Of course, my beloved wife, Pavithra, and my little daughter, Dinadi, supported me throughout this process. Pavithra wanted me to write this book even more than I wanted to write it. If I say she is the driving force behind this book, it's no exaggeration. She simply went beyond just feeding me with encouragement—she also helped immensely in reviewing the book and developing samples. She was always the first reader. Thank you very much, Pavithra.

My parents and my sister have been the driving force behind me since my birth. If not for them, I wouldn't be who I am today. I am grateful to them for everything they have done for me. Last but not least, my wife's parents—they were amazingly helpful in making sure that the only thing I had to do was to write this book, taking care of almost all the other things that I was supposed to do.

The point is that although writing a book may sound like a one-man effort, it's the entire team behind it who makes it a reality. Thank you to everyone who supported me in many different ways.

Introduction

APIs are becoming increasingly popular for exposing business functionalities to the rest of the world. According to an infographic published by Layer 7, 86.5% of organizations will have an API program in place in the next five years. Of those, 43.2% already have one. APIs are also the foundation of building communication channels in the Internet of Things (IoT). From motor vehicles to kitchen appliances, countless items are beginning to communicate with each other via APIs. Cisco estimates that as many as 50 billion devices could be connected to the Internet by 2020.

This book is about securing your most important APIs. As is the case with any software system design, people tend to ignore the security element during the API design phase. Only at deployment or at the time of integration do they start to address security.

Security should never be an afterthought—it's an integral part of any software system design, and it should be well thought out from the design's inception. One objective of this book is to educate you about the need for security and the available options for securing an API.

The book also guides you through the process and shares best practices for designing APIs for rock-solid security. API security has evolved a lot in the last five years. The growth of standards has been exponential. OAuth 2.0 is the most widely adopted standard. But it's more than just a standard—it's a framework that lets people build standards on top of it. The book explains in depth how to secure APIs, from traditional HTTP Basic Authentication to OAuth 2.0 and the standards built around it, such as OpenID Connect, User Managed Access (UMA), and many more.

JSON plays a major role in API communication. Most of the APIs developed today support only JSON, not XML. This book also focuses on JSON security. JSON Web Encryption (JWE) and JSON Web Signature (JWS) are two increasingly popular standards for securing JSON messages. The latter part of this book covers JWE and JWS in detail.

Another major objective of this book is to not just present concepts and theories, but also explain each of them with concrete examples. The book presents a comprehensive set of examples that work with APIs from Google, Twitter, Facebook, Yahoo!, Salesforce, Flickr, and GitHub.

The evolution of API security is another topic covered in the book. It's extremely useful to understand how security protocols were designed in the past and how the drawbacks discovered in them pushed us to where we are today. The book covers some older security protocols such as Flickr Authentication, Yahoo! BBAuth, Google AuthSub, Google ClientLogin, and ProtectServe in detail.

I hope this book effectively covers this much-needed subject matter for API developers, and I hope you enjoy reading it.

CHAPTER 1

Managed APIs

Enterprise API adoption has exceeded predictions. According to an infographic published by Layer 7 (`http://www.layer7tech.com/infographic/img/inf-2-download.jpg`), 86.5% of organizations will have an API program in place in the next five years. Of those, 43.2% already have one. APIs are also the foundation of building communication channels in the Internet of Things (IoT). From motor vehicles to kitchen appliances, countless items will start communicating with each other via APIs. Cisco estimates that as many as 50 billion devices could be connected to the Internet by 2020.

The world is more connected than ever. You can log in to Yahoo! with Facebook credentials, share photos from Instagram in Facebook, share a location from Foursquare in Twitter, and publish tweets to your Facebook wall. The list of connections is limitless. All this is made possible only because of public APIs, which have proliferated in the last couple of years. In 2013, 90% of Expedia's business was coming through its API. Salesforce generates almost 50% of its annual $3 billion in revenue through APIs. APIs have become the coolest way of exposing business functionalities to the outside world.

The API Evolution

API stands for application programming interface. If you've worked with Java, .NET, or any other programming language, you've probably written code against an API. Java provides Java Database Connectivity (JDBC) as an API to talk to different heterogeneous database management systems (DBMSs), as shown in Figure 1-1. The JDBC API encapsulates the logic for how your application connects to the database; thus the application logic doesn't need to change whenever it connects to different databases. The database's connectivity logic is wrapped in a JDBC driver and exposed as an API. To change the database, you need to pick the right JDBC driver.

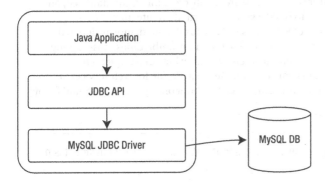

Figure 1-1. *JDBC API*

An API itself is an interface. It's the interface for clients that interact with the system. Clients should only know about the interface and nothing about its implementation. There can be more than one implementation for a given interface; the clients written against the interface can switch between implementations seamlessly and painlessly.

The client application and the API implementation can be running in the same process or in different processes. If they're running in the same process, then the call between the client and the API is a native one—if not, it's a remote call. In the case of the JDBC API, it's a native call. The Java client application directly invokes the JDBC API, implemented by a JDBC driver running in the same process.

APIs can also be exposed for remote access. To invoke an API remotely, you need to have a protocol defined for interprocess communication. Java RMI, CORBA, .NET Remoting, SOAP, and REST (over HTTP) are some protocols that facilitate interprocess communication. Java RMI provides the infrastructure-level support to invoke a Java API remotely from a non-local Java virtual machine (JVM, which runs in a different process than the one that runs the Java API). All the requests from the client are serialized into the wire by the RMI infrastructure at the client side (also known as *marshalling*) and are deserialized into Java objects at the server side by its RMI infrastructure (also known as *unmarshalling*); see Figure 1-2. This marshalling/unmarshalling technique is specific to Java. It must be a Java client to invoke an API exposed over Java RMI—and it's language dependent.

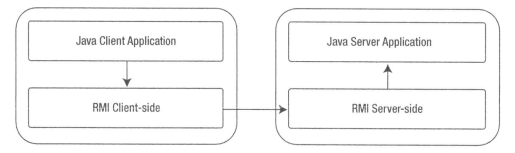

Figure 1-2. *Java RMI*

SOAP-based web services provide a way to build and invoke a hosted API in a language- and platform-neutral manner. A message from one end to the other is passed as an XML payload. SOAP is very structured and is backed by a large number of specifications. The request/response protocol between the client and the server is defined in the SOAP specification. The way you describe a SOAP service is defined in Web Services Description Language (WSDL). The WS-Security, WS-Trust, and WS-Federation specifications describe how to secure a SOAP-based service. WS-Policy provides a framework to build quality-of-service expressions around SOAP services. WS-SecurityPolicy defines the security requirements of a SOAP service in a standard way, built on top of the WS-Policy framework. The list goes on and on. Due to the nature of SOAP-based services, which are highly decoupled, standardized, and governed based on policies, they're the preferred ingredient to build a service-oriented architecture (SOA).

At least, that was the story a decade ago. The popularity of SOAP-based APIs has declined, mostly due to the inherent complexity of the WS-* standards. SOAP promised interoperability, but many ambiguities arose among different implementation stacks. To overcome this issue and promote interoperability between implementation stacks, the Web Services Interoperability (WS-I) organization came up with the Basic Profile for web services. The Basic Profile helps removing ambiguities in web service standards. An API design built on top of SOAP should follow the guidelines defined in the Basic Profile.

■ **Note** SOAP was initially an acronym that stood for Simple Object Access Protocol. From SOAP 1.2 onward, it is no longer an acronym.

In contrast to SOAP, REST is a design paradigm, rather than a rule set. Even though Roy Fielding, who first described REST in his PhD thesis (http://www.ics.uci.edu/~fielding/pubs/dissertation/top.htm.), did not couple REST to HTTP, 99% of RESTful services or APIs today are based on HTTP. For the same reason, we could easily argue, REST is based on the rule set defined in the HTTP specification. The Web 2.0 trend emerged in 2006-2007 and set a course to a simpler, less complex architectural style for building APIs. Web 2.0 is a set of economic, social, and technology trends that collectively formed the basis for the next generation of Internet computing. It was built by tens of millions of participants. The platform built around Web 2.0 was based on the simple, lightweight, yet powerful AJAX-based programming languages and REST—and it started to move away from SOAP-based services.

Modern APIs have their roots in both SOAP and REST. Salesforce launched its public API in 2000, and it still has support for both SOAP and REST. Amazon launched its web services API in 2002 with support for both REST and SOAP, but the early adoption rate of SOAP was very low. By 2003, it was revealed that 85% of Amazon API usage was on REST. ProgrammableWeb, a registry of web APIs, has tracked APIs since 2005. In 2005, ProgrammableWeb tracked 105 APIs, including Google, Salesforce, eBay, and Amazon. The number increased six-fold by 2008 to 601 APIs, with growing interest from social and traditional media companies to expose data to external parties. There were 2,500 APIs by the end of 2010. The online clothing and shoe shop Zappos published a REST API, and many government agencies and traditional brick-and-mortar retailers joined the party. The British multinational grocery and merchandise retailer Tesco allowed ordering via APIs. The photo-sharing application Instagram became the Twitter for pictures. The Face introduced facial recognition as a service. Twilio allowed anyone to create telephony applications in no time. The number of public APIs rose to 5,000 by 2011; and as of this writing, there are more than 11,000 APIs registered by ProgrammableWeb. At the same time, the trend toward SOAP has nearly died: 73% of the APIs on ProgrammableWeb today use REST, while SOAP is far behind with only 27%.

The term *API* has existed for decades, but only recently has it been caught up in the hype and become a popular buzzword. The modern definition of an API mostly focused on a hosted, web-centric (over HTTP), public-facing API to expose useful business functionalities to the rest of the world. Salesforce, Amazon, eBay, Dropbox, Facebook, Twitter, LinkedIn, Google, Flickr, Yahoo, and most of the key players doing business online have an API platform to expose business functionalities.

API vs. Managed API

The Twitter API can be used to tweet, get timeline updates, list followers, update profiles, and do many other things. None of these operations can be performed anonymously—you need to authenticate first. Let's take a concrete example (you need to have cURL installed to try this, or you can use the Chrome Advanced REST client browser plug-in):

```
curl https://api.twitter.com/1.1/statuses/home_timeline.json
```

This API is supposed to list all the tweets published by the authenticated user and his or her followers. If you just invoke it, it returns an error code, specifying that the request isn't authenticated:

```
{"errors":[{"message":"Bad Authentication data","code":215}]}
```

All the Twitter APIs are secured for legitimate access with OAuth 1.0 (which is discussed in detail in Chapter 6). Even with proper access credentials, you can't invoke the API as you wish. Twitter enforces a rate limit on each API call: within a given time window, you can only invoke a Twitter API a fixed number of times. This precaution is required for all public-facing APIs to minimize any possible denial of service (DoS) attacks. In addition to securing and rate-limiting its APIs, Twitter also closely monitors them. Twitter API Health (https://dev.twitter.com/status) shows the current status of each API. Security, rate limiting (throttling), and monitoring are key aspects of a managed business API. It also must have the ability to scale up and down for high availability based on traffic.

Life-cycle management is another key differentiator between a naked API and a managed API. A managed API has a life cycle from its creation to its retirement. A typical API life cycle might flow through Created, Published, Deprecated, and Retired stages, as illustrated in Figure 1-3. To complete each life-cycle stage, there can be a checklist to be verified. For example, to promote an API from Created to Published, you need to make sure the API is secured properly, the documentation is ready, throttling rules are enforced, and so on. A naked business API, which only worries about business functionalities, can be turned into a managed API by building these quality-of-service aspects around it.

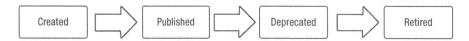

Figure 1-3. *API life cycle*

API vs. Service

Going back to the good old days, there was an unambiguous definition for *API* vs. *service*. An API is the interface between two parties or two components. These two parties/components can communicate within a single process or between different processes. A service is a concrete implementation of an API using one of the technologies/ standards available. An API that is exposed over SOAP is a SOAP service. Similarly, the same API can be exposed as REST, and then it becomes a RESTful service.

Today, the topic of API vs. service is debatable, because there are many overlapping areas. One popular definition is that an API is external facing whereas a service is internal facing (see Figure 1-4). An enterprise uses an API whenever it wants to expose useful business functionality to the outside world through the firewall. This, of course, raises another question: why would a company want to expose its precious business assets to the outside world through an API? Twitter once again is the best example. It has a web site that lets users log in and tweet from there. At the same time, anything that can be done through the web site can also be done via Twitter's API. As a result, third parties develop applications against the Twitter API; there are mobile apps, browser plug-ins, and desktop apps. This has drastically reduced traffic to the Twitter web site. Even today, the web site doesn't have a single advertisement. If there was no public API, Twitter could easily have built an advertising platform around the web site, just as Facebook did. However, having a public API helped build a strong ecosystem around Twitter.

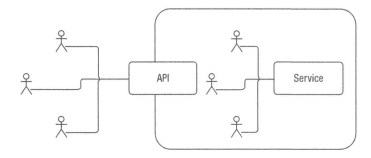

Figure 1-4. *API vs. service. An API is external facing*

Exposing corporate data via an API adds value. Not just corporate stakeholders, but also a larger audience, have access to the data. Limitless innovative ideas may pop up and, in the end, add value to the data. Say you're a pizza dealer with an API that returns the number of calories for a given pizza type and the size. You can develop an application to find out how many pizzas a person would have to eat per day to reach a body mass index (BMI) in the obesity range.

Discovering and Describing APIs

APIs are public facing, and that raises the need for the API description to be extremely useful and meaningful. At the same time, APIs need to be published somewhere to be discovered. A comprehensive API management platform needs to have at least three main components: a publisher, a store, and a gateway.

The API publisher provides tooling support to create and publish APIs. When an API is created, it needs to be associated with API documentation and other related quality-of-service controls. Then it's published into the API store and deployed into the API gateway. Application developers can discover APIs from the store. ProgrammableWeb (www.programmableweb.com) is a popular API store that has more than 11,000 APIs at the time of this writing. You could also argue that ProgrammableWeb is simply a directory, rather than a store. A store goes beyond just listing APIs (which is what ProgrammableWeb does): it lets API consumers and application developers subscribe to APIs, and it manages API subscriptions. There are many open source and proprietary API management products out there that provide support for a comprehensive API store.

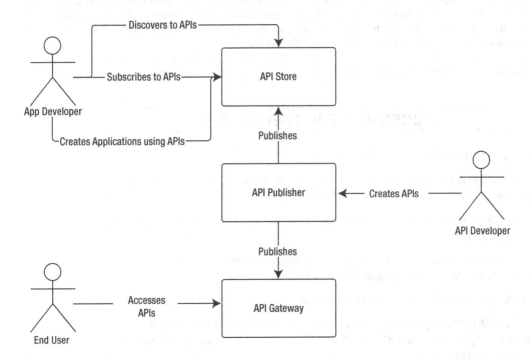

Figure 1-5. *API management platform*

In the SOAP world, there are two major standards for service discovery. Universal Description, Discovery and Integration (UDDI) was popular, but it's extremely bulky and didn't perform to the level it was expected to. UDDI is almost dead today. The second standard is WS-Discovery, which provides a much more lightweight approach. Most modern APIs are REST friendly. For RESTful services or APIs, there is no widely accepted standard means of discovery at the time of this writing. Most API stores make discovery simple via searching and tagging.

Describing a SOAP-based web service is standardized through Web Service Definition Language (WSDL). WSDL describes what operations are exposed through the web service and how to reach them. For RESTful services and APIs, there are two popular standards for description: Web Application Description Language (WADL, www.w3.org/Submission/wadl/) and Swagger (https://helloreverb.com/developers/swagger). WADL is an XML-based standard to describe RESTful or HTTP-based services. Just as in WSDL, WADL describes the API and its expected request/response messages. Swagger is a specification and a complete framework implementation for describing, producing, consuming, and visualizing RESTful web services.

Managed APIs in Practice

Most of the APIs offered by popular cloud service providers and other social neworking sites are managed APIs. Twitter, Salesforce, Amazon, Google, Microsoft, and Yahoo! all provide managed APIs.

Twitter API

Twitter provides a rich API for application developers that generates more than 90% of Twitter traffic. It has a REST API as well as a Streaming API.

The REST API allows developers to access core Twitter data like status data and user information. It also lets developers update the Twitter timeline. The REST API has another part, which is for Twitter search. This separate API for search is due to historical reasons: Twitter acquired Summize Inc., which before the acquisition was an independent company that provided search functionality over Twitter data.

The Streaming API is another RESTful service, which allows developers to get near-real-time updates by specifying filtering criteria. All Twitter APIs from version 1.1 onward are secured with OAuth 1.0.

ACCESSING THE TWITTER API

In this exercise, you see how to invoke the Twitter API:

1. First you need to generate OAuth keys. To do so, you need to create a Twitter app. Go to `https://dev.twitter.com/apps`, and click Create New App.

2. Once the app is created, go to `https://dev.twitter.com/apps` and click the link to the app that you just created.

3. Go to Permissions, check Read and Write, and click Update Settings at the bottom of the page. Allow some time for the changes to be updated.

4. Go to API Keys, and click Create My Access Token under Token Actions.

5. Refresh API Keys (token generation takes some time; you may need to refresh the page few times), and copy the values of the following attributes. You need these values to create the app against the Twitter API:

    •   API Key (listed under Application Settings)

    •   API Secret (listed under Application Settings)

    •   Access Token (listed under Your Access Token)

    •   Access Token Secret (listed under Your Access Token)

6. Click the Test OAuth button in the top left corner, and then paste the following in the Request URI text box while keeping the Request Type as GET. Then click the See OAuth Signature For This Request button:

    `https://api.twitter.com/1.1/statuses/home_timeline.json`

    This API lists the tweets published by the authenticated user and his or her followers.

7. Copy the generated text against the cURL command, and execute it in the command line. Here's an example cURL command:

```
curl --get 'https://api.twitter.com/1.1/statuses/home_timeline.json'
    --header 'Authorization: OAuth
    oauth_consumer_key="mSMOiaAm9xPMJJjjY1KsKqhXM",
    oauth_nonce="a776b23996cb162cd5b8d9abd2ef2876",
    oauth_signature="HSr0%2BQo3q5ROvoXf5a3akYK%2FSL4%3D",
    oauth_signature_method="HMAC-SHA1",
    oauth_timestamp="1403248335",
    oauth_token="10963912-Wwfbz5RjU1LOSFObQR3ZYh8BOmvanQh2Elgok8oe6",
    oauth_version="1.0"' --verbose
```

This returns the tweets published by the authenticated user and his or her followers in JSON format. To format the JSON response, you can copy the JSON payload and paste it at http://jsonformatter.curiousconcept.com/.

8. Try out the same cURL command few times until you see the following error. This indicates you've exceeded the default rate limit, which is 15 requests per user per time window. At the time of this writing, the default time window is 15 minutes:

```
{"errors":[{"message":"Rate limit exceeded","code":88}]}
```

Let's tryout another simple API, this time tweeting via cURL:

1. Click the Test OAuth button, and then paste the following in the Request URI text box while setting the Request Type to POST:

```
https://api.twitter.com/1.1/statuses/update.json
```

In the Request Query text box, type status="Having fun with Twitter API", and click See OAuth Signature For This Request.

2. Copy the generated text against the cURL command, and execute it in the command line. Here's an example cURL command:

```
curl --request 'POST' ' https://api.twitter.com/1.1/statuses/update.json '
    --data 'status=%E2%80%9DHaving+fun+with+Twitter+API%E2%80%9D'
    --header 'Authorization: OAuth
    oauth_consumer_key="mSMOiaAm9xPMJJjjY1KsKqhXM",
    oauth_nonce="930f8fdf2f819bcc6e8e2eda8ee8d4df",
    oauth_signature="lziGgiz3cvWMWML%2F%2F8VB4jl2doI%3D",
    oauth_signature_method="HMAC-SHA1",
    oauth_timestamp="1403248803",
    oauth_token="10963912-Wwfbz5RjU1LOSFObQR3ZYh8BOmvanQh2Elgok8oe6",
    oauth_version="1.0"' -verbose
```

If you see the following error, it means your token has expired:

```
{"errors":[{"message":"Invalid or expired token","code":89}]}
```

You need to regenerate a new token. Go to API Keys, and click Regenerate API Keys.

This is just an appetizer. You learn more about the Twitter API and OAuth 1.0 in Chapter 6.

Salesforce API

Force.com has a comprehensive REST API that identifies each resource by a named URI and is accessible through standard HTTP methods (HEAD, GET, POST, PATCH, DELETE). To interact with a Salesforce or Force.com organization, you use a resource. The following are some things you can do with the Salesforce API (the complete REST API developer guide from Salesforce is available at www.salesforce.com/us/developer/docs/api_rest/api_rest.pdf):

- Retrieve summary information about the API versions available to you

- Obtain detailed information about Salesforce objects, such as Accounts or custom objects

- Obtain detailed information about Force.com objects, such as Users or custom objects

- Perform a query or search

- Update or delete records

ACCESSING THE SALESFORCE API

In this exercise, you go through a couple of scenarios step by step to see how the Salesforce API is secured:

1. Create a Salesforce account if you don't have one yet. You can create a free developer account at http://developer.force.com.

2. After logging in to your Salesforce developer account, you need to create an application to represent the application you'll develop to consume Salesforce APIs. Make sure you're logged in to the Developer Account. If not, click the drop-down under your login name and select My Developer Account. To create an application, click Setup next to your Salesforce logged-in name, click Create under Build, and then click Apps. Under Connected Apps, click New. Fill in the required details, and check Enable OAuth Settings.

3. Type an HTTPS URL as the Callback URL. For the moment, this can be anything—even something that doesn't exist will work. In this example, you aren't going to use it; this is needed only if you try to authenticate via a browser. Also pick Full Access as the OAuth scope. Then save the changes. Now the OAuth Consumer Key and the Consumer Secret are generated for your application; copy them for future use.

4. Unlike Twitter, Salesforce enforces more security controls over API access. To access an API using the generated keys, you need to whitelist the IP addresses where you run your application. This is extremely useful in cases where you need to make sure the APIs are accessed only from your corporate domain/network. But keep in mind that IP addresses can be spoofed.

5. If you want your Salesforce APIs to be accessible from anywhere, you need to create a security token. To do so, under your Salesforce logged-in name, click My Settings; then, choose under Personal ➤ Reset My Security Token ➤ Reset Security Token. You receive the token via your registered e-mail account. Copy it; you need it in future steps.

You've finished setting up your Salesforce account to access APIs. Next you need to see how to invoke APIs securely. For Twitter, you used cURL. But here you use a different tool: the Advanced Rest Client Chrome App (available from https://chrome.google.com/webstore/detail/advanced-rest-client/hgmloofddffdnphfgcellkdfbfbjeloo):

1. After installing the Advanced Rest Client Chrome App, launch it via extension://hgmloofddffdnphfgcellkdfbfbjeloo/RestClient.html from the Chrome browser. Simply type this URL in the browser address bar.

2. Type https://login.salesforce.com/services/oauth2/token in the URL box, and select POST as the HTTP method.

3. You need to construct the HTTP request body required to retrieve the OAuth key or access token. Use the following as a template, and replace the values in square brackets with your own values:

```
grant_type=password&
username=[your salesforce username]&
password=[your salesforce password][your salesforce security token]&
client_id=[salesforce consumer key for your app]&
client_secret=[salesforce consumer secret for your app]
```

Notice the way you generate the password. You need to concatenate your Salesforce password with the security token you got via e-mail. If your password was *foo* and the security token was *bar*, then the password for API access would be *foobar*.

After you replace this template with your actual values, copy and paste the complete line in the Advanced Rest Client as a Raw payload. Click Form as the payload type.

4. Copy and paste the following line as a Raw HTTP header:

```
Content-Type: application/x-www-form-urlencoded;charset=UTF-8
```

5. Click Send to get an access token to access APIs. You receive the access token in a JSON response. Copy and keep the value of the access token; you need it to invoke the Salesforce APIs.

6. You're all set. Type the following API in the URL text box, and select GET as the HTTP method:

```
https://na1.salesforce.com/services/data/v20.0/
```

7. Copy and paste the following line as a Raw HTTP header. Make sure you replace [access_token] with the value of the access token you received previously:

```
Authorization: Bearer [access_token]
```

8. Click Send to invoke the API. This returns a list of available Salesforce resources in a JSON response:

```
{
    sobjects: "/services/data/v20.0/sobjects"
    licensing: "/services/data/v20.0/licensing"
    identity: "https://login.salesforce.com/id/00D90000000v28SEAQ/005900000026oRVAAY"
```

```
          connect: "/services/data/v20.0/connect"
          search: "/services/data/v20.0/search"
          query: "/services/data/v20.0/query"
          tooling: "/services/data/v20.0/tooling"
          chatter: "/services/data/v20.0/chatter"
          recent: "/services/data/v20.0/recent"
      }
```

9. To get more information about the authenticated user, set the value of the `identity` attribute from the JSON response in the URL box and, with the same access token, click Send:

    ```
    https://login.salesforce.com/id/00D90000000m0ZiEAI/00590000001QHFEAA4
    ```

This is once again just an appetizer. You learn more about the Salesforce API and OAuth 2.0 in Chapter 7.

Summary

This chapter discussed the evolution of APIs and how managed APIs are different from naked APIs. Most cloud service providers today expose public managed APIs. The later part of the chapter focused on building two examples around Twitter and Salesforce APIs.

   In the next chapter, we will take a closer look at the basic principles everyone should know when doing a security design.

CHAPTER 2

■ ■ ■

Security by Design

Security isn't an afterthought. It has to be an integral part of any development project and also for APIs. It starts with requirements gathering and proceeds through the Design, Development, Testing, Deployment, and Monitoring phases.

Design Challenges

Security brings a plethora of challenges into system design. It's hard to build a 100% secured system, at least in theory. The only thing you can do is to make the attacker's job harder.

User Comfort

The most challenging thing in any security design is to find and maintain the right balance between security and the user comfort. Say you have the most complex password policy ever, which can never be broken by any brute-force attack. A password has to have more than 20 characters, with mandatory uppercase and lowercase letters, numbers, and special characters. Who on Earth is going to remember their password? Either you'll write it on a piece of paper and keep it in your wallet, or you'll add it as a note in your mobile device. Either way, you lose the ultimate objective of the strong password policy. Why would someone carry out a brute-force attack when the password is written down and kept in a wallet? The principle of psychological acceptability, discussed later in this chapter, states that security mechanisms should not make the resource more difficult to access than if the security mechanisms were not present.

> *It is essential that the human interface be designed for ease of use, so that users routinely and automatically apply the protection mechanisms correctly. Also, to the extent that the user's mental image of his protection goals matches the mechanisms he must use, mistakes will be minimized. If he must translate his image of his protection needs into a radically different specification language, he will make errors.*

> —Jerome Saltzer and Michael Schoeder

Performance

Performance is another key criterion. What is the cost of the overhead you add to your business operations to protect them from intruders? Say you have an API secured with a key, and each API call must be digitally signed. If the key is compromised, an attacker can use it to access the API. How do you minimize the impact? You can make the key valid only for a very short period; so, whatever the attacker can do with the stolen key is limited to its lifetime. What kind of impact will this have on legitimate day-to-day business operations? Each API call should first check the validity period of the key and, if it has expired, make another call to the authorization server to generate a new key. If you make the lifetime too short, then for each API call, there will be another call to the authorization server to generate a new key. That kills performance—but drastically reduces the impact of an intruder getting access to the API key.

Weakest Link

A proper security design should include all the communication links in the system. Your system is no stronger than its weakest link. In 2010, it was discovered that since 2006, a gang of robbers equipped with a powerful vacuum cleaner had stolen more than 600,000 euros from the Monoprix supermarket chain in France. The most interesting thing was the way they did it. They found out the weakest link in the system and attacked it. To transfer money directly into the store's cash coffers, cashiers slid tubes filled with money through pneumatic suction pipes. The robbers realized that it was sufficient to drill a hole in the pipe near the trunk and then connect a vacuum cleaner to capture the money. They didn't have to deal with the coffer shield.

Defense in Depth

A layered approach is preferred for any system being tightened for security. This is also known as *defense in depth*. Most international airports, which are at a high risk of terrorist attacks, follow a layered approach in their security design. On November 1, 2013, a man dressed in black walked into the Los Angeles International Airport, pulled a semi-automatic rifle out of his bag, and shot his way through a security checkpoint, killing a TSA screener and wounding at least two other officers. This was the first layer of defense. In case someone got through it, there has to be another to prevent the gunman from entering a flight and taking control. If there had been a security layer before the TSA, maybe just to scan everyone who entered the airport, it would have detected the weapon and probably saved the life of the TSA officer.

The number of layers and the strength of each layer depend on which assets you want to protect and the threat level associated with them. Why would someone hire a security officer and also use a burglar alarm system to secure an empty garage?

Insider Attacks

Insider attacks are less powerful and less complicated, but highly effective. From the confidential US diplomatic cables leaked by WikiLeaks to Edward Snowden's disclosure about the National Security Agency's secret operations, are all insider attacks. Both Snowden and Bradley Manning were insiders who had legitimate access to the information they disclosed. Most organizations spend the majority of their security budget to protect their systems from external intruders; but approximately 60% to 80% of network misuse incidents originate from inside the network, according to the Computer Security Institute (CSI) in San Francisco.

■ **Note** Insider attacks are identified as a growing threat in the military. To address this concern, the US Defense Advanced Research Projects Agency (DARPA) launched a project called Cyber Insider Threat (CINDER) in 2010. The objective of this project was to develop new ways to identify and mitigate insider threats as soon as possible.

Security by Obscurity

Kerckhoffs' Principle[1] emphasizes that a system should be secured by its design, not because the design is unknown to an adversary. Microsoft's NTLM design was kept secret for some time, but at the point (to support interoperability between Unix and Windows) Samba engineers reverse-engineered it, they discovered security vulnerabilities caused by the protocol design itself. In a proper security design, it's highly recommended not to use any custom-developed algorithms or protocols. Standards are like design patterns: they've been discussed, designed, and tested in an open forum. Every time you have to deviate from a standard, should think twice—or more.

Design Principles

Jerome Saltzer and Michael Schroeder produced one of the most widely cited research papers in the information security domain.[2] The paper, "The Protection of Information in Computer Systems," put forth eight design principles for securing information in computer systems, as described in the following sections.

Least Privilege

The principle of least privilege states that an entity should only have the required set of permissions to perform the actions for which they are authorized, and no more. Permissions can be added as needed and should be revoked when no longer in use. This limits the damage that can result from an accident or error.

■ **Note**   The *need to know* principle is popular in military security. This states that even if someone has all the necessary security clearance levels to access information, they should not be granted access unless there is a real/proven need.

Fail-Safe Defaults

This principle highlights the importance of making a system safe by default. A user's default access level to any resource in the system should be "denied" unless they've been granted a "permit" explicitly. The Java Security Manager implementation follows this principle—once engaged, none of the components in the system can perform any privileged operations unless explicitly permitted.

Economy of Mechanism

This principle highlights the value of simplicity. The design should be as simple as possible. All the component interfaces and the interactions between them should be simple enough to understand.

---

[1]In 1883, Auguste Kerckhoffs published two journal articles on La Cryptographie Militaire in which he emphasized six design principles for military ciphers. This resulted in the well-known Kerckhoffs' Principle: *A cryptosystem should be secured even if everything about the system, except the key, is public knowledge.*
[2]"The Protection of Information in Computer Systems," http://web.mit.edu/Saltzer/www/publications/protection/, October 11, 1974.

Complete Mediation

With complete mediation, a system should validate access rights to all its resources to ensure that they're allowed. Most systems do this once at the entry point to build a cached permission matrix. Each subsequent operation validates the resource permission against the permission matrix. If the access level to a given resource is being revoked, but that isn't reflected in the permission matrix, it would violate this principle.

Open Design

This principle highlights the importance of building a system in an open manner—with no secret, confidential algorithms. This is the opposite of security by obscurity, discussed earlier in the section "Design Challenges."

Separation of Privilege

The principle of separation of privilege states that granting permissions to an entity should not be purely based on a single condition. For example, say a reimbursement claim can be submitted by any employee but can only be approved by the manager. What if the manager wants to submit a reimbursement? According to this principle, the manager should not be granted the right to approve his or her own reimbursement claims.

Least Common Mechanism

The principle of least common mechanism concerns the risk of sharing state among different components. If one can corrupt the shared state, it can then corrupt all the other components that depend on it.

Psychological Acceptability

The principle of psychological acceptability states that security mechanisms should not make the resource more difficult to access than if the security mechanisms were not present. Microsoft introduced Information Cards in 2006 as a new paradigm for authentication to fight against phishing. But the user experience was bad, with a high setup cost, for people who were addicted to username/password-based authentication. It went down in history as another unsuccessful initiative from Microsoft.

Confidentiality, Integrity, Availability (CIA)

Confidentiality, integrity, and availability are three key factors used in benchmarking information systems security, as discussed next.

Confidentiality

Confidentiality means protecting data from unintended recipients, both at rest and in transit. You achieve confidentiality by protecting transport channels and storage with encryption. For APIs, where the transport channel is HTTP, you can use Transport Level Security (TLS), which is HTTPS. For storage, you can use disk-level encryption or application-level encryption. Channel encryption or transport-level encryption isn't 100% secure. In contrast, there is message-level encryption, which happens at the application level and has no dependency on the transport channel. If you secure data with message-level encryption, then you can use HTTP as the transport channel. Transport-level encryption only provides point-to-point protection and truncates from where the connection ends. As soon as data leaves the transport channel, it's no longer secured. At the same time, when you connect to an API gateway through a proxy, the data could be in cleartext while inside the proxy.

A TLS connection from the client to the gateway can be established in two ways: either with SSL bridging or with SSL tunneling. Almost all proxy servers support both modes. For a highly secured deployment, SSL tunneling is recommended. In SSL bridging (see Figure 2-1), the initial connection truncates from the proxy server, and a new connection to the gateway is established from there. That means the data is in cleartext in the proxy server. Any intruder who can plant malware in the proxy server can intercept traffic that passes through. With SSL tunneling (see Figure 2-2), the proxy server facilitates creating a direct channel between the client machine and the gateway. The data flow through this channel is invisible to the proxy server.

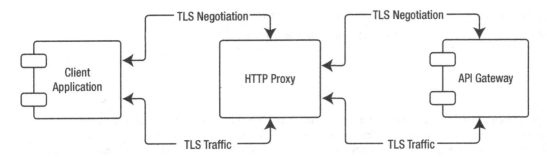

Figure 2-1. *SSL bridging*

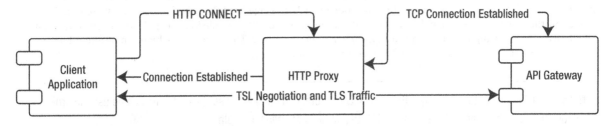

Figure 2-2. *SSL tunneling*

■ **Note** Secure Socket Layer (SSL) and Transport Layer Security (TLS) are often used interchangeably, but in pure technical terms they aren't the same. TLS is the successor of SSL 3.0. TLS 1.0, which is defined under the IETF RFC 2246, is based on the SSL 3.0 protocol specification, which was published by Netscape. The differences between TLS 1.0 and SSL 3.0 aren't dramatic, but they're significant enough that TLS 1.0 and SSL 3.0 don't interoperate.

Message-level encryption, on the other hand, is independent from the underlying transport. It's the application developers' responsibility to encrypt and decrypt messages. Because this is application specific, it hurts interoperability and builds tight couplings between the sender and the receiver. Each has to know how to encrypt/decrypt data beforehand—which will not scale up in a distributed system. To overcome this challenge, there have been some concentrated efforts to build standards around message-level encryption. XML Encryption is one such effort, led by the W3C. It standardizes how to encrypt an XML payload. Similarly, the IETF JavaScript Object Signing and Encryption (JOSE) working group is in the process of building a set of standards for JSON payloads. JSON Web Encryption and JSON Web Signature are discussed in Chapter 13.

Transport-level security encrypts the entire message. Because it relies on the underlying channel for protection, application developers have no control over which part of the data to encrypt and which part not to. Partial encryption isn't supported by transport-level security, but it is supported by message-level security. The Table 2-1 summarizes the key differences between transport-level security and message-level security.

Table 2-1. *Transport-Level Security vs. Message-Level Security*

Transport-Level Security	Message-Level Security
Relies on the underlying transport	No dependency on the underlying transport
Point-to-point	End-to-end
Partial encryption not supported	Partial encryption supported
High performance	Relatively less performance

Integrity

Integrity is a guarantee of data's correctness and trustworthiness and the ability to detect any unauthorized modifications. It ensures that data is protected from unauthorized or unintentional alteration, modification, or deletion. The way to achieve integrity is twofold: preventive measures and detective measures. Both measures have to take care of data in transit as well as data at rest.

To prevent data from alteration while in transit, you should use a confidential channel that only intended parties can read. TLS is the recommended approach for transport-level encryption. TLS itself has a way of detecting data modifications. It sends a message-authentication code in each message from the initial handshake, which can be verified by the receiving party to make sure the data has not been modified while in transit. For data at rest, you can calculate the message digest periodically and keep it in a secured place. The audit logs, which can be altered by an intruder to hide suspicious activities, need to be protected for integrity.

■ **Note** HTTP Digest Authentication with the quality of protection (qop) value set to `auth-int` can be used to protect messages for integrity. Chapter 3 discusses HTTP Digest Authentication in depth.

Availability

Making a system available for legitimate users to access all the time is the ultimate goal of any system design. Security isn't the only aspect to look into, but it plays a major role in keeping the system up and running. The goal of the security design should be to make the system highly available by protecting it from illegal access attempts. Doing so is extremely challenging. Attacks, especially on a public API, can vary from an attacker planting malware in the system to a highly organized distributed denial of service (DDoS) attack.

DDoS attacks are hard to eliminate fully, but with a careful design they can be minimized to reduce their impact. In most cases, DDoS attacks must be detected at the network perimeter level—so, the application code doesn't need to worry too much. But vulnerabilities in the application code can be exploited to bring a system down. The research paper "A New Approach towards DoS Penetration Testing on Web Services" by Christian Mainka, Juraj Somorovsky, Jorg Schwenk, and Andreas Falkenberg (https://www.nds.rub.de/media/nds/veroeffentlichungen/2013/07/19/ICWS_DoS.pdf) discusses eight types of DoS attacks that can be carried out against SOAP based APIs with XML payloads:

■ **Note** According to eSecurity Planet, the largest-ever DDoS attack hit the Internet in March 2013 and targeted the CloudFlare network with 120 Gbps. The upstream providers were hit by 300 Gbps DDoS at the peak of the attack.

- *Coercive parsing attack*: The attacker sends an XML document with a deeply nested XML structure. When a DOM-based parser processes the XML document, an out-of-memory exception or a high CPU load can occur.

- *SOAP array attack:* Forces the attacked web service to declare a very large SOAP array. This can exhaust the web service's memory.

- *XML element count attack:* Attacks the server by sending a SOAP message with a high number of non-nested elements.

- *XML attribute count attack:* Attacks the server by sending a SOAP message with a high attribute count.

- *XML entity expansion attack:* Causes a DoS attack by forcing the server to recursively resolve entities defined in a document type definition (DTD). This attack is also known as an *XML bomb* or a *billion laughs attack.*

- *XML external entity DoS attack:* Causes a DoS attack by forcing the server to resolve a large external entity defined in a DTD. If an attacker is able to execute the external entity attack, an additional attack surface may appear.

- *XML overlong name attack:* Injects overlong XML nodes in the XML document. Overlong nodes can be overlong element names, attribute names, attribute values, or namespace definitions.

- *Hash collision attack (HashDoS):* Different keys result in the same bucket assignments, causing a collision. A collision leads to resource-intensive computations in the bucket. When a weak hash function is used, an attacker can intentionally create hash collisions that lead to a DoS attack.

Most of these attacks can be prevented at the application level. For CPU- or memory-intensive operations, you can keep threshold values. For example, to prevent a coercive parsing attack, the XML parser can enforce a limit on the number of elements. Similarly, if your application executes a thread for a longer time, you can set a threshold and kill it. Aborting any further processing of a message as soon as it's found to be not legitimate is the best way to fight against DoS attacks. This also highlights the importance of having authentication/authorization checks closest to the entry point of the system.

There are also DoS attacks carried out against JSON vulnerabilities. CVE-2013-0269 explains a scenario in which a carefully crafted JSON message can be used to trigger the creation of arbitrary Ruby symbols or certain internal objects, to result in a DoS attack.

Security Controls

The CIA triad (confidentiality, integrity, and availability) is one of the core principles of information security. In achieving CIA, *authentication, authorization, nonrepudiation,* and *auditing* play a vital role.

Authentication

Authentication is the process of validating user-provided credentials to prove that users are who they claim to be. It can be single factor or multifactor. Something you know, something you are, and something you have are the well-known three factors of authentication. For multifactor authentication, a system should use a combination of at least two factors. Combining two techniques that fall under the same category isn't considered multifactor authentication. For example, entering a username and a password and then a PIN number isn't considered multifactor authentication.

■ **Note**   Google two-step verification falls under multifactor authentication. First you need to provide a username and a password (something you know), and then a PIN number is sent to your mobile phone. Knowing the PIN number verifies that the registered mobile phone is under your possession: it's something you have.

Something You Know

Passwords, passphrases, and PIN numbers belong to the category of *something you know*. This has been the most popular form of authentication not just for decades, but for centuries. It goes back to the 18th century. In the Arabian folk tale "Ali Baba and the Forty Thieves" from *One Thousand and One Nights*, Ali Baba uses the passphrase "open sesame" to open the door to a hidden cave. Since then, this has become the most popular form of authentication. Unfortunately, it's also the weakest form of authentication. Password-protected systems can be broken in several ways. Going back to the Ali Baba's story, his brother-in-law got stuck in the same cave without knowing the password and tried shouting all the words he knew. This, in modern days, is known as a *brute-force attack*. The first known brute-force attack took place in the 18th century. Since then, it has become a popular way of breaking password-secured systems.

■ **Note**   In April 2013, WordPress was hit with a brute-force attack of massive scale. The average scans per day in April were more than 100,000. See "The WordPress Brute Force Attack Timeline" by Daniel Cid, `http://blog.sucuri.net/2013/04/the-wordpress-brute-force-attack-timeline.html`, April 16, 2013.

There are different forms of brute-force attacks. The dictionary attack is one of them, where the brute-force attack is carried out with a limited set of inputs based on a dictionary of commonly used words. This is why you should have a corporate password policy that should enforce strong passwords with mixed alphanumeric characters that aren't found in dictionaries. Most public web sites enforce a captcha after few failed login attempts. This makes automated/tool-based brute-force attacks harder to execute.

Something You Have

Certificates and smart card-based authentication fall into the category of *something you have*. This is a much stronger form of authentication than something you know. SSL mutual authentication is the most popular way of securing APIs with client certificates; this is covered in detail in Chapter 4.

Something You Are

Fingerprints, eye retinas, facial recognition, and all other biometric-based authentication techniques fall into the category of *something you are*. This is the strongest form of authentication.

Authorization

Authorization is the process of validating what actions an authenticated user can perform in the system. Authorization happens with the assumption that the user is already authenticated. Discretionary Access Control (DAC) and Mandatory Access Control (MAC) are two modes to control access.

Discretionary Access Control (DAC) vs. Mandatory Access Control (MAC)

With DAC, the user can be the owner of the data and, at their discretion, can transfer rights to another user. Most operating systems support DAC, including Unix, Linux, and Windows. When you create a file in Linux, you can decide who should be able to read, write to, and execute it. Nothing prevents you from sharing it with any user or a group of users. There is no centralized control—which can easily bring security flaws into the system.

With MAC, only designated users are allowed to grant rights. Once rights are granted, users can't transfer them. SELinux, Trusted Solaris, and TrustedBSD are some of the operating systems that support MAC.

■ **Note**   SELinux is an NSA research project that added a MAC architecture to the Linux kernel, which was then merged into the mainstream version of Linux in August 2003. It utilizes a Linux 2.6 kernel feature called the Linux Security Modules (LSM) interface.

The difference between DAC and MAC lies in who owns the right to delegate. In either case, you need to have a way to represent access-control rules, or the access matrix. Authorization tables, access-control lists (see Figure 2-3), and capabilities are three ways of representing access-control rules.

	File-1	File-2	File-3
Tom	Read	Write	Read
Peter	Write	Write	Read
Jene	Read	Read	Write

Figure 2-3. *Access-control list*

An authorization table is a three-column table with subject, action, and resource. The subject can be an individual user or a group. With access-control lists, each resource is associated with a list, indicating, for each subject, the actions that the subject can exercise on the resource. With capabilities, each subject has an associated list called a capability list, indicating, for each resource, the actions that the user is allowed to exercise on the resource. A locker key can be considered a capability: the locker is the resource, and the user holds the key to the resource.

At the time the user tries to open the locker with the key, you only have to worry about the capabilities of the key—not the capabilities of its owner. An access-control list is resource driven, whereas capabilities are subject driven.

These three types of representations are very coarse grained. One alternative is to use policy-based access control. With policy-based access control, you can have authorization policies with fine granularity. In addition, capabilities and access-control lists can be dynamically derived from policies. eXtensible Access Control Markup Language (XACML) is the de facto standard for policy-based access control.

■ **Note**   XACML is an XML-based open standard for policy-based access control developed under the OASIS XACML Technical Committee. The latest XACML 3.0 specification was standardized in January 2013. See `www.oasis-open.org/committees/tc_home.php?wg_abbrev=xacml`.

XACML provides a reference architecture (see Figure 2-4), a request response protocol, and a policy language. Under the reference architecture, it talks about a Policy Administration Point (PAP), a Policy Decision Point (PDP), a Policy Enforcement Point (PEP), and a Policy Information Point (PIP). This is a highly distributed architecture in which none of the components are tightly coupled with each other. The PAP is the place where you author policies. The PDP is the place where policies are evaluated. While evaluating policies, if there is any missing information that can't be derived from the XACML request, the PDP calls the PIP. The role of the PIP is to feed the PDP any missing information, which can be user attributes or any other required details. The policy is enforced through the PEP, which sits between the client and the service and intercepts all requests. From the client request, it extracts certain attributes such as the subject, the resource, and the action; then it builds a standard XACML request and calls the PDP. Then it gets a XACML response from the PDP. That is defined under the XACML request/response model. The XACML policy language defines a schema to create XACML policies for access control.

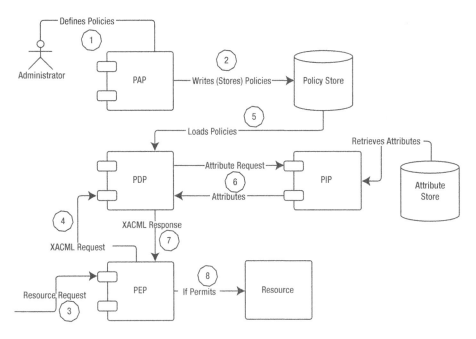

Figure 2-4. *XACML reference architecture*

■ **Note** With the increasing popularity and adaptation of APIs, it becomes crucial for XACML to be easily understood in order to increase the likelihood it will be adopted. XML is often considered too verbose. Developers increasingly prefer a lighter representation using JSON, the JavaScript Object Notation. The profile "Request / Response Interface Based on JSON and HTTP for XACML 3.0" aims at defining a JSON format for the XACML request and response. See https://www.oasis-open.org/committees/document.php?document_id=47775.

Nonrepudiation

Whenever you do a business transaction via an API by proving your identity, later you should not be able to reject it or repudiate it. The property that ensures the inability to repudiate is known as *nonrepudiation*. You do it once—you own it forever. Nonrepudiation should provide proof of the origin and the integrity of data, both in an unforgeable manner, which a third party can verify at any time. Once a transaction is initiated, none of its content—including user identity, date and time, and transaction details—should be altered while in transit to maintain transaction integrity and allow future verifications. One has to ensure that the transaction is unaltered and logged after it's committed and confirmed. Logs must be archived and properly secured to prevent unauthorized modifications. Whenever there is a repudiation dispute, transaction logs along with other logs or data can be retrieved to verify the initiator, date and time, transaction history, and so on.

■ **Note** TLS ensures authentication (by verifying the certificates), confidentiality (by encrypting the data with a secret key), and integrity (by digesting the data), but not the nonrepudiation. In TLS, the Message Authentication Code (MAC) value of the data transmitted is calculated with a shared secret key, known to both the client and the server. Shared keys can't be used to achieve nonrepudiation.

Digital signatures provide a strong binding between the user (who initiates the transaction) and the transaction the user performs. A key known only to the user should sign the complete transaction, and the server (or the service) should be able to verify the signature through a trusted broker that vouches for the legitimacy of the user's key. This trusted broker can be a certificate authority (CA). Once the signature is verified, the server knows the identity of the user and can guarantee the integrity of the data. For nonrepudiation purposes, the data must be stored securely for any future verification.

■ **Note** The paper "Non-Repudiation in Practice," by Chii-Ren Tsai of Citigroup (http://www.researchgate.net/publication/240926842_Non-Repudiation_In_Practice), discusses two potential nonrepudiation architectures for financial transactions using challenge-response one-time password tokens and digital signatures.

Auditing

There are two aspects of auditing: keeping track of all legitimate access attempts, to facilitate nonrepudiation; and keeping track of all illegal access attempts, to identify possible threats. There can be cases where you're permitted to access a resource, but it should be with a valid purpose. For example, a mobile operator is allowed to access a user's call history, but it should not do so without a request from the corresponding user. If someone frequently accesses a user's call history, this can be detected by proper audit trails. Audit trails also play a vital role in fraud detection. An administrator must define fraud-detection patterns, and the audit logs should be evaluated in near real time. Complex event processing is a popular technique used for fraud detection.

Security Patterns

Patterns provide solutions for common problems in a way similar to sharing industry best practices. Having a broader understanding of security patterns can help you design solutions. The solutions proposed in security patterns are widely recognized and well tested; hence you need not worry about reinventing the wheel.

Direct Authentication Pattern

An API can be open for anonymous access or protected for limited/restricted access. If it's anonymous, you need not worry about authentication. Twitter API version 1.0 had a couple of open APIs. The `https://api.twitter.com/1/statuses/public_timeline.json` API, which returned the public timeline of a given Twitter user, was an open API. From version 1.1 onward, all Twitter APIs were made protected. If you make a public API open, be sure you enforce proper rate limits. Otherwise, this could be an invaluable source to carry out a DoS attack.

A public API can be secured for authentication with HTTP Basic/Digest Authentication. Chapter 3 digs into more about HTTP Basic/Digest Authentication. Until then, it's a way of accessing a protected API by sending a username and a password in the HTTP Authorization header, along with the API invocation request. The limitation here is, you need to own and maintain the user base or the user store. In other words, if your API is available for public access, you also need to have a registration process to bring users into the system, and you own and maintain that user store. HTTP Basic Authentication won't work in a federated scenario where you want to give access to the users not owned by you. This pattern of authentication is known as *Direct Authentication*.

Both public and private APIs can be secured with HTTP Basic/Digest Authentication. The difference is in the deployment, where you carry out the authentication check. In the case of a public API, you should carry out the authentication check inside the demilitarized zone (DMZ).

In Figure 2-5, there are three firewalls used to overcome the challenge of enabling access to the user store or the LDAP from the DMZ. It's a best practice to not to put any databases or user stores into the DMZ. The figure introduces another secured zone called the *yellow zone*. The user store is inside the yellow zone, which is protected by two firewalls. One firewall is between the DMZ and the yellow zone, and it only allows inbound connections from the API gateway in the DMZ to the yellow zone. The other one is between the green zone and the yellow zone. This only allows inbound connections from the green zone to the yellow zone. With this approach, you share the same user store, having both internal corporate users and external users, with the two API gateways in the DMZ and the green zone. But you never let a connection propagate from the DMZ to the green zone except through ports 80 and 443 to access the application server. The actual API implementation is hosted in the application server.

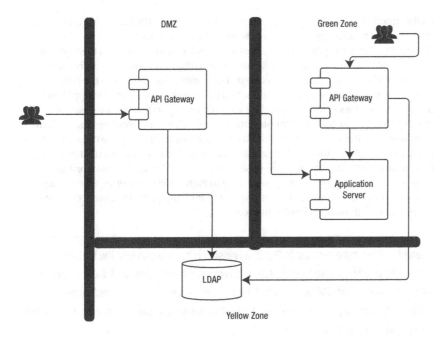

Figure 2-5. *Direct authentication with layered defense in security*

▓ **Note** A DMZ is a physical or logical separation between the internal network and the services exposed for a larger, untrusted environment—usually the Internet. In a typical setup, the DMZ has two firewalls: one between the DMZ and the public Internet and the other between the DMZ and the internal network (LAN).

Managing Credentials

In a system protected with HTTP Basic Authentication, you need to be concerned about the confidentiality of credentials. Credentials can be leaked at two stages: while in transit and at rest. To secure credentials in transit, you must use an encrypted channel. For API calls carrying user credentials, you can use HTTP over TLS (HTTPS). Securing the API call isn't sufficient. A system is secured only to the level of the strength of its weakest link. You also need to think about how the API gateway connects to the user store. In the case of LDAP, you should use LDAP over TLS (LDAPS); and in the case of JDBC, you should use JDBC over TLS.

How do you store passwords? Ideally, passwords should only be known by the owners. They should not even be known by system administrators or people having full access to the system—at the database level. Passwords can be encrypted and stored in the user store. That prevents any attacker from getting access to the user store and seeing user credentials. But system administrators would be able to see passwords in cleartext, given that they have access to the key used to encrypt passwords. Using one-way hashing can prevent this. With hashing, you can pick whatever hashing algorithm you need and apply it to the password in cleartext. That results in a fixed-length hash, which isn't reversible. In other words, given the hash and the hashing algorithm, you can't derive the password. Also note that hashing doesn't involve a key.

How does this make your password safe? Anyone having access to the user store can see the hashes, but they can never derive passwords from them. Keep in mind—you can't log in with a hashed password. But is this safe enough? A hacker who has access to the user store can still replace the hashed password with a hash calculated with a cleartext known to the attacker. Then the attacker can log in to the corresponding account with the cleartext known to him or her—because it's verified against the hash value the attacker replaced in the database.

Hashing alone is never safe. Whenever you store anything in cleartext as a hashed value, you need to store it as a *salted* hash. In cryptography, a salt comprises random bits that are used as one of the inputs to a key-derivation function. The other input is usually a password or a passphrase in cleartext. The application calculates the hash value of both the password in cleartext and the salt value and stores the salted hash in the database. The application also has to store the salt value. As a best practice, the salt value should be kept secret, separate from the password database. When a user enters their password for login, the application retrieves the salt value, calculates the hash over both the salt and the entered password, and matches the result with the hash value stored in the password database.

If a hacker has access to the database and replaces the user's password with a hash value of a cleartext password known to the attacker, the password verification will fail, because the hash isn't calculated with the password alone. It's from both the password and the salt value. In this case, if the hacker wants to gain access to user accounts, they must break into the database, which stores salt values as well. The bottom line is, hashing alone is never secure, and salted hashing is much more secure—but all that makes it is harder to break.

■ **Note**   LinkedIn provides a good example of insecure hashes. In 2012, a Russian hacker broke into the LinkedIn network and got access to more than 6.5 million user accounts with their passwords. All the passwords were securely stored with a SHA-1 hash, but none of them were salted. Using rainbow tables, attackers managed to crack around 300,000 passwords. Rainbow tables provide a directory of precalculated hashes against cleartext passwords. If you know the hash, you can find the corresponding word in cleartext.

Biometric Authentication

Biometric authentication implements the Direct Authentication pattern. Let's take a fingerprint time-clock attendance recorder as an example (see Figure 2-6). This scans the user's fingerprint and calls an API at the backend system to authenticate the user. Once the user is authenticated, the recorder has to update another backend system with the date and the time. This also can be done in a single step. The fingerprint scanner directly calls the API of the time-recording system with the fingerprint. The fingerprint goes as binary data on the wire. When it hits the API gateway, it extracts the fingerprint and calls the API of the biometric system to validate the fingerprint. If all goes well, the user's time is recorded, and the user is granted access to the building.

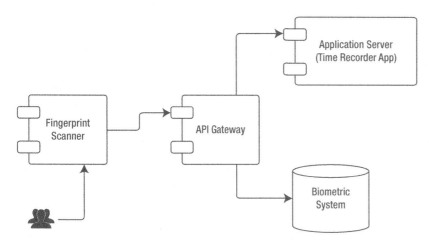

Figure 2-6. *Biometric authentication*

To prevent any sort of spoofing between the fingerprint scanner and the biometric system, you need to make sure the channel between the scanner and the API gateway, as well as the channel between the API gateway and the biometric system, are on TLS. The API gateway should connect to a biometric database or to a biometric system to complete the authentication process. There are vendors who specifically focus on building biometric systems for authentication, and they do expose APIs that other systems can call.

Sealed Green Zone Pattern

In Figure 2-5, given the way the deployment is layered, the DMZ has an open connection to the green zone via ports 80/443. Some system administrators are extremely strict about connections between the DMZ and the green zone, whereas others don't worry about opening ports 443 and 80 to the green zone. For extremely tight security, you should not open any inbound ports to the green zone. That leaves you with a challenge: how do you access any services running in the green zone from the DMZ?

In Figure 2-7, no ports are open toward the green zone. That restricts anyone from making connections into the green zone. To facilitate communication between API gateway in the DMZ and the application server in the green zone, you use a message broker. The message broker has a queue, and whenever the API gateway gets a request, it authenticates the request first and publishes the message into the queue. The application server from the green zone subscribes to the same queue to receive messages. This is possible because it's okay to open outbound connections from the green zone to the DMZ. A similar channel is used to send back the responses to the API gateway in the DMZ.

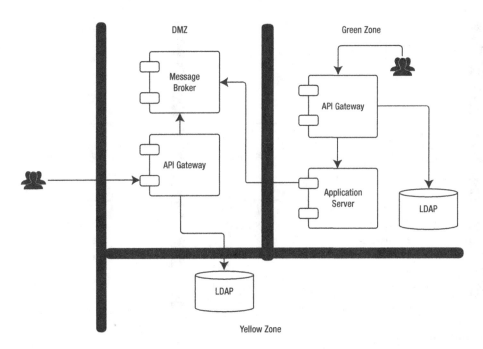

Figure 2-7. *Sealed Green Zone pattern and Least Common Mechanism pattern*

Least Common Mechanism Pattern

In Figure 2-5, both the internal and external user accounts are in the same user store. It's always recommended that you keep external user accounts in a different user store. Ideally, this should be a separate physical user store, as in Figure 2-7. Then you don't need a connection between the green zone and the yellow zone, because you can keep the user store with internal users in the green zone. The principle of least common mechanism concerns the risk of sharing infrastructure among different components.

Brokered Authentication Pattern

Password-based authentication only facilitates the Direct Authentication pattern, where you need to have control over the user store under you. Certificate-based authentication supports both the Direct Authentication pattern as well as the Brokered Authentication pattern. In direct authentication, each user in your system has a certificate stored in the user store against their name. Once the validation process (or the handshake) in SSL mutual authentication is completed, the system checks whether it has a user with that given certificate. The system looks for each individual certificate during the authentication process. With the Brokered Authentication pattern, you don't need to look for each individual certificate. You only go through the validation process in SSL mutual authentication and then check whether the CA that signed the client certificate is trusted. If the certificate is from a trusted CA, the system lets the user in. Figure 2-8 illustrates the Brokered Authentication pattern with certificates.

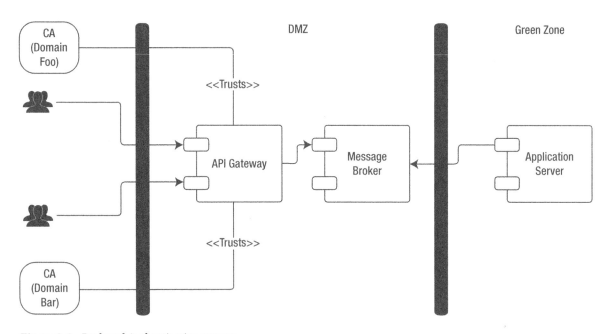

Figure 2-8. Brokered Authentication pattern

■ **Note** SSL mutual authentication is covered in detail in Chapter 4.

Policy-Based Access Control Pattern

The deployment in Figure 2-9 illustrates how to enforce XACML-based authorization on APIs. Just as with authentication, for external inbound calls, you also need to enforce authorization checks in the DMZ. That makes sure only legitimate requests pass through to the green zone.

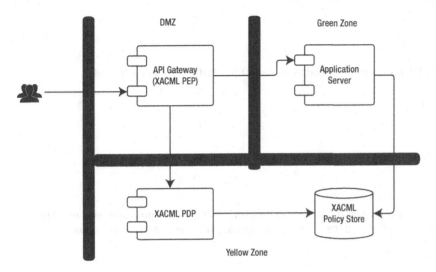

Figure 2-9. *Policy-Based Access Control pattern with XACML*

The request from the end user hits the API gateway first and completes the authentication process to identify the user who invokes the API. Then it creates a XACML request using the identified user as the subject, the context of the API as the resource, and the HTTP method as the action, and calls the XACML PDP. The XACML PDP evaluates the request against the policies loaded from the XACML Policy Store. After the evaluation, it returns the decision in a XACML response.

Listing 2-1 shows a sample XACML request generated from the API gateway. It has foo as the subject, GET as the action, and http://api.gateway/bar as the resource.

Listing 2-1. Sample XACML Request

```
<Request>
    <Attributes Category="urn:oasis:names:tc:xacml:1.0:subject-category:access-subject">
        <Attribute AttributeId="urn:oasis:names:tc:xacml:1.0:subject:subject-id">
            <AttributeValue
                DataType=http://www.w3.org/2001/XMLSchema#string>foo</AttributeValue>
        </Attribute>
    <Attributes>
    <Attributes Category="urn:oasis:names:tc:xacml:3.0:attribute-category:action">
        <Attribute AttributeId="urn:oasis:names:tc:xacml:1.0:action:action-id">
            <AttributeValue
                DataType="http://www.w3.org/2001/XMLSchema#string">GET</AttributeValue>
        </Attribute>
    </Attributes>
```

```
        <Attributes Category="urn:oasis:names:tc:xacml:3.0:attribute-category:resource">
            <Attribute AttributeId="urn:oasis:names:tc:xacml:1.0:resource:resource-id">
                <AttributeValue
                    DataType="http://www.w3.org/2001/XMLSchema#string">
                            http://api.gateway/bar
                </AttributeValue>
            </Attribute>
        </Attributes>
</Request>
```

Listing 2-2 shows a sample XACML response generated from the XACML PDP. The result is "Permit".

Listing 2-2. Sample XACML Response

```
<Response>
    <Result>
        <Decision>Permit</Decision>
    </Result>
</Response>
```

Listing 2-3 shows the sample XACML policy corresponding to the previous XACML request and response. The policy returns "Permit" for any user doing a GET on http://api.gateway/bar. All other actions will be denied.

Listing 2-3. Sample XACML Policy

```
<Policy>
    <Target>
        <AnyOf>
            <AllOf>
                <Match MatchId="urn:oasis:names:tc:xacml:1.0:function:string-equal">
                    <AttributeValue
                        DataType="http://www.w3.org/2001/XMLSchema#string">
                                http://api.gateway/bar</AttributeValue>
                    <AttributeDesignator MustBePresent="false"
                        Category="urn:oasis:names:tc:xacml:3.0:attribute-category:resource"
                        AttributeId="urn:oasis:names:tc:xacml:1.0:resource:resource-id"
                        DataType=http://www.w3.org/2001/XMLSchema#string />
                </Match>
            </AllOf>
        </AnyOf>
    </Target>
    <Rule RuleId="permit_rule" Effect="Permit">
        <Target>
            <AnyOf>
                <AllOf>
                    <Match MatchId="urn:oasis:names:tc:xacml:1.0:function:string-equal">
                        <AttributeValue
                            DataType="http://www.w3.org/2001/XMLSchema#string">
                                    GET</AttributeValue>
```

```
            <AttributeDesignator MustBePresent="false"
                    Category="urn:oasis:names:tc:xacml:3.0:attribute-category:action"
                    AttributeId="urn:oasis:names:tc:xacml:1.0:action:action-id"
                    DataType=http://www.w3.org/2001/XMLSchema#string />
            </Match>
        </AllOf>
      </AnyOf>
    </Target>
  </Rule>
  <Rule RuleId="deny_rule" Effect="Deny">
  </Rule>
</Policy>
```

When you're building authorization policies, there are two main concepts you should take into consideration: the principle of least privilege and segregation of duties. When giving users access rights to resources in the system, you should give them only the bare minimum set of permissions to perform the expected actions, and no more. With segregation of duties, you need to make sure the ability to complete a critical task is divided between more than one person. For example, the person responsible for adding users to the system should be different from the person responsible for approving such actions. Being compliant with these two concepts will minimize security vulnerabilities that could creep into the system due to human errors.

■ **Note**   Everything discussed so far has been related to direct access control. There is another derivation from this: *delegated access control.* OAuth is the de facto standard for delegated access control. Chapter 7 talks more about OAuth and how XACML can be integrated with it. Delegated access control is all about giving someone else access to a resource you own so that they can perform actions on your behalf.

Threat Modeling

Threat modeling is a methodical, systematic approach to identifying possible security threats and vulnerabilities in a system deployment. First you need to identify all the assets in the system. *Assets* are the resources you have to protect from intruders. These can be user records/credentials stored in an LDAP, data in a database, files in a file system, CPU power, memory, network bandwidth, and so on. Identifying assets also means identifying all their interfaces and the interaction patterns with other system components. For example, the data stored in a database can be exposed in multiple ways. Database administrators have physical access to the database servers. Application developers have JDBC-level access, and end users have access to an API.

Once you identify all the assets in the system to be protected and all the related interaction patterns, you need to list all possible threats and associated attacks. Threats can be identified by observing interactions, based on the CIA triad. In Figure 2-10, you see three communication links or interactions. From the application server to the database is a JDBC connection. A third party can eavesdrop on that connection to read or modify the data flowing through it. That's a threat. How does the application server keep the JDBC connection username and password? If they're kept in a configuration file, anyone having access to the application server's file system can find them and then access the database over JDBC. That's another threat. The JDBC connection is protected with a username and password, which can potentially be broken by carrying out a brute-force attack. Another threat.

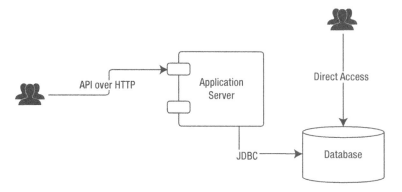

Figure 2-10. *Assets and interactions*

Administrators have direct access to the database servers. How do they access the servers? If access is open for SSH via username/password, then a brute-force attack is likely a threat. If it's based on SSH keys, where those keys are stored? Are they stored on the physical personal machines of administrators or uploaded to a key server? Losing SSH keys to an intruder is another threat. How about the ports? Have you opened any ports to the database servers, where some intruder can telnet and get control or carry out an attack on an open port to exhaust system resources? Can the physical machine running the database be accessed from outside the corporate network? Is it only available over VPN? All these questions lead you to identifying possible threats against the database server.

End users have access to the data via the API. This is a public API, which is exposed from the corporate firewall. A brute-force attack is always a threat if the API is secured with HTTP Basic/Digest Authentication. Having broken the authentication layer, anyone could get free access to the data. Another possible threat is an attacker getting access to the confidential data that flows through the transport channels. Executing a man-in-the-middle attack can do this. DoS is also a possible threat. An attacker can send carefully crafted, malicious, extremely large payloads to exhaust server resources.

STRIDE is a popular technique to identify threats associated with a system in a methodical manner. STRIDE stands for Spoofing, Tampering, Repudiation, Information disclosure, Denial of service, Escalation of privileges. Table 2-2 compares STRIDE with the security properties discussed at the start of the chapter.

Table 2-2. *Security Properties vs. Threats*

Security Properties	Threats
Authentication	Spoofing
Integrity	Tampering
Nonrepudiation	Repudiation
Confidentiality	Information disclosure
Availability	Denial of service
Authorization	Escalation of privileges

Once you've identified all the possible threats and associated attacks, you can start planning attacks. This requires tooling support. You have to identify what tools would be used to carry out a brute-force attack, a DoS attack, and so on. Once the test matrix is planned against all possible threats, you can begin executing. At the end of the test, you can identify all possible vulnerabilities in your system. Then you need to think about countermeasures to mitigate them.

Threat modeling is an exercise that must be carried out against any serious enterprise deployment before moving to production. A proper threat-modeling exercise includes business analysts, solution architects, system architects, developers, and testers. Each one has a role to play. The challenge faced by the moderator is to capture all the bits and pieces, resolve any contradictions, and come up with all possible data-flow diagrams. A single missing data-flow diagram could easily put your company on the news the day after you move to production—which could result in a huge loss in customer confidence.

Summary

This chapter focused on building a solid foundation for the rest of the book by introducing core security principles. It covered security principles, design challenges, security patterns and best practices, security properties, and threat-modeling techniques.

In the next chapter, we are going to discuss HTTP basic and digest authentication as means of securing APIs for legitimate access.

■ ■ ■

CHAPTER 3

HTTP Basic/Digest Authentication

HTTP Basic Authentication and Digest Authentication are popular for protecting resources on the web. Both are based on usernames and passwords. HTTP/1.0 includes the specification for the Basic Access Authentication scheme, which takes the username and password over the network in cleartext. Hence it isn't considered to be a secured way of authenticating users, unless it's used over an externally secured system such as Transport Level Security (TLS). RFC 2617 defines the specification for HTTP's authentication framework (the original Basic Access Authentication scheme) and Digest Access Authentication, which is based on cryptographic hashes. Unlike Basic Authentication, Digest Authentication doesn't take the user's password over the wire in cleartext.

■ **Note** The HTTP/1.0 specification is defined under RFC 1945. It's available at `www.rfc-base.org/txt/rfc-1945.txt`.

HTTP Basic Authentication

The HTTP/1.0 specification first defined the scheme for HTTP Basic Authentication. With this model, users must authenticate themselves with the corresponding username and password for each realm. A given user can belong to multiple realms simultaneously. The value of the realm is shown to the user at the time of authentication. It allows the resources on the server to be partitioned into a set of protection domains, each with its own authentication scheme and/or authorization database. The realm value is a string, which is assigned by the authentication server. Once the request hits the server with Basic Authentication credentials, the server will accept the request only if it can validate the username and the password for the protected resource.

ACCESSING THE GITHUB API WITH HTTP BASIC AUTHENTICATION

The GitHub REST API is protected with HTTP Basic Authentication. Before you proceed any further, you need to create a GitHub account at `https://github.com`.

■ **Note** Complete documentation about the GitHub API is available at `http://developer.github.com/v3/`.

Let's try to invoke the following GitHub API with cURL. It's an open API that doesn't require any authentication and returns pointers to all available resources:

```
curl -v https://api.github.com/users/{github-user}

e.g. :
curl -v https://api.github.com/users/prabath
```

Now let's try out another API. Here you create a GitHub repository with the following API call. This returns a negative response with the HTTP status code "401 Unauthorized." The API is secured with HTTP Basic Authentication, and you need to provide credentials to access it:

```
curl -i  -X POST -H 'Content-Type: application/x-www-form-urlencoded'
     -d '{"name": "my_github_repo"}'
     https://api.github.com/user/repos
```

Let's invoke the same API with proper GitHub credentials. Replace $GitHubUserName and $GitHubPassword with your values:

```
curl  -i  -v -u $GitHubUserName:$GitHubPassword
     -X POST -H 'Content-Type: application/x-www-form-urlencoded'
     -d '{"name": "my_github_repo"}'
     https://api.github.com/user/repos
```

Next, let's look at the HTTP request generated from the above cURL command:

```
POST /user/repos HTTP/1.1
Authorization: Basic cHewemFOaDpwdsdsdsdE5ODc=
```

The HTTP Authorization header in the request is generated from the username and the password you provided. The formula is simple: `Basic Base64Encode(username:password)`. Any Base64-encoded text is no better than cleartext—it can be decoded quite easily back to the cleartext. That is why HTTP Basic Authentication on HTTP isn't secured. It must be used in conjunction with an external secure system such as TLS.

■ **Note**   To add HTTP Basic Authentication credentials to a request generated from a cURL client, you use the option **–u username:password**. This creates the Base64-encoded HTTP Basic Authorization header. **–i** is used to include HTTP headers in the output, and **–v** is used to run cURL in verbose mode. **–H** is used to set HTTP headers in the outgoing request, and **–d** is used to post data to the endpoint.

Observing the response from GitHub for the unauthenticated API call to create a repository, it looks as though the GitHub API isn't fully compliant with the HTTP 1.1 specification at the time of this writing. According to the HTTP 1.1 specification, whenever the server returns a 401 status code, it also must return the HTTP header `WWW-Authenticate`.

HTTP Digest Authentication

HTTP Digest Authentication was proposed by RFC 2617 to overcome some limitations in HTTP Basic Authentication. It works in a challenge/response mode without sending the password over the wire. Because the password is never sent over the wire with the request, TLS isn't a must. Anyone intercepting the traffic won't be able to discover the password in cleartext.

■ **Note**   RFC 2617, which defines Basic and Digest Authentication, is available at `www.ietf.org/rfc/rfc2617.txt`.

To initiate Digest Authentication, the client has to send a request to the protected resource with no authentication information, which results in a challenge (in the response). Following is an example of how to initiate a Digest Authentication handshake from cURL:

```
curl -k --digest -u userName:password -v https://localhost:8443/recipe
```

> ■ **Note** To add HTTP Digest Authentication credentials to a request generated from a cURL client, use the option **--digest -u username:password**.

Let's look at the HTTP headers in the response. The first response is a 401 with the HTTP header WWW-Authenticate, which contains a challenge:

```
HTTP/1.1 401 Unauthorized
WWW-Authenticate: Digest realm="cute-cupcakes.com", qop="auth",

nonce="1390781967182:c2db4ebb26207f6ed38bb08eeffc7422",
opaque="F5288F4526B8EAFFC4AC79F04CA8A6ED"
```

> ■ **Note** You learn more about the Recipe API and how to deploy it locally as you proceed through this chapter. The "Securing the Recipe API with HTTP Digest Authentication" exercise at the end of the chapter explains how to secure an API with Digest Authentication.

The challenge consists of four main elements. Each of these elements is defined in RFC 2617:

- realm: A string to be displayed to users so they know which username and password to use. This string should contain at least the name of the host performing the authentication and may additionally indicate the collection of users who may have access.

- nonce: A server-specified data string, which should be uniquely generated each time a 401 response is made. The content of the nonce is implementation dependent.

- opaque: A string of data, specified by the server, that should be returned by the client unchanged in the Authorization header of subsequent requests with URIs in the same protection space (which is the realm).

- qop: The "quality of protection" options applied to the response by the server. The value auth indicates authentication while auth-int indicates authentication with integrity protection.

Once the client gets the response with the challenge, it has to respond back. Here's the HTTP request with the response to the challenge:

```
Authorization: Digest username="prabath", realm="cute-cupcakes.com",
                nonce="1390781967182:c2db4ebb26207f6ed38bb08eeffc7422",
                uri="/recipe", cnonce="MTM5MDc4", nc=00000001, qop="auth",
                response="f5bfb64ba8596d1b9ad1514702f5a062",
                opaque="F5288F4526B8EAFFC4AC79F04CA8A6ED"
```

Let's have a look at the definition of each parameter:

- `username`: The identity of the user who's going to invoke the API

- `realm/qop/nonce/opaque`: The same as in the challenge

- `response`: The response to the challenge calculated by the client

The value of `response` is calculated in the following manner. Digest Authentication supports multiple algorithms. RFC 2617 recommends using MD5 or MD5-sess (MD5-session). If no algorithm is specified in the server challenge, MD5 is used. Digest calculation is done with two types of data: security-related data (A1) and message-related data (A2).

If you use MD5 as the hashing algorithm, then you define security-related data (A1) in the following manner:

```
A1 = username:password:realm
```

If you use MD5-sess as the hashing algorithm, then you define security-related data (A1) in the following manner. `cnonce` is an opaque quoted string value provided by the client and used by both client and server to avoid chosen plaintext attacks. The value of `nonce` is the same as in the server challenge:

```
A1 = MD5 (username:password:realm):nonce:cnonce
```

RFC 2617 defines message-related data (A2) in two ways, based on the value of `qop` in the server challenge. If the value is `auth` or `undefined`, then the message-related data (A2) is defined in the following manner. `request-method` is `GET`, `POST`, `PUT`, `DELETE`, or any HTTP verb, and `uri-directive-value` is the request URI from the request line:

```
A2 = request-method:uri-directive-value
```

If the value of `qop` is `auth-int`, then you need to protect the integrity of the message, in addition to authenticating. A2 is derived in following manner. When you have MD5 or MD5-sess as the hashing algorithm, H is MD5:

```
A2 = request-method:uri-directive-value:H(request-entity-body)
```

The final value of the digest is calculated in the following way, based on the value of `qop`. If `qop` is set to `auth` or `auth-int`, then the final digest value is as shown next. The `nc` value is the hexadecimal count of the number of requests (including the current request) that the client has sent with the `nonce` value in this request. This directive helps the server detect replay attacks. The server maintains its own copy of `nonce` and the nonce count (`nc`); if any are seen twice, that indicates a possible replay attack:

```
MD5(MD5(A1):nonce:nc:cnonce:qop:MD5(A2))
```

If `qop` is undefined, then the final digest value is

```
MD5(MD5(A1):<nonce>:MD5(A2))
```

Table 3-1 provides a comparison between HTTP basic authentication and digest authentication.

Table 3-1. *HTTP Basic Authentication vs. HTTP Digest Authentication*

HTTP Basic Authentication	HTTP Digest Authentication
Sends credentials in cleartext over the wire	Credentials are never sent in cleartext. A digest derived from the cleartext password is sent over the wire.
Should be used in conjunction with some external security systems like TLS	Doesn't depend on transport-level security or external security systems.
Only performs authentication	Can be used to protect the integrity of the message, in addition to authentication (with qop=auth-int).
User store can store passwords as a salted hash	User store should store passwords in cleartext or should store the hash value of username:password:realm.

■ **Note**   With HTTP Digest Authentication, most user stores store either the password in cleartext or the hashed value of username:password:realm. This is required because the server has to validate the digest sent from the client, which is derived by the cleartext password (or the hash of username:password:realm). Neither option is safe. If you use Digest Authentication, it's recommended that you encrypt and store the hash of username:password:realm.

CUTE-CUPCAKE FACTORY: DEPLOYING THE RECIPE API IN APACHE TOMCAT

In this example, you deploy a prebuilt web application with the Recipe API in Apache Tomcat. The Recipe API is hosted and maintained by the Cute-Cupcake factory. It's a public API with which the customers of Cute-Cupcake can interact.

You can download the latest version of Apache Tomcat from http://tomcat.apache.org. All the examples discussed in this book use Tomcat 7.0.50.

The Recipe API supports following five operations:

- GET /recipe: Returns all the recipes in the system
- GET /recipe/{$recipeNo}: Returns the recipe with the given recipe number
- POST /recipe: Creates a new recipe in the system
- PUT /recipe: Updates the recipe in the system with the given details
- DELETE /recipe/{$recipeNo}: Deletes the recipe from the system with the given recipe number

To deploy the API, download recipe.war from https://svn.wso2.org/repos/wso2/people/prabath/api-security/recipe and copy it to [TOMCAT_HOME]\webapps. To start Tomcat, run the following from the [TOMCAT_HOME]\bin directory:

```
[Linux] sh catalina.sh run
[Windows] catalina.bat run
```

Once the server is started, use cURL to execute the following command. Here it's assumed that Tomcat is running on its default HTTP port 8080:

```
curl  http://localhost:8080/recipe
```

This returns all the recipes in the system as a JSON payload:

```
{
    "recipes":[
        {
            "recipeId":"10001",
            "name":"Lemon Cupcake",
            "ingredients":"lemon zest, white sugar,unsalted butter, flour,salt, milk",
            "directions":"Preheat oven to 375 degrees F (190 degrees C). Line 30 cupcake pan
cups with paper liners...."
        },
        {
            "recipeId":"10002",
            "name":"Red Velvet Cupcake",
            "ingredients":"cocoa powder, eggs, white sugar,unsalted butter, flour,salt, milk",
            "directions":" Preheat oven to 350 degrees F. Mix flour, cocoa powder,
                                baking soda and salt in medium bowl. Set aside...."
        }
    ]
}
```

To get the recipe of any given cupcake, use the following cURL command, where 10001 is the ID of the cupcake you just created:

```
curl  http://localhost:8080/recipe/10001
```

This returns the following JSON response:

```
{
            "recipeId":"10001",
            "name":"Lemon Cupcake",
            "ingredients":"lemon zest, white sugar,unsalted butter, flour,salt, milk",
            "directions":"Preheat oven to 375 degrees F (190 degrees C). Line 30 cupcake pan
cups with paper liners...."
}
```

To create a new recipe, use the following cURL command:

```
curl  -X POST -H 'Content-Type: application/json'
      -d '{"name":"Peanut Butter Cupcake",
          "ingredients":"peanut butter, eggs, sugar,unsalted butter, flour,salt, milk",
          "directions":"Preheat the oven to 350 degrees F (175 degrees C).
           Line a cupcake pan with paper liners, or grease and flour cups..."
          }' http://localhost:8080/recipe
```

This returns the following JSON response:

```
{
        "recipeId":"10003",
        "location":"http://localhost:8080/recipe/10003",
}
```

To update an existing recipe, use the following cURL command:

```
curl  -X PUT -H 'Content-Type: application/json'
      -d '{"name":"Peanut Butter Cupcake",
          "ingredients":"peanut butter, eggs, sugar,unsalted butter, flour,salt, milk",
          "directions":"Preheat the oven to 350 degrees F (175 degrees C). Line a cupcake
pan with
          paper liners, or grease and flour cups..."
          }' http://localhost:8080/recipe/10003
```

This returns the following JSON response:

```
{
        "recipeId":"10003",
        "location":"http://localhost:8080/recipe/10003",
}
```

To delete an existing recipe, use the following cURL command:

```
curl  -X DELETE http://localhost:8080/recipe/10001
```

■ **Note** To do remote debugging with Apache Tomcat, start the server as [Linux] `sh catalina.sh jdpa run` or [Windows] `catalina.bat jdpa run`. This opens port 8000 for remote-debugging connections.

CONFIGURING APACHE DIRECTORY SERVER (LDAP)

Apache Directory Server is an open source LDAP server distributed under Apache 2.0 license. You can download the latest version from `http://directory.apache.org/studio/`. It's recommended that you download the Studio itself, because it comes with a set of very useful tools to configure LDAP. This book uses Apache Directory Studio 2.0.0.

■ **Note** Refer to the Apache Directory Studio user guide for setup and getting-started instructions: `http://directory.apache.org/studio/users-guide/apache_directory_studio/`.

These steps are needed only if you don't have an LDAP server set up to run. First you need to start Apache Directory Studio. This provides a management console to create and manage LDAP servers and connections. Then proceed as follows:

1. From Apache Directory Studio, go to the LDAP Servers view. If it's not there already, go to Window ➤ Show View ➤ LDAP Servers.

2. Right-click LDAP Servers View, choose New ➤ New Server, and select ApacheDS 2.0.0. Give any name to the server in the Server Name text box, and click Finish.

3. The server you created appears in the LDAP Servers view. Right-click the server, and select Run. If it's started properly, State is updated to Started.

4. To view or edit the configuration of the server, right-click it and select Open Configuration. By default, the server starts on LDAP port 10389 and LDAPS port 10696.

Now you have an LDAP server up and running. Before you proceed any further, let's create a test connection to it from the Apache Directory Studio:

1. From Apache Directory Studio, go to the Connections view. If it's not there already, go to Window ➤ Show View ➤ Connections.

2. Right-click Connections View, and select New Connection.

3. In the Connection Name text box, give a name to the connection.

4. The Host Name field should point to the server where you started the LDAP server. In this case, it's `localhost`.

5. The Port field should point to the port of your LDAP server, which is 10389 in this case.

6. Keep Encryption Method set to No Encryption for the time being. Click Next.

7. Type `uid=admin,ou=system` as the Bind DN and `secret` as the Bind Password, and click Finish. These are the default Bind DN and password values for Apache Directory Server.

8. The connection you just created appears in the Connections view. Double-click it, and the data retrieved from the underlying LDAP server appears in the LDAP Browser view.

In the sections that follow, you need some users and groups in the LDAP. Let's create a user and a group. First you need to create an organizational unit (OU) structure under the `dc=example,dc=com` domain in Apache Directory Server:

1. In Apache Directory Studio, go to the LDAP browser by clicking the appropriate LDAP connection in the Connections view.

2. Right-click `dc=example,dc=com`, and choose New ➤ New Entry ➤ Create Entry From Scratch. Pick organizationalUnit from Available Object Classes, click Add, and then click Next. Select `ou` for the RDN, and give it the value `groups`. Click Next and then Finish.

3. Right-click `dc=example,dc=com`, and choose New ➤ New Entry ➤ Create Entry From Scratch. Pick organizationalUnit from Available Object Class, click Add, and then click Next. Select `ou` for the RDN, and give it the value `users`. Click Next and then Finish.

4. Right-click `dc=example,dc=com` / `ou=users`, and choose New ➤ New Entry ➤ Create Entry From Scratch. Pick inetOrgPerson from Available Object Classes, click Add, and then click Next. Select `uid` for the RDN, give it a value, and click Next. Complete the empty fields with appropriate values. Right-click the same pane, and choose New Attribute. Select userPassword as the Attribute Type, and click Finish. Enter a password, select SSHA-256 as the hashing method, and click OK.

5.   The user you created appears under dc=example,dc=com / ou=users in the LDAP browser.

6.   To create a group, right-click dc=example,dc=com / ou=groups ➤ New ➤ New Entry
      ➤ Create Entry From Scratch. Pick groupOfUniqueNames from Available Object Classes, click
      Add, and click Next. Select cn for the RDN, give it a value, and click Next. Give the DN of the
      user created in the previous step as the uniqueMember (for example,
      uid=prabath,ou=users,ou=system), and click Finish.

7.   The group you created appears under dc=example,dc=com / ou=groups in the LDAP browser.

CONNECTING APACHE TOMCAT TO APACHE DIRECTORY SERVER (LDAP)

You've already deployed the Recipe API in Apache Tomcat. Let's see how you can configure Apache Tomcat to talk
to the LDAP server you configured:

1.   Shut down the Tomcat server if it's running.

2.   By default, Tomcat finds users from the conf/tomcat-users.xml file via org.apache.
      catalina.realm.UserDatabaseRealm.

3.   Open [TOMCAT_HOME]\conf\server.xml, and comment out the following line in it:

```
<Resource
        name="UserDatabase" auth="Container"
        type="org.apache.catalina.UserDatabase"
        description="User database that can be updated and saved" factory="org.apache.
        catalina.users.MemoryUserDatabaseFactory"
        pathname="conf/tomcat-users.xml" />
```

4.   In [TOMCAT_HOME]\conf\server.xml, comment out the following line, which points to the
      UserDatabaseRealm:

```
<Realm   className="org.apache.catalina.realm.UserDatabaseRealm"
        resourceName="UserDatabase"/>
```

5.   To connect to the LDAP server, you should use JNDIRealm. Copy and paste the following
      configuration into [TOMCAT_HOME]\conf\server.xml just after <Realm className="org.
      apache.catalina.realm.LockOutRealm">:

```
<Realm   className="org.apache.catalina.realm.JNDIRealm"
        debug="99"
        connectionURL="ldap://localhost:10389"
        roleBase="ou=groups , dc=example, dc=com"
        roleSearch="(uniqueMember={0})"
        roleName="cn"
        userBase="ou=users, dc=example, dc=com"
        userSearch="(uid={0})"/>
```

SECURING AN API WITH HTTP BASIC AUTHENTICATION

The Recipe API that you deployed in Apache Tomcat is still an open API. Let's see how to secure it with HTTP Basic authentication. You want to authenticate users against the corporate LDAP and also use access control based on HTTP operations (GET, POST, DELETE, PUT):

1. Shut down the Tomcat server if it's running, and make sure connectivity to the LDAP server works correctly.

2. Open [TOMCAT_HOME]\webapps\recipe\WEB-INF\web.xml and add the following under the root element <web-app>. The security-role element at the bottom lists all the roles that are allowed to access this web application:

```
<security-constraint>
    <web-resource-collection>
        <web-resource-name>Secured Recipe API</web-resource-name>
        <url-pattern>/*</url-pattern>
    </web-resource-collection>
    <auth-constraint>
        <role-name>admin</role-name>
    </auth-constraint>
</security-constraint>

<login-config>
    <auth-method>BASIC</auth-method>
    <realm-name>cute-cupcakes.com</realm-name>
</login-config>

<security-role>
    <role-name>admin</role-name>
</security-role>
```

This configuration will protect the complete Recipe API from unauthenticated access attempts. A legitimate user should have an account in the corporate LDAP and also should be in the admin group. If you don't have a group called admin, change the configuration appropriately.

3. You can further enable fine-grained access control to the Recipe API by HTTP operation. You need to have a <security-constraint> for each scenario. The following two blocks will let any user belonging to the admin group perform GET/POST/PUT/DELETE on the Recipe API, whereas a user belonging to the user group can only do a GET. When you define an http-method inside a web-resource-collection, only those methods are protected. The rest can be invoked by anyone if no other security constraint has any restrictions on those methods. For example, if you only had the second block, then any user would be able to do a POST. Because you have the first block that controls POST, only allowed users can do it. The security-role element at the bottom lists all the roles that are allowed to access this web application:

```
<security-constraint>
    <web-resource-collection>
        <web-resource-name>Secured Recipe API</web-resource-name>
        <url-pattern>/*</url-pattern>
        <http-method>GET</http-method>
```

```
            <http-method>PUT</http-method>
            <http-method>POST</http-method>
            <http-method>DELETE</http-method>
        </web-resource-collection>
        <auth-constraint>
            <role-name>admin</role-name>
        </auth-constraint>
</security-constraint>

<security-constraint>
        <web-resource-collection>
            <web-resource-name>Secured Recipe API</web-resource-name>
            <url-pattern>/*</url-pattern>
            <http-method>GET</http-method>
        </web-resource-collection>
        <auth-constraint>
            <role-name>user</role-name>
        </auth-constraint>
</security-constraint>

<login-config>
        <auth-method>BASIC</auth-method>
        <realm-name>cute-cupcakes.com</realm-name>
</login-config>

<security-role>
        <role-name>admin</role-name>
        <role-name>user</role-name>
</security-role>
```

ENABLING TLS IN APACHE TOMCAT

The way you configured HTTP Basic Authentication in the previous exercise isn't secure enough. It uses HTTP to transfer credentials. Anyone who can intercept the channel can see the credentials in cleartext. Let's see how to enable TLS in Apache Tomcat and restrict access to the Recipe API only via TLS:

1. To enable TLS, first you need to have a keystore with a public/private key pair. You can create a keystore using Java keytool. It comes with the JDK distribution, and you can find it in [JAVA_HOME]\bin. The following command creates a Java keystore with the name catalina-keystore.jks:

■ **Note** JAVA_HOME refers to the directory where you've installed the JDK. To run the keytool, you must have Java installed in your system.

```
keytool   -genkey -alias localhost -keyalg RSA -keysize 1024
          -dname "CN=localhost"
          -keypass catalina123
          -keystore catalina-keystore.jks
          -storepass catalina123
```

This command uses `catalina123` as the keystore password as well as the private key password.

2. Copy `catalina-keystore.jks` to `[TOMCAT_HOME]\conf`, and add the following element to `[TOMCAT_HOME]\conf\server.xml` under the `<Service>` parent element. Replace the values of `keystoreFile` and `keystorePass` appropriately:

```
<Connector
    port="8443"
    maxThreads="200"
    scheme="https"
    secure="true"
    SSLEnabled="true"
    keystoreFile="absolute/path/to/catalina-keystore.jks"
    keystorePass="catalina123"
    clientAuth="false"
    sslProtocol="TLS"/>
```

3. Start the Tomcat server, and execute the following cURL command to validate the TLS connectivity. Make sure you replace the values of `username` and `password` appropriately. They must come from the underlying user store:

```
curl -k   -u userName:password   https://localhost:8443/recipe
```

You've configured Apache Tomcat to work with TLS. Next you should make sure the Recipe API only accepts connections over TLS.

Open `[TOMCAT_HOME]\webapps\recipe\WEB-INF\web.xml`, and add the following under each **<security-constraint>** element. This makes sure only TLS connections are allowed:

```
<user-data-constraint>
    <transport-guarantee>CONFIDENTIAL</transport-guarantee>
</user-data-constraint>
```

SECURING THE RECIPE API WITH HTTP DIGEST AUTHENTICATION

At the time of this writing, the Tomcat `JNDIRealm` that you used previously to connect to LDAP doesn't support HTTP Digest Authentication. If you need that support, you have to write your own `Realm`, extending Tomcat `JNDIRealm`, and override the `getPassword()` method. To see how to secure an API with Digest Authentication, switch back to the Tomcat `UserDatabaseRealm`:

1. Open `[TOMCAT_HOME]\conf\server.xml`, and make sure the following line is there. If you commented this out during a previous exercise, revert it back:

```
<Resource
        name="UserDatabase"
        auth="Container"
        type="org.apache.catalina.UserDatabase"
        description="User database that can be updated and saved"
        factory="org.apache.catalina.users.MemoryUserDatabaseFactory"
        pathname="conf/tomcat-users.xml" />
```

2. In `[TOMCAT_HOME]\conf\server.xml`, make sure the following line, which points to `UserDatabaseRealm`, is there. If you commented it out during a previous exercise, revert it back:

```
<Realm  className="org.apache.catalina.realm.UserDatabaseRealm"
        resourceName="UserDatabase"/>
```

3. Open `[TOMCAT_HOME]\webapps\recipe\WEB-INF\web.xml`, and add the following under the root element `<web-app>`:

```
<security-constraint>
    <web-resource-collection>
        <web-resource-name>Secured Recipe API</web-resource-name>
        <url-pattern>/* </url-pattern>
    </web-resource-collection>
    <auth-constraint>
        <role-name>admin</role-name>
    </auth-constraint>
</security-constraint>

<login-config>
    <auth-method>DIGEST</auth-method>
    <realm-name>cute-cupcakes.com</realm-name>
</login-config>

<security-role>
    <role-name>admin</role-name>
</security-role>
```

4. Open [TOMCAT_HOME]\conf\tomcat-users.xml, and add the following under the root element. This adds a role and a user to Tomcat's default file system–based user store:

    ```
    <role rolename="admin"/>
    <user username="prabath" password="prabath123" roles="admin"/>
    ```

5. Invoke the API with the cURL command shown next. The --digest -u userName:password option used here generates the password in digest mode and adds it to the HTTP request. Replace userName:password with appropriate values:

    ```
    curl -k -v --digest -u userName:password https://localhost:8443/recipe
    ```

Summary

HTTP Basic Authentication and Digest Authentication are the most-used authentication schemes for many APIs prior to the OAuth era. This chapter covered both of these authentication schemes in depth. It also discussed how to secure an API deployed in Apache Tomcat and having an Apache Directory Server user store.

In the next chapter, we are going to take a deep look into Transport Layer Security (TLS) and its applications in API security.

CHAPTER 4

■ ■ ■

Mutual Authentication with TLS

Transport Layer Security (TLS) mutual authentication, also known as client authentication or two-way Secure Socket Layer (SSL), is part of the TLS handshake process. In one-way TLS, only the server proves its identity to the client; this is mostly used in e-commerce to win consumer confidence by guaranteeing the legitimacy of the e-commerce vendor. In contrast, mutual authentication authenticates both parties—the client and the server.

Evolution of TLS

TLS has its roots in SSL. Netscape Communications introduced SSL in 1994 to build a secured channel between the Netscape browser and the web server it connects to. This was an important need at that time, just prior to the dot-com bubble. The SSL 1.0 specification was never released to the public, because it was heavily criticized for the weak crypto algorithms that were used. In November 1994, Netscape released the SSL 2.0 specification with many improvements.[1] Most of its design was done by Kipp Hickman, with much less participation from the public community. Even though it had its own vulnerabilities, it earned the trust and respect of the public as a strong protocol. The very first deployment of SSL 2.0 was in Netscape Navigator 1.1.

In January 1996, Ian Goldberg and David Wagner discovered a vulnerability in the random-number-generation logic in SSL 2.0.[2] Mostly due to US export regulations, Netscape had to weaken its encryption scheme to use 40-bit long keys. This limited all possible key combinations to a million million, which were tried by a set of researchers in 30 hours with many spare CPU cycles; they were able to recover the encrypted data.

Because SSL 2.0 was completely under the control of Netscape, Microsoft responded to its weaknesses by developing its own variant of SSL in 1995, called Private Communication Technology (PCT).[3] PCT fixed many security vulnerabilities uncovered in SSL 2.0 and simplified the SSL handshake with fewer round trips required to establish a connection.

Netscape released SSL 3.0 in 1996, and Paul Kocher was the key architect. In fact, Netscape hired Paul Kocher to work with its own Phil Karlton and Allan Freier to build SSL 3.0 from scratch. SSL 3.0 introduced a new specification language as well as a new record type and new data encoding, which made it incompatible with SSL 2.0. It fixed issues in its predecessor, introduced due to MD5 hashing. The new version used a combination of the MD5 and SHA-1 algorithms to build a hybrid hash. SSL 3.0 was the most stable of all. In 1996, Microsoft came up with a new proposal to merge SSL 3.0 and its own SSL variant PCT 2.0 to build a new standard called Secure Transport Layer Protocol (STLP).[4]

---

[1]Adam Shostack, the well-known author of *The New School of Information Security,* provides an overview of SSL 2.0 at www.homeport.org/~adam/ssl.html.

[2]Ian Goldberg and David Wagner, "Randomness and the Netscape Browser: How Secure Is the World Wide Web?" www.cs.berkeley.edu/~daw/papers/ddj-netscape.html, January 1996.

[3]Microsoft proposed PCT to the IETF in October 1995: http://tools.ietf.org/html/draft-benaloh-pct-00. This was later superseded by SSL 3.0 and TLS.

[4]"Microsoft Strawman Proposal for a Secure Transport Layer Protocol ('STLP')," http://cseweb.ucsd.edu/~bsy/stlp.ps.

Due to the interest shown by different vendors in solving the same problem in different ways, in 1996 the IETF initiated the TLS working group to standardize all vendor-specific implementations. All the major vendors, including Netscape and Microsoft, met under the chairmanship of Bruce Schneier in a series of IETF meetings to decide the future of TLS. TLS 1.0 (RFC 2246) was the result; it was released by the IETF in January 1999. The differences between TLS 1.0 and SSL 3.0 aren't dramatic, but they're significant enough that TLS 1.0 and SSL 3.0 don't interoperate. TLS 1.0 was quite stable and stayed unchanged for seven years, until 2006. In April 2006, RFC 4346 introduced TLS 1.1, which made few major changes to 1.0. Two years later, RFC 5246 introduced TLS 1.2, which is the latest at the time of this writing.

How TLS Works

In its design, TLS can be divided into two phases: the handshake and the data transfer. During the handshake phase, both client and server get to know about each other's cryptographic capabilities and establish cryptographic keys to protect the data transfer. The data transfer happens at the end of the handshake. The data is broken down into a set of records, protected with the cryptographic keys established in the first phase, and transferred between the client and the server. Figure 4-1 shows various TLS protocol layers built on top of TCP/IP.

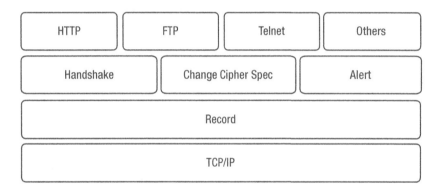

Figure 4-1. *TLS protocol layers*[5]

TLS Handshake

The client initiates the TLS handshake. Let's do a quick cURL request to https://www.google.com to observe the message flow in a TLS handshake:

```
curl -v https://www.google.com

Connected to www.google.com (74.125.128.99) port 443 (#0)
SSLv3, TLS handshake, Client hello (1):
SSLv3, TLS handshake, Server hello (2):
SSLv3, TLS handshake, CERT (11):
SSLv3, TLS handshake, Server finished (14):
SSLv3, TLS handshake, Client key exchange (16):
SSLv3, TLS change cipher, Client hello (1):
```

---

[5]A detailed description of the TLS protocol layers is available in "Overview of SSL/TLS Encryption," http://technet.microsoft.com/en-us/library/cc781476(v=ws.10).aspx, July 31, 2003.

```
SSLv3, TLS handshake, Finished (20):
SSLv3, TLS change cipher, Client hello (1):
SSLv3, TLS handshake, Finished (20):
SSL connection using RC4-SHA
Server certificate:
        subject: C=US; ST=California; L=Mountain View; O=Google Inc; CN=www.google.com
        start date: 2014-06-04 08:58:29 GMT
        expire date: 2014-09-02 00:00:00 GMT
        subjectAltName: www.google.com matched
        issuer: C=US; O=Google Inc; CN=Google Internet Authority G2
        SSL certificate verify ok.
```

■ **Note** The TLS handshake phase includes three subprotocols: the *Handshake protocol*, the *Change Cipher Spec protocol*, and the *Alert protocol*. The Handshake protocol is responsible for building an agreement between the client and the server on cryptographic keys to be used to protect the application data. Both the client and the server precede the Change Cipher Spec protocol to indicate to the other party that it's going to switch to a cryptographically secured channel for further communication. The Alert protocol is responsible for generating alerts and communicating them to the parties involved in the TLS connection. For example, the certificate_revoked alert can be generated from the client when the server certificate it receives during the TLS handshake is a revoked one.

Client hello is the first message from the client to the server. This includes the highest version of TLS it supports, a random number generated by the client, cipher suites, the compression algorithm supported by the client, and an optional session identifier. The session identifier can be used to resume an existing session rather than doing the handshake again from scratch. The TLS handshake is very CPU intensive, but with the support for session resumption, this overhead can be minimized.

■ **Note** TLS session resumption has a direct impact on performance. The master key–generation process in the TLS handshake is extremely costly. With session resumption, the same master secret from the previous session is reused. It has been proven through several academic studies that the performance enhancement resulting from TLS session resumption can be up to 20%. Session resumption also has a cost, which is mostly handled by servers. Each server has to maintain the TLS state of all its clients and also to address high-availability aspects; it needs to replicate this state across different nodes in the cluster.

Server hello is the first message from the server to the client. It includes the highest version of TLS that both the client and the server can support, a random number generated by the server, the strongest cipher suite, and the compression algorithm that both the client and the server can support. Both parties use the random numbers generated by the client and the server independently to generate the master secret. This master secret will be used later to derive encryption keys. To generate a session identifier, the server has several options. If no session identifier is included in the Client hello, the server generates a new one. Even the client includes one; but if the server can't resume that session, then once again a new identifier is generated. If the server is capable of resuming the TLS session corresponding to the session identifier specified in the Client hello, then the server includes it in the Server hello. The server may also decide not to include any session identifiers for any new sessions that it's not willing to resume in the future.

■ **Note** In the history of TLS, several attacks have been reported against the TLS handshake. Cipher suite rollback and version rollback are a couple of them. This could be a result of a man-in-the-middle attack, where the attacker intercepts the TLS handshake and downgrades either the cipher suite or the TLS version, or both. The problem was fixed from SSL 3.0 onward with the introduction of the Change Cipher Spec message. This requires both parties to share the hash of all TLS handshake messages up to the Change Cipher Spec message, exactly as each party read them. Each has to confirm that they read the messages from each other in the same way.

Once it's finished with the Server hello, the server sends its public certificate, along with other certificates, up to the root certificate authority (CA) in the certificate chain. The client must validate these certificates to accept the identity of the server. It uses the public key from the server certificate to encrypt the premaster secret key later. The *premaster key* is a shared secret between the client and the server to generate the master secret. If the public key in the server certificate isn't cable of encrypting the premaster secret key, then the TLS protocol mandates another extra step, known as the *server key exchange*. During this step, the server has to create a new key and send it to the client. Later it will be used to encrypt the premaster secret key.

If the server demands TLS mutual authentication, then the next step is for the server to request the client certificate. The client certificate request message from the server includes a list of certificate authorities trusted by the server and the type of certificate. After the last two optional steps, the server sends the Server hello done message to the client. This is an empty message that only indicates to the client that the server has completed its initial phase in the handshake.

If the server demanded the client certificate, now the client sends its public certificate along with all other certificates in the chain up to the CA required to validate the client certificate. Next would be the Client key exchange message, which includes the TLS protocol version as well as the premaster secret key. The TLS protocol version must be the same as specified in the initial Client hello message. This is a guard against any rollback attacks to force the server to use an unsecured TLS/SSL version. The premaster secret key included in the message should be encrypted with the server's public key obtained from the server certificate or with the key passed in the Server key exchange message.

The Certificate verify message is next in line. This is optional and is needed only if the server demands client authentication. The client has to sign the entire set of TLS handshake messages that have taken place so far with its private key and send the signature to the server. The server validates the signature using the client's public key, which was shared in a previous step. The signature-generation process varies depending on which signing algorithm you pick. If RSA is being used, then the hash of all the previous handshake messages is calculated with both MD5 and SHA-1. Then the concatenated hash is encrypted using the client's private key. For Digital Signature Standard (DSS), only a SHA-1 hash is used, and it's encrypted using the client's private key.

At this point, the client and the server have exchanged all the required materials to generate the master secret. The master secret is generated using the client random number, the server random number, and the premaster secret. The client now sends the Change cipher spec message. This indicates to the server that all messages generated from here onward are protected with the keys already established.

The Finished message is the last one from the client to the server. It's the hash of the complete handshake message flow. This message is hashed and encrypted using the already-established keys. Once it's received at the server end, the server also sends the Change cipher spec message. This indicates to the client that the server will start communicating with the secret keys already established. Finally, the Finished message is sent from the server. This is the same as the Finished message generated by the client and includes the hash of the complete handshake message flow encrypted by the generated cryptographic keys.

■ **Note** The research paper "Lessons Learned from Previous SSL/TLS Attacks: A Brief Chronology of Attacks and Weaknesses," by Christopher Meyer and Jorg Schwenk, explains several attacks carried out against SSL, for more than 15 years until 2013.

Application Data Transfer

After the TLS handshake phase is complete, sensitive application data can be exchanged between the client and the server using the TLS Record protocol. This protocol is responsible for breaking all outgoing messages into blocks and assembling all incoming messages. Each outgoing block is compressed, a message authentication code (MAC) is calculated, and the block is encrypted. Each incoming block is decrypted, decompressed, and MAC verified.

CRYPTOGRAPHIC KEYS IN TLS

During the TLS handshake, each side derives a master secret using the client-generated random key, the server-generated random key, and the client-generated premaster secret. The master secret is never transferred over the wire. Using the master secret, each side generates four more keys. The client uses first key to calculate the MAC for each outgoing message. The server uses the same key to validate the MAC of all incoming messages from the client. The server uses the second key to calculate the MAC for each out going message. The client uses the same key to validate the MAC of all incoming messages from the server. The client uses the third key to encrypt outgoing messages, and the server uses the same key to decrypt all incoming messages. The server uses the fourth key to encrypt outgoing messages, and the client uses the same key to decrypt all incoming messages.

■ **Note** Before you begin working on the examples in this chapter, be sure you have set up the example "Cute-Cupcake Factory: Deploying the Recipe API in Apache Tomcat," in Chapter 3.

SECURING AN API WITH TLS MUTUAL AUTHENTICATION

You've already deployed the Recipe API from the Cute-Cupcake factory in Apache Tomcat. Let's see how you can configure Apache Tomcat to secure the API with mutual authentication:

1. To enable TLS in Apache Tomcat, first you need to have a keystore with a public/private key pair. You can create a keystore using Java `keytool`, which comes with the JDK distribution and is in `[JAVA_HOM]\bin`. The following command creates a Java keystore named `catalina-keystore.jks`:

```
keytool  -genkey -alias localhost -keyalg RSA -keysize 1024
            -dname "CN=localhost"
            -keypass catalina123
            -keystore catalina-keystore.jks
            -storepass catalina123
```

This uses `catalina123` as the keystore password as well as the private key password.

2. To enable TLS mutual authentication, you also need to have a keystore to hold trusted client certificates. The following command creates a Java keystore named `catalina-truststore.jks`:

```
keytool -genkey -alias localhost -keyalg RSA -keysize 1024
        -dname "CN=localhost"
        -keypass catalina123
        -keystore catalina-truststore.jks
        -storepass catalina123
```

This uses `catalina123` as the keystore password as well as the private key password.

3. You need a key pair for the client that invokes the secured API. The following command creates a Java keystore named `client-keystore.jks`:

```
keytool -genkey -alias client -keyalg RSA -keysize 1024
                        -dname "CN=client"
                        -keypass client23
                        -keystore client-keystore.jks
                        -storepass client123
```

This uses `client123` as the keystore password as well as the private key password.

4. To ask Tomcat to trust your API client, you need to export the public certificate from `client-keystore.jks` and import it into `catalina-truststore.jks`. The following `keytool` command exports the public certificate from `client-keystore.jks` and saves it in the file `client.cert`:

```
keytool -export -file client.cert
                -keystore client-keystore.jks
                -alias client
                -storepass client123
```

5. The following `keytool` command imports the public certificate `client.cert` from the previous step into `catalina-truststore.jks`:

```
keytool -import -file client.cert
                -keystore catalina-truststore.jks
                -alias client
                -storepass catalina123
```

■ **Note** client-trustore.jks should only include the public certificates of trusted CAs. You don't need to import each and every user certificate. Every user can have a certificate signed by the trusted CA.

---

6. Copy `catalina-keystore.jks` and `catalina-truststore.jks` to `[TOMCAT_HOME]\conf`, and add the following element to `[TOMCAT_HOME]\conf\server.xml` under the `<Service>` parent element. Change the values of keystoreFile, keystorePass, truststoreFile, and truststorePass appropriately:

```
<Connector
        port="8443"
        maxThreads="200"
        scheme="https"
        secure="true"
        SSLEnabled="true"
        keystoreFile="absolute/path/to/catalina-keystore.jks"
        keystorePass="catalina123"
        truststoreFile="absolute/path/to/catalina-truststore.jks"
        truststorePass="catalina123"
        clientAuth="false"
        sslProtocol="TLS"/>
```

By setting the `clientAuth` attribute to `true`, you can enable TLS mutual authentication support at the container level in Apache Tomcat. That will affect all the APIs and web applications deployed in Tomcat. You set this to `false` here and enable it only for the Recipe API later.

7. Open `[TOMCAT_HOME]\conf\server.xml`, and make sure the following line is there. If you commented it out during a previous exercise, revert it back:

```
<Resource name="UserDatabase" auth="Container"
          type="org.apache.catalina.UserDatabase"
          description="User database that can be updated and saved"
          factory="org.apache.catalina.users.MemoryUserDatabaseFactory"
          pathname="conf/tomcat-users.xml" />
```

8. In `[TOMCAT_HOME]\conf\server.xml`, make sure the following line (which points to UserDatabaseRealm) is there. If you commented this out during a previous exercise, revert it back:

```
<Realm className="org.apache.catalina.realm.UserDatabaseRealm"
                            resourceName="UserDatabase"/>
```

9. Open `[TOMCAT_HOME]\webapps\recipe\WEB-INF\web.xml`, and add the following under the root element:

```
<security-constraint>
    <web-resource-collection>
        <web-resource-name>Secured Recipe API</web-resource-name>
        <url-pattern>/*</url-pattern>
    </web-resource-collection>
    <auth-constraint>
        <role-name>admin</role-name>
    </auth-constraint>
```

```
        <user-data-constraint>
            <transport-guarantee>CONFIDENTIAL</transport-guarantee>
        </user-data-constraint>
    </security-constraint>

    <login-config>
        <auth-method>CLIENT-CERT</auth-method>
        <realm-name>cute-cupcakes.com</realm-name>
    </login-config>

    <security-role>
        <role-name>admin</role-name>
    </security-role>
```

This configuration sets `auth-method` to `CLIENT-CERT`, which secures the Recipe API with TLS mutual authentication. Because you've set `transport-guarantee` to `CONFIDENTIAL`, no one can access the API via cleartext. It must be a confidential channel. `auth-constraint` is set to a `role-name`, which means a user authenticating with the certificate should belong to the *admin* role.

■ **Note** The `auth-constraint` `<role-name>admin</role-name>` limits API access to anyone having the role *admin*. If you want to make the API accessible to anyone who has authenticated into the system with a certificate, belonging to any role, use * for the `role-name` : `<role-name>*</role-name>`.

---

10. Open `[TOMCAT_HOME]\conf\tomcat-users.xml`, and add the following under the root element. This adds a role and a user to Tomcat's default file system–based user store. The user name is identified by the value of `Subject` in the client certificate, which in this case is CN=client:

```
<role rolename="admin"/>
<user username="CN=client" roles="admin"/>
```

INVOKING A SECURED API WITH TLS MUTUAL AUTHENTICATION VIA CURL

You've secured the Recipe API with TLS mutual authentication. Let's see how to invoke it with cURL:

1. The private key and the public key of the client should be exported from the client keystore (`client-keystore.jks`) in Privacy-enhanced Electronic Mail(PEM) format. This can be done using KeyStore Explorer.

■ **Note**   KeyStore Explorer is a free tool for Java keystore management. It runs on Windows, Mac OS, and Linux, and is available from `http://keystore-explorer.sourceforge.net/`. Before running KeyStore Explorer, you have to patch the JDK, allowing it to use much longer key lengths for encryption. To patch the JDK, download the Java Cryptography Extension (JCE) unlimited-strength jurisdiction policy files corresponding to your JDK version, and copy the two jar files in the zip file to `JAVA_HOME/lib/security` to replace the existing jar files. For Java 6, the download link is www.oracle.com/technetwork/java/javase/downloads/jce-6-download-429243.html, and for Java 7 it's www.oracle.com/technetwork/java/javase/downloads/jce-7-download-432124.html.

---

2.   Launch KeyStore Explorer, and select Open An Existing KeyStore. Point to `client-keystore.jks` to load it. KeyStore Explorer asks for the keystore password at the time of loading, which is *client123*.

3.   Right-click the available key entry, and select Export ➤ Export Private Key. Type the private key password, which is *client123*, select PKCS #8, and click OK.

4.   You can export the private key as an encrypted key or in cleartext. If you don't want the key to be encrypted, uncheck Encrypt.

5.   Be sure to check PEM, give an export file path (`client.key`), and click Export.

6.   In the same way, you can export the public key in PEM format. Right-click the available key entry, and select Export ➤ Export Public Key.

7.   Be sure to check PEM, give an export file path (`client.cert`), and click Export.

8.   You've exported both the public and private keys. Concatenate them into a single file, and name that file `client.cert`. In Linux/Unix/Mac, you can use the following command from the shell:

```
cat client.cert client.key > client.pem
```

9.   You're all set. Use the following cURL command to invoke the API. –k is used here to accept any server certificate. Otherwise, you have to specify the CA certificate corresponding to the server's public certificate. --cert specifies the concatenated public and private keys of the client:

```
curl  -k --cert client.pem  https://localhost:8443/recipe
```

■ **Note**   PKCS is a set of standards for public-key cryptography that focuses on 15 areas, from PKCS #1 to PKCS #15. PKCS #8 talks about syntax for keeping private-key information in a standard manner, and PKCS #12 talks about an archive file format to keep multiple cryptographic elements, such as private keys and X.509 certificates, in a single file. A summary of the PKCS standards is available at `http://coitweb.uncc.edu/~yonwang/papers/pkcs.pdf`.

JKS VS. PKCS #12

Java KeyStore (JKS) and PKCS #12 are two types of popular keystore formats. A *keystore* in general is a container for certificates and private keys. JKS is a Java-specific keystore format, mostly used by application servers written in Java, such as Apache Tomcat. PKCS #12 keystores are mostly used by the Apache web server and tools built on top of Microsoft technologies. PKCS #12 keystores carry the extension `.p12` or `.pfx`. JKS is language dependent, whereas PKCS #12 is language neutral.

Java `keytool` supports both types of keystores. To convert a JKS keystore to a PKCS #12 keystore, use the following `keytool` command:

```
keytool -importkeystore
        -srckeystore client-keystore.jks -srcstoretype jks -srcstorepass client123
        -destkeystore client-keystore.p12 -deststoretype pkcs12 -deststorepass client123
```

ENCODING RULES

Abstract Station Notation One (ASN.1) is a standard that provides a set of notations for encoding/decoding and transmitting data over communication networks. The X.690 standard specifies a set of ASN.1 encoding rules: Basic Encoding Rules (BER), Distinguished Encoding Rules (DER), and Canonical Encoding Rules (CER). When you export a public certificate from a Java keystore, by default it is a DER-encoded file:

```
keytool -export -file client.cert -keystore client-keystore.jks -alias client -storepass
client123
```

`client.cert` is the DER-encoded X.509 certificate. It can be viewed using KeyStore Explorer. PEM is the Base64-encoded DER. Do the following to convert the DER-encoded certificate into PEM or ANS.1:

1. Launch KeyStore Explorer, and select Examine Certificate. Point to `client.cert` to load it.

2. To convert the DER-encoded certificate into PEM or ANS.1, click the appropriate button.

REVERSE-ENGINEERING TLS

For each session, TLS creates a master secret and derives four keys from it for hashing and encryption. What if the private key of the server leaked out? If all the data transferred between clients and the server is being recorded, can it be decrypted? Yes, it can. If the TLS handshake is recorded, you can decrypt the premaster secret if you know the server's private key. Then, using the client-generated random number and the server-generated random number, you can derive the master secret—and then the other four keys. Using these keys, you can decrypt the entire set of recorded conversations.

Using perfect forward secrecy (PFS) can prevent this. With PFS, just as in TLS, a session key is generated, but the session key can't later be derived back from the server's master secret. This eliminates the risk of losing the confidentiality of the data if a private key leaks out. To add support for PFS, both the server and the client participating in the TLS handshake should support a cipher suite with ephemeral Diffie-Hellman (DHE) or the elliptic-curve variant (ECDHE).

■ **Note**   Google enabled forward secrecy for Gmail, Google+, and Search in November 2011.

CONFIGURING APACHE TOMCAT FOR PERFECT FORWARD SECRECY

In this exercise, we will be configuring Apache Tomcat to support perfect forward secrecy with the following steps:

1. Open [TOMCAT_HOME]\conf\server.xml, and find the following Connector configuration for HTTPS. If you don't see this section, follow the exercise "Securing an API with TLS Mutual Authentication" earlier in this chapter:

   ```
   <Connector
           port="8443"
           maxThreads="200"
           scheme="https"
           secure="true"
           SSLEnabled="true"
           keystoreFile="absolute path to catalina-keystore.jks"
           keystorePass="catalina123"
           truststoreFile="absolute path to catalina-truststore.jks"
           truststorePass="catalina123"
           clientAuth="false"
           sslProtocol="TLS"/>
   ```

2. To enable PFS support in Tomcat, you need to configure the appropriate cipher suite and disable all other weak cipher suites. Add the following cipher suite and protocol as attributes to the Tomcat HTTPS Connector configuration. TLS in the name of the protocol suite says to use TLS. ECDHE specifies elliptic curve Diffie-Hellman with ephemeral keys as the key agreement protocol. ECDSA is the elliptic curve digital signature algorithm used during the TLS handshake. AES_128_CBC uses AES as the symmetric encryption algorithm with 128-bit cipher-block chaining to encrypt application data. SHA is the hashing algorithm:

   ```
   ciphers="TLS_ECDHE_ECDSA_WITH_AES_128_CBC_SHA256"
   protocol="org.apache.coyote.http11.Http11NioProtocol"
   ```

3. You need to create a new keystore with a compatible key algorithm. If you're on Oracle JDK 1.6_*, you need to install a crypto provider that supports elliptic curve encryption. Download the Bouncycastle crypto provider from www.bouncycastle.org/download/ bcprov-ext-jdk15on-150.jar, and copy it to JAVA_HOME/lib/ext. Then add the following entry to JAVA_HOME/lib/security/java.security file. Replace the value of N appropriately; it has to be a number:

   ```
   security.provider.N=org.bouncycastle.jce.provider.BouncyCastleProvider
   ```

▪ **Note** SSL debugging can be enabled in Tomcat 7 by adding the entry `javax.net.debug=all` to the
`CATALINA_HOME/conf/catalina.properties` file.

---

4. To generate a keystore with the elliptic curve key algorithm, use the following `keytool`
   command, and replace the current Tomcat keystore file with the new one. Here you're using
   `EC` as the `keyalg`:

```
keytool  -genkey -alias localhost
                 -keyalg EC
                 -keysize 256
                 -dname "CN=localhost"
                 -keypass catalina123
                 -keystore catalina-keystore.jks
                 -storepass catalina123
```

5. By default, cURL doesn't include `TLS_ECDHE_ECDSA_WITH_AES_128_CBC_SHA256` as a cipher
   suite in its `Client hello`. This can be forcefully included via the `--ciphers` parameter.

```
curl  -k --cert client.pem  -v
         --ciphers TLS_ECDHE_ECDSA_WITH_AES_128_CBC_SHA256 https://localhost:8443
```

▪ **Note** Qualys SSL Labs provides a free online service to analyze the SSL configuration of a given public web site.
It's available at `https://www.ssllabs.com/ssltest/analyze.html`.

Summary

TLS mutual authentication is a strong form of client authentication. This chapter focused on building a foundation
related to TLS and its evolution. The later part of the chapter explained how to secure an API deployed in Apache
Tomcat with TLS mutual authentication.

In the next chapter, we will take a deeper look at distinct identity delegation models, which laid the path to the
popular OAuth 2.0 standard.

CHAPTER 5

Identity Delegation

Identity delegation plays a key role in enterprise security. You could be the owner but not the direct consumer of the API. There may be a third party who wants to access it on your behalf. Sharing credentials with a third party who wants to access a resource you own on your behalf is an anti-pattern. Most web-based applications and APIs developed prior to 2006 utilized credential sharing to facilitate identity delegation. Post-2006, many vendors started developing their own proprietary ways to address this concern without credential sharing. Yahoo BBAuth, Google AuthSub, and Flickr Authentication are some of the implementations that became popular.

Any identity-delegation model has three main roles: *delegator*, *delegate*, and *service provider*. The delegator owns the resource and is also known as the *resource owner*. The delegate wants to access a service on behalf of the delegator. The delegator delegates a limited set of privileges to the delegate to access the service. The service provider hosts the protected service and validates the legitimacy of the delegate. The service provider is also known as the *resource server*.

Direct Delegation vs. Brokered Delegation

Let's take a step back and look at a real-world example (see Figure 5-1). Flickr is a popular cloud-based service for storing and sharing photos. Photos stored in Flickr are the resources, and Flickr is the resource server or the service provider. Say you have a Flickr account: you're the resource owner (or the delegator) of the photos under your account. You also have a Snapfish account. Snapfish is a web-based photo-sharing and photo-printing service that is owned by Hewlett-Packard. How can you print your Flickr photos from Snapfish? To do so, Snapfish has to first import those photos. To do that, Snapfish should have the following privileges, which should be delegated to Snapfish by you. You're the delegator, and Snapfish is the delegate. Other than the allowed actions, Snapfish won't be able to do anything with your Flickr photos (such as delete them).

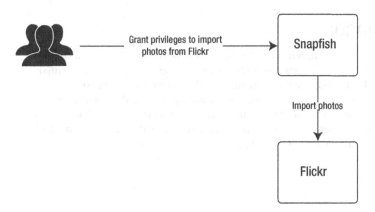

Figure 5-1. *Direct delegation*

- Access your Flickr account (including private content)

- Upload, edit, and replace photos and videos in the account

- Interact with other members' photos and videos (comment, add notes, favorite)

Snapfish can now access your Flickr account on your behalf with the delegated privileges. This model is called *direct delegation*: the delegator directly delegates a subset of his or her privileges to a delegate. The other model is called *indirect delegation*: the delegator first delegates to an intermediate delegate, and that delegate delegates to another delegate. This is also known as *brokered delegation* (see Figure 5-2).

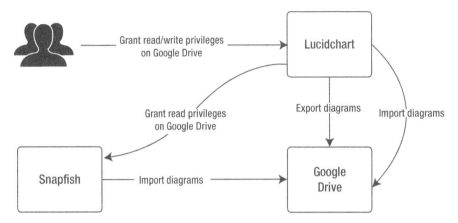

Figure 5-2. Brokered delegation

Let's say you have a Lucidchart account. Lucidchart is a cloud-based design tool that you can use to draw a wide variety of diagrams. It also integrates with Google Drive. From your Lucidchart account, you have the option to publish completed diagrams to your Google Drive. To do that, Lucidchart needs privileges to access the Google Drive API on your behalf, and you need to delegate the relevant permissions to Lucidchart. If you want to print something from Lucidchart, it invokes the Snapfish printing API. Snapfish needs to access the diagrams stored in your Google Drive. Lucidchart has to delegate a subset of the permissions you delegated to it, to Snapfish. Even though you granted read/write permissions to Lucidchart, it only has to delegate read permission to Snapfish to access your Google Drive and print the selected drawing.

Evolution of Identity Delegation

The modern history of identity delegation can be divided into two eras: pre-2006 and post-2006. Credential sharing mostly drove identity delegation prior to 2006. Twitter, SlideShare, and almost all web applications used credential sharing to access third-party APIs. As shown in Figure 5-3, when you created a Twitter account prior to 2006, Twitter asked for your e-mail account credentials so it could access your e-mail address book and invite your friends to join Twitter. Interestingly, it displayed the message "We don't store your login, your password is submitted securely, and we don't email without your permission" to win user confidence. But who knows—if Twitter wanted to read all your e-mails or do whatever it wanted to your e-mail account, it could have done so quite easily.

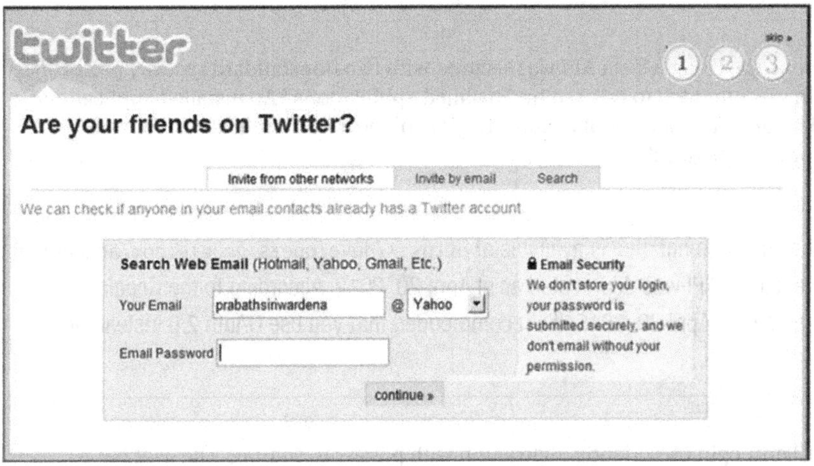

Figure 5-3. *Twitter, pre-2006*

SlideShare did the same thing. SlideShare is a cloud-based service for hosting and sharing slides. Prior to 2006, if you wanted to publish a slide deck from SlideShare to a Blogger blog, you had to give your Blogger username and password to SlideShare, as shown in Figure 5-4. SlideShare used Blogger credentials to access its API to post the selected slide deck to your blog. If SlideShare had wanted to, it could have modified published blog posts, removed them, and so on.

Figure 5-4. *SlideShare, pre-2006*

These are just two examples. The pre-2006 era was full of such applications. Google Calendar, introduced in April 2006, followed a similar approach. Any third-party application that wanted to create an event in your Google Calendar first had to request your Google credentials and use them to access the Google Calendar API. This wasn't tolerable in the Internet community, and Google was pushed to invent a new and, of course, better way of securing its APIs. Google AuthSub was introduced toward the end of 2006 as a result. This was the start of the post-2006 era of identity delegation.

Google ClientLogin

In the very early stages of its deployment, the Google Data API was secured with two nonstandard security protocols: ClientLogin and AuthSub. ClientLogin was intended to be used by "installed applications." An installed application can vary from a simple desktop application to a mobile application—but it can't be a web application. For web applications, the recommended way was to use AuthSub.

■ **Note** The complete Google ClientLogin documentation is available at https://developers.google.com/accounts/docs/AuthForInstalledApps. The ClientLogin API was deprecated as of April 20, 2012. According to the Google deprecation policy, it will operate the same until April 20, 2015. It's recommended that you use OAuth 2.0 instead of ClientLogin, where appropriate.

As shown in Figure 5-5, Google ClientLogin uses identity delegation with password sharing. The user has to supply their Google credentials to the installed application in the first step. Then the installed application creates a request token out of the credentials, and it calls the Google Accounts Authorization service. After the validation, a CAPTCHA challenge is sent back as the response. The user must respond to the CAPTCHA and is validated again against the Google Accounts Authorization service. Once the user is validated successfully, a token is issued to the application. Then the application can use the token to access Google services.

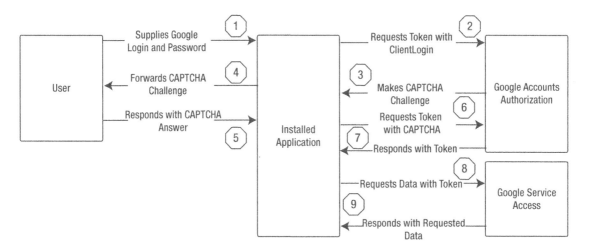

Figure 5-5. *Google ClientLogin*

■ **Note** Some of the APIs used in this chapter could be deprecated or retired by the time you try them. One of the objectives of this chapter is to provide a comprehensive overview of the evolution of API security; hence, those examples are included. Knowing the history will definitely help you design in the future.

GOOGLE CLIENTLOGIN WITH CURL

In this example, you invoke the Google Calendar API with a token obtained via Google ClientLogin. Once you know the Google username and the corresponding password of the end user, you can execute the following cURL command:

```
curl https://www.google.com/accounts/ClientLogin
    -d "accountType=GOOGLE"
    -d "Email=siriwardena.prabath@gmail.com"
    -d "Passwd=mypassword"
    -d "service=cl"
    -d "source=api-security-book"
```

Each Google service has its own identifier. In the previous cURL command, you're using cl, for the Google Calendar service. The value of the source attribute can be anything—and it's used only for logging purposes. As the response to the cURL command, you get the following:

```
SID=DQAAANEAAAADjFMd_40nS-9L363Js1cN7kh5_ZnPSVCKQ8efFk
    ndPQ4vVwJrEMWrdHcDD3MBcNlPx6FFThBpeAWjbZ3vyP

LSID=DQAAANQAAAAhJOFgebk3sC77NAvcxuGZXAKcNoGhqqu9e1I3e
    Cbw063zV-2EX1gwWbz8xYMXySvV_Mq320goUKjLS4hWmHSnM
    l6pje2BKVOLZgoEpr89iQ-

Auth=DQAAANMAAAAhJOFgebk3sC77NAvcxuGZXAKcNoGhqqu9e1I3e
    Cbw063zV-2EX1gwWbz8xYMXySvV_Mq320goUKjLS4hWmHSn8_
    R9OdKbZyhF2FcpHiaZmOm5dmBy2
```

This response includes three tokens: SID, LSID, and Auth. Auth token should be used with all the API calls. The other two aren't active—you can ignore them for the moment.

Before you can use the Auth token to invoke the Google Calendar API, the installed application must have an API project created in Google. To create an API project, follow these steps:

1. Go to https://code.google.com/apis/console/. If this is your first time, you get a welcome message; click Continue.

2. Click APIs and Auth.

3. Click the Off button by Calendar API to switch it on.

4. Click APIs and Auth ➤ Credentials.

5. Click Public API Access ➤ Create New Key ➤ Server Key ➤ Create.

6. Copy the value of the API key.

■ **Note** Creating an API project in Google or registering the installed application to obtain an API key is not a must. Google allows nonregistered applications to use its APIs—but it has a very low daily rate limit. If you want to obtain a higher quota, you need to register your application.

To access an API on behalf of the end user, the installed application needs two tokens: `Auth` and the API key:

```
curl -H "Authorization : GoogleLogin
            auth=DQAAANMAAAAhJOFgesdsdWeNAvcxuGZXAKcNo
                Ghqqu9e1I3eCbwO63zV2EX1gwWbz8xYMXySvV_M
                q32OgOUKjwEdWmHSn8_R9OdKbZyhF2FcpHiaZmOm5dmBy2"
            https://www.googleapis.com/calendar/v3/users/me/calendarList?
            key=AIzaSewBhq7Pewzxk4kXzN_lyAx72WIX7wKGWF4
```

The `Auth` token should be set in the HTTP Authorization header with the prefix `GoogleLogin`. The API key goes in the query parameters with the identifier key. The previous command returns the following JSON response:

```
{
 "kind": "calendar#calendarList",
 "etag": "\"-kteSF26GsdKQ5bfmcd4H3_-u3g/BGBvKnAdZF_NzImEmH7Eq1FIK8Q\"",
 "items": [
  {
   "kind": "calendar#calendarListEntry",
   "etag": "\"-kteSF26GsdKQ5bfmcd4H3_-u3g/XWbZkPYJb1_3zLlJugl9SxzKPRU\"",
   "id": "siriwardena.prabath@gmail.com",
   "summary": "Prabath Siriwardena",
   "timeZone": "Asia/Colombo",
   "colorId": "17",
   "backgroundColor": "#9a9cff",
   "foregroundColor": "#000000",
   "selected": true,
   "accessRole": "owner",
   "defaultReminders": [
    {
     "method": "sms",
     "minutes": 30
    },
    {
     "method": "popup",
     "minutes": 30
    }
   ],
   "primary": true
  }
 ]
}
```

■ **Note** The complete reference for the Google Calendar API is available at
https://developers.google.com/google-apps/calendar/v3/reference/.

Google AuthSub

Google AuthSub was the recommended authentication protocol to access Google APIs via web applications in the post-2006 era. Unlike ClientLogin, AuthSub doesn't require credential sharing. Users don't need to provide credentials for a third-party web application—instead, the application provides credentials directly to Google, along with a temporary token with a limited set of privileges. The third-party application uses the temporary token to access Google APIs. Figure 5-6 explains the protocol flow in detail.

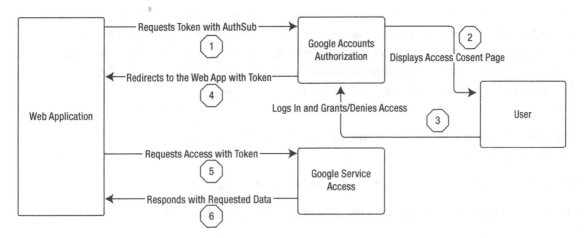

Figure 5-6. *Google AuthSub*

The end user initiates the protocol flow by visiting the web application. The web application redirects the user to the Google Accounts Authorization service with an AuthSub request. Google notifies the user of the access rights requested by the application, and the user can approve the request by logging in. Once approved by the user, Google Accounts Authorization service provides a temporary token to the web application. Now the web application can use that temporary token to access Google APIs.

■ **Note**   The complete Google AuthSub documentation is available at https://developers.google.com/accounts/ docs/AuthSub. How to use AuthSub with the Google Data API is explained at https://developers.google.com/gdata/ docs/auth/authsub. The AuthSub API was deprecated as of April 20, 2012. According to the Google deprecation policy, it will operate the same until April 20, 2015. It's recommended that you use OAuth 2.0 instead of AuthSub, where appropriate.

GOOGLE AUTHSUB WITH CURL

In this example, you invoke the Google Calendar API from a token obtained via Google AuthSub. Before proceeding any further, make sure you've created an API project in Google and have an API key readily available for your application, as explained in the previous exercise.

The first step in AuthSub is to redirect the user to the Google Accounts Authorization service to get a token authorized by the end user. Usually this must be initiated by a web application. Because you're using cURL here, you use a workaround.

Copy and paste the following URL in the browser, replacing the value of **key** with your API key value:

```
http://google.com/accounts/AuthSubRequest?
            next=http://mywebapp/&
            scope=http://www.google.com/calendar/feeds/default/allcalendars/full&
            session=1&secure=0&
            key=AIzaSyDGmwx3sMDkxAJfpk9Rqv3yW5fD1ftbcSM
```

> ■ **Note**   Each Google service defines its own set of scopes. A *scope* is a way of reducing /limiting access to a service. At the time the end user grants access to a service, access rights are only granted to the requested scope by the third-party application. The current exercise uses the scope `http://www.google.com/calendar/feeds/default/allcalendars/full`, which restricts API access to the `allcalendars/full` feed.

You're prompted to log in to Google and authorize the request. Once authorized, you're redirected to `http://mywebaap` on browser:

```
http://mywebapp/?token=1%2FVv7CI1DjmFjtcoPbx7eatWpuO2vEVBY4n3DyZ-tcqWY
```

Copy the value of `token`, and decode it with a URL decoder. Keep the decoded value of the token—you'll need it in the future.

> ■ **Note**   An online URL Decoder is available at `http://meyerweb.com/eric/tools/dencoder/`.

The token you got in the previous step is a short-lived, single-use token. You need to exchange it for a session token. Use the following cURL command to exchange the token for a session token:

```
curl -H "Authorization : AuthSub
        token=1/zeWLOQENk6PL49NOUoypvmTZvChq4KOgT8g9ajVWKsU"
        https://www.google.com/accounts/AuthSubSessionToken?
        key=AIzaSyDGmwx3sMDkxAJfpk9Rqv3yW5fD1ftbcSM
```

Here you have the decoded token in the HTTP Authorization header, prefixed with `AuthSub`. As in the previous case, you also need to specify the application's API key as a query parameter. This returns the session token in the response:

```
Token=1/N9oTDOX3si1bCsRKhvRmbX-HuRclCKeGOEsr951tFsA
```

Now you can use the session token to access the Google Calendar API. The value of the token is added to the HTTP Authorization header, prefixed with `AuthSub`. You also need to specify the application's API key as a query parameter:

```
curl -H "Authorization : AuthSub
        token=1/N9oTDOX3si1bCsRKhvRmbX-HuRclCKeGOEsr951tFsA"
        https://www.googleapis.com/calendar/v3/users/me/calendarList?
        key=AIzaSyDGmwx3sMDkxAJfpk9Rqv3yW5fD1ftbcSM
```

This returns the following JSON response:

```json
{
 "kind": "calendar#calendarList",
 "etag": "\"-kteSF26GsdKQ5bfmcd4H3_-u3g/BGBvKnAdZF_NzImEmH7Eq1FIK8Q\"",
 "items": [
  {
   "kind": "calendar#calendarListEntry",
   "etag": "\"-kteSF26GsdKQ5bfmcd4H3_-u3g/XWbZkPYJb1_3zLlJugl9SxzKPRU\"",
   "id": "siriwardena.prabath@gmail.com",
   "summary": "Prabath Siriwardena",
   "timeZone": "Asia/Colombo",
   "colorId": "17",
   "backgroundColor": "#9a9cff",
   "foregroundColor": "#000000",
   "selected": true,
   "accessRole": "owner",
   "defaultReminders": [
    {
     "method": "sms",
     "minutes": 30
    },
    {
     "method": "popup",
     "minutes": 30
    }
   ],
   "primary": true
  }
 ]
}
```

Flickr Authentication API

Flickr is a popular image/video hosting service owned by Yahoo!. Flickr was launched in 2004 (before the acquisition by Yahoo! in 2005), and toward 2005 it exposed its services via a public API. It was one of the very few companies at that time that had a public API; this was even before the Google Calendar API. Flickr was one of the very few applications that followed an identity delegation model without credential sharing prior to 2006. Most of the implementations that came after that were highly influenced by the Flickr Authentication API. Unlike in Google AuthSub or ClientLogin, the Flickr model was signature based. Each request should be signed by the application from its application secret.

FLICKR AUTHENTICATION API WITH CURL

In this example, you invoke a Flickr API on behalf of a user and get information about the user's photos stored in Flickr. The API is invoked with a token obtained via the Flickr Authentication API.

First you need to create a Flickr app:

1. Go to `www.flickr.com/services/apps/create/noncommercial/`, provide the appropriate information, and submit.

2. Note the key and the secret generated for your application.

3. Go to `www.flickr.com/services/apps`, and click the link to the application you just created.

4. Click the Edit link, provide `http://mywebapp` as the Callback URL, and save the changes.

5. To access a Flickr API on behalf of a user, you need to obtain a token from Flickr that is authorized by the user. Copy and paste the following URL into the browser; it redirects you to Flickr, and there you can log in and authorize the app. The URL only requests read access to your Flickr account. Replace the value of `api_key` with the value of the key you got for your Flickr application:

   ```
   http://www.flickr.com/services/auth/?
       api_key=96b77823e5006334db4374785659d287&
       perms=read&
       api_sig=8E356554D9F885DC8346CED4982A46BE
   ```

The value of `api_sig` is calculated in the following manner:

Put all query parameters in ascending order (except `api_sig`):

`api_key=96b77823e5006334db4374785659d287&perms=read`

Remove all & signs and = signs:

`api_key96b77823e5006334db4374785659d287permsread`

Append the value of the Flickr application secret at the beginning:

`186d6af54ad46ca0api_key96b77823e5006334db4374785659d287permsread`

Calculate the MD5 of the previous string: that is the value of `api_sign`.

■ **Note** You can calculate the MD5/SHA1/SHA-256 of a given string or file from `http://onlinemd5.com/`.

---

6. Once you authorize the app, Flickr redirects you to the callback URL associated with your application, with a temporary single-use token:

   `http://mywebapp/?frob=72157641727374043-d603b924a9cb2447-45865350`

   Copy the value of `frob`, and decode it with a URL decoder. Keep the decoded value of the token—you'll need it in the future.

7. Now you need to exchange this token for a session token:

```
curl http://flickr.com/services/rest
          -d "api_key=96b77823e5006334db4374785659d287"
          -d "frob=72157641727236925-29a09296309f597e-45865350"
          -d "method=flickr.auth.getToken"
          -d "api_sig=08CED6B68FA49C13A9D3E21CB6F97AC6"
```

Replace the value of api_key with the value of the key you got for your Flickr application, replace the value of frob with the decoded value of frob obtained in the previous step, and set the method to flickr.auth.getToken.

The value of api_sig needs to be calculated the same way as before:

Order all query parameters in ascending order (except api_sig):

```
api_key=96b77823e5006334db4374785659d287&
frob=72157641727236925-29a09296309f597e-45865350&
method=flickr.auth.getToken
```

Remove all & signs and = signs (no line breaks):

```
api_key96b77823e5006334db4374785659d287
frob72157641727236925-29a09296309f597
e-45865350methodflickr.auth.getToken
```

Append the value of the Flickr application secret at the beginning (no line breaks):

```
186d6af54ad46ca0
api_key96b77823e5006334db4374785659d287
frob72157641727236925-29a09296309f597
e-45865350methodflickr.auth.getToken
```

Calculate the MD5 of this string: that is the value of api_sign.

The previous cURL request returns the following response. Copy the value of token, which you use in the next step:

```
<rsp stat="ok">
<auth>
    <token>72157641727374033-f3a12f2cb198cfda</token>
    <perms>read</perms>
    <user nsid="45910672@N06" username="prabathsiriwardena" fullname="Prabath Siriwardena" />
</auth>
</rsp>
```

Now you're all set to access the Flickr API. Use the following cURL command, and replace the values appropriately. api_key is the value of the key you got for your Flickr application. The value of auth_token is the token you obtained in the previous step. The method has to be `flickr.activity.userPhotos`, and `api_sig` should be calculated in the same way as you did before:

```
curl http://flickr.com/services/rest
         -d "api_key=96b77823e5006334db4374785659d287"
         -d "auth_token=72157641727374033-f3a12f2cb198cfda"
         -d "method=flickr.activity.userPhotos"
         -d "api_sig=A34696A187E477BE0F875E1EB5DE14E2"
```

This cURL request returns the following response:

```
<rsp stat="ok">
<items page="1" pages="0" perpage="10" total="0" />
</rsp>
```

▪ **Note** `flickr.activity.userPhotos` returns the list of activities on photos belonging to the corresponding user. The complete Flickr API specification is available at `www.flickr.com/services/api/`.

Yahoo! Browser-Based Authentication (BBAuth)

Yahoo! BBAuth was launched in September 2006 as a generic way of granting third-party applications access to Yahoo! data with a limited set of privileges. Yahoo! photos and Yahoo Mail were the first two services to support BBAuth. BBAuth, like Google AuthSub, borrowed the same concept used in Flickr (see Figure 5-7).

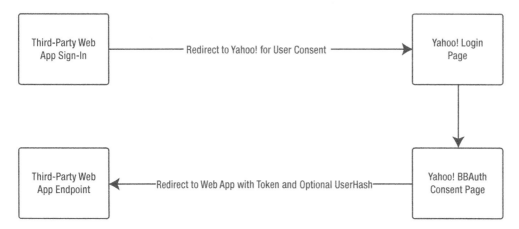

Figure 5-7. *Yahoo! BBAuth*

The user first initiates the flow by visiting the third-party web application. The web application redirects the user to Yahoo!, where user has to log in and approve the access request from the third-party application. Once approved by the user, Yahoo! redirects the user to the web application with a temporary token. Now the third-party web application can use the temporary token to access the user's data in Yahoo! with limited privileges.

▪ **Note** A complete guide to Yahoo! BBAuth is available at `http://developer.yahoo.com/bbauth/`.

YAHOO! BBAUTH WITH CURL

This exercise shows you how to invoke Yahoo! data APIs from a token obtained via Yahoo! BBAuth. First you need to create a BBAuth application at the following URL. During the registration process, you must also confirm ownership of the domain where you're going to host your application:

```
https://developer.apps.yahoo.com/wsregapp/
```

Once you complete the registration flow, go to `https://developer.apps.yahoo.com/projects`. Under the application you just created are an application ID and a shared secret:

```
Your application id is RbISImHIkYOTFeGwcaIPqhco42xvVQQr66Dz.H95SufRHA–
Your shared secret is dc214c1a0f6bcf0163038109fb32a536
```

To obtain the BBAuth token, the third-party web application has to redirect the user to the following Yahoo! URL. This request must be initiated from the confirmed domain name:

```
https://api.login.yahoo.com/WSLogin/V1/wslogin?
    appid=RbISImHIkYOTFeGwcaIPqhco42xvVQQr66Dz.H95SufRHA--&
    ts=1393746700 dc214c1a0f6bcf0163038109fb32a536&
    sig=92B453643462AD71AB32B5DB829FDEDC
```

`appid` is the application ID you obtained after registration, and `ts` is the timestamp in seconds since January 1, 1970 GMT. The signature is calculated in the following manner:

```
sig= MD5 ("/WSLogin/V1/wslogin?appid=application_id&ts=timestamp" + secret);
```

For example:

```
sig= MD5 ("/WSLogin/V1/wslogin?
    appid=RbISImHIkYOTFeGwcaIPqhco42xvVQQr66Dz.H95SufRHA--&
    ts=1393746700" + "dc214c1a0f6bcf0163038109fb32a536");
```

Once the end user has confirmed that they want to share permissions with the third-party application, Yahoo! returns a token that is valid for 14 days in its response to the web application.

To invoke Yahoo! data APIs on behalf of the user, the third-party application has to exchange the token it obtained in the previous step for an `auth` cookie and a Web Service Session Identifier (WSSID).

The following cURL command gets you back the `auth` cookie and the corresponding WSSID in the response:

```
curl -G https://api.login.yahoo.com/WSLogin/V1/wspwtoken_login?
    appid= RbISImHIkYOTFeGwcaIPqhco42xvVQQr66Dz.H95SufRHA--&
    ts=1393748700&
    token=EKEaFUMk4DdfbBcgMWESUw70JGIdHWVRbpqYItcM--&
    sig=8f43ccb0eea8a7676cd4a16891f84e7b
```

`appid` is the application ID you obtained after registration, and `ts` is the timestamp in seconds since January 1, 1970 GMT. The signature is calculated in the following manner:

```
sig= MD5 ("/WSLogin/V1/ wspwtoken_login?
    appid=application_id&
    token=token_value&ts=timestamp" + secret);
```

For example:

```
sig= MD5 ("/WSLogin/V1/wslogin?
    appid=RbISImHIkYoTFeGwcaIPqhcO42xvVQQr66Dz.H95SufRHA--&
    token=EKEaFUMk4DdfbBcgMWESUw7OJGIdHWVRbpqYItcM--&
    ts=1393746700" + "dc214c1a0f6bcf0163038109fb32a536");
```

This returns the `auth` cookie and the corresponding WSSID in the response as an XML message. To invoke a Yahoo! business service on behalf of the user, the application ID and the WSSID should be passed as query parameters, and the `auth` cookie must be set as the HTTP `Cookie` header:

```
curl -H "Cookie:Y=DsdeHjhjdsdskDdsdseDWdet"
    -d @soap-reuqest.xml https://someservice.yahooapis.com/webservice?&
    appid= RbISImHIkYoTFeGwcaIPqhcO42xvVQQr66Dz.H95SufRHA-&
    WSSID=jsdaklj9a
```

■ **Note** Complete documentation for the Yahoo! BBAuth authentication protocol is available at `http://developer.yahoo.com/bbauth/user.html`. Documentation for making authenticated service calls is available at `http://developer.yahoo.com/bbauth/authcalls.html`.

Google AuthSub, Yahoo BBAuth, Flickr Authentication all made considerable contributions to initiate a dialog to build a common standardized delegation model. OAuth 1.0 was the first step toward identity delegation standardization. The roots of OAuth go back to November 2006, when Blaine Cook started developing an OpenID implementation for Twitter. In parallel, Larry Halff of Magnolia (a social bookmarking site) was thinking about integrating an authorization model with OpenID (around this time, OpenID began gaining more traction in the Web 2.0 community). Larry started discussing the use of OpenID for Magnolia with Twitter and found out there is no way to delegate access to Twitter APIs through OpenID. Blaine and Larry, together with Chris Messina, DeWitt Clinton, and Eran Hammer, started a discussion group in April 2007 to build a standardized access-delegation protocol—which later became OAuth. The access-delegation model proposed in OAuth 1.0 wasn't drastically different from what Google, Yahoo, and Flickr already had.

■ **Note** OpenID is a standard developed by the OpenID Foundation for decentralized single sign-on. The OpenID 2.0 final specification is available at `http://openid.net/specs/openid-authentication-2_0.html`.

The OAuth 1.0 core specification was released in December 2007. Later, in 2008, during the 73rd Internet Engineering Task Force (IETF) meeting, a decision was made to develop OAuth under the IETF. Although it took sometime to be established in the IETF, OAuth 1.0a was released as a community specification in June 2009 to fix a security issue related to a session-fixation attack. In April 2010, OAuth 1.0 was released as RFC 5849 under the IETF. Chapter 6 talks about OAuth 1.0 in detail.

■ **Note**　The OAuth 1.0 community specification is available at `http://oauth.net/core/1.0/`, and 1.0a is at `http://oauth.net/core/1.0a/`.

In November 2009, during the Internet Identity Workshop (IIW), Dick Hardt of Microsoft, Brian Eaton of Google, and Allen Tom of Yahoo! presented a new draft specification for access delegation. It was called Web Resource Authorization Profiles (WRAP), and it was built on top of the OAuth 1.0 model to address some of its limitations. In December 2009, WRAP was deprecated in favor of OAuth 2.0. Chapter 6 discusses WRAP in detail.

■ **Note**　The WRAP specification contributed to the IETF OAuth working group is available at `http://tools.ietf.org/html/draft-hardt-oauth-01`.

While OAuth was being developed under the OAuth community and the IETF working group, the OpenID community also began to discuss a model to integrate OAuth with OpenID. This effort, initiated in 2009, was called OpenID/OAuth hybrid extension. This extension describes how to embed an OAuth approval request into an OpenID authentication request to allow combined user approval. For security reasons, the OAuth access token isn't returned in the OpenID authentication response. Instead, a mechanism to obtain the access token is provided.

■ **Note**　The finalized specification for OpenID/OAuth extension is available at `http://step2.googlecode.com/svn/spec/openid_oauth_extension/latest/openid_oauth_extension.html`.

OAuth 1.0 provided a good foundation for access delegation. However, criticism arose against OAuth 1.0, mainly targeting its usability and extensibility. As a result, OAuth 2.0 was developed as an authorization framework, rather than a standard protocol. OAuth 2.0 became RFC 6749 in October 2012 under the IETF. Chapter 7 discusses OAuth 2.0 in detail.

Summary

The identity delegation model discussed in this chapter is the foundation for almost all delegated access-control models used at present. The chapter focused on building the foundation through the evolution of identity delegation models. The Google ClientLogin, Google AuthSub, Flickr Authentication, and Yahoo BBAuth models were discussed later with examples. Some of the APIs used in this chapter may be deprecated or retired by the time you try them; but one of the objectives of this chapter was to give you a comprehensive overview of the evolution of API security. Knowing history will help you design in the future.

In the next chapter, we will dive deeper into OAuth 1.0.

■ ■ ■

CHAPTER 6

OAuth 1.0

As discussed in the last section of Chapter 5, OAuth 1.0 was the first step toward the standardization of identity delegation. OAuth involves three parties in an identity delegation transaction. The delegator, also known as the user, assigns access to his or her resources to a third party. The delegate, also known as the consumer, accesses a resource on behalf of its user. The application that hosts the actual resource is known as the service provider. This terminology was introduced in the first release of the OAuth 1.0 specification under oauth.net. It changed a bit when the OAuth specification was brought into the IETF working group. In OAuth 1.0, RFC 5849, the user (delegator) is known as the *resource owner*, the consumer (delegate) is known as the *client*, and the service provider is known as the *server*.

■ **Note** The OAuth 1.0 community specification is available at http://oauth.net/core/1.0/, and 1.0a is at http://oauth.net/core/1.0a/. OAuth 1.0, RFC 5849, made OAuth 1.0 (community version) and 1.0a obsolete. RFC 5849 is available at http://tools.ietf.org/html/rfc5849.

The Token Dance

Token-based authentication goes back to 1994, when the Mosaic Netscape 0.9 beta version added support for cookies. For the first time, cookies were used to identify whether the same user was revisiting a given web site. Even though it's not a strong form of authentication, this was the first time in history that a cookie was used for identification. Later, most browsers added support for cookies and started using them as a form of authentication. To log in to a web site, the user gives his or her username and password. Once the user is successfully authenticated, the web server creates a session for that user, and the session identifier is written into a cookie. To reuse the already authenticated session for each request from then onward, the user must attach the cookie. This is the most widely used form of token-based authentication.

■ **Note** RFC 6265 defines the cookie specification in the context of HTTP: see http://tools.ietf.org/html/rfc6265.

> *Token: A unique identifier issued by the server and used by the client to associate authenticated requests with the resource owner whose authorization is requested or has been obtained by the client. Tokens have a matching shared-secret that is used by the client to establish its ownership of the token, and its authority to represent the resource owner.*
>
> —OAuth 1.0 RFC 5849

This chapter helps you digest the formal definition given for *token* by RFC 5849. OAuth uses tokens at different phases in its protocol flow (see Figure 6-1). Three main phases are defined in OAuth 1.0 handshake: the temporary-credential request phase, the resource-owner authorization phase, and the token-credential request phase.

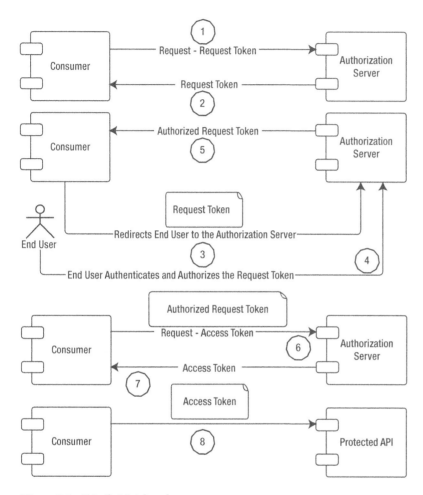

Figure 6-1. *OAuth 1.0 token dance*

▧ **Note**   All three phases in the OAuth 1.0 token dance *must* happen over TLS.

Temporary-Credential Request Phase

During the temporary-credential request phase, the OAuth client sends an HTTP POST to the temporary-credential request endpoint hosted in the resource server:

```
POST /oauth/request-token HTTP/1.1
Host: server.com
Authorization: OAuth realm="simple",
```

```
oauth_consumer_key="dsdsddDdsdsds",
oauth_signature_method="PLAINTEXT",
oauth_callback="http://client.net/client_cb",
oauth_signature="dsDSdsdsdsdddsdsdsd"
```

The authorization header in the request is constructed with following parameters:

- OAuth: The keyword used to identify the type of the authorization header. It must have the value OAuth.

- realm: An identifier known to the resource server. Looking at the realm value, the resource server can find out how to authenticate the OAuth client. The value of realm here serves the same purpose as in HTTP Basic Authentication.

- oauth_consumer_key: A unique identifier issued to the OAuth client by the resource server. This key is associated with a secret key that is known both to the client and to the resource server.

- oauth_signature_method: The method used to generate the oauth_signature. This can be PLAINTEXT, HMAC-SHA1, or RSA-SHA1. PLAINTEXT means no signature, HMAC-SHA1 means a shared key has been used for the signature, and RSA-SHA1 means an RSA private key has been used for the signature. The OAuth specification doesn't mandate any signature method. The resource server can enforce any signature method, based on its requirements.

- oauth_signature: The signature, which is calculated according to the method defined in oauth_signature_method.

▪ **Note** With PLAINTEXT as the oauth_signature_method, the oauth_signature is the consumer secret followed by &. For example, if the consumer secret associated with the corresponding consumer_key is Ddedkljlj878dskjds, then the value of oauth_signature is Ddedkljlj878dskjds&.

- oauth_callback: An absolute URI that is under the control of the client. In the next phase, once the resource owner has authorized the access request, the resource server has to redirect back to this oauth_callback URI. If this is preestablished between the client and the resource server, the value of oauth_callback should be set to oob to indicate that it is out of band.

The temporary-credential request authenticates the client. The client must be a registered entity at the resource server. The client-registration process is outside the scope of the OAuth specification. This is a direct HTTP POST request from the client to the resource server, and the user isn't aware of this phase. The client gets the following in response to the temporary-credential request. Both the temporary credential request and the response must be over TLS:

```
HTTP/1.1 200 OK
Content-Type: application/x-www-form-urlencoded
oauth_token=bhgdjgdds&
oauth_token_secret=dsdasdasdse&
oauth_callback_confirmed=true
```

Let's examine the definition of each parameter.

- oauth_token: An identifier generated by the resource server. This is used to identify the value of the oauth_token_secret in future requests made by the client to the resource server. This identifier links the oauth_token_secret to the oauth_consumer_key.

- oauth_token_secret: A shared secret generated by the resource server. The client will use this in future requests to generate the oauth_signature.

- oauth_callback_confirmed: This must be present and set to true. It helps the client to confirm that the resource server received the oauth_callback sent in the request.

To initiate the temporary-credential request phase, the client must first be registered with the resource server and have a consumer key / consumer secret pair. At the end of this phase, the client will have an oauth_token and an oauth_token_secret.

Resource-Owner Authorization Phase

During the resource-owner authorization phase, the client must get the oauth_token received in the previous phase authorized by the user or the resource owner. The client redirects the user to the resource server with the following HTTP GET request. The oauth_token received in the previous phase is added as a query parameter. Once the request hits the resource server, the resource server knows the client corresponding to this token and displays it to the user on its login page. The user must authenticate first and then authorize the token:

```
GET /authorize_token?oauth_token= bhgdjgdds HTTP/1.1
Host: server.com
```

After the resource owner's approval, the resource server redirects the user to the oauth_callback URL corresponding to the client:

```
GET /client_cb?x=1&oauth_token=dsdsdsdd&oauth_verifier=dsdsdsds HTTP/1.1
Host: client.net
```

Let's examine the definition of each parameter.

- oauth_token: An identifier generated by the resource server. It's used to identify the value of the oauth_token_verifier in future requests made by the client to the resource server. This identifier links the oauth_token_verifier to the oauth_consumer_key.

- oauth_token_verifier: A shared verification code generated by the resource server. The client will use this in future requests to generate oauth_signature.

■ **Note** If no oauth_callback URL is registered by the client, the resource server displays a verification code to the resource owner. The resource owner must take it and provide it to the client manually. The process by which the resource owner provides the verification code to the client is outside the scope of the OAuth specification.

To initiate the resource-owner authorization phase, the client must have access to the oauth_token and the oauth_token_secret. At the end of this phase, the client has a new oauth_token and an oauth_verifier.

Token-Credential Request Phase

During the token-credential request phase, the client makes a direct HTTP POST or a GET request to the access-token endpoint hosted at the authorization server:

```
POST /access_token HTTP/1.1
Host: server.com
Authorization: OAuth realm="simple",
oauth_consumer_key="dsdsddDdsdsds",
oauth_token=" bhgdjgdds ",
oauth_signature_method="PLAINTEXT",
oauth_verifier=" dsdsdsds",
oauth_signature="fdfsdfdfdfdfsfffdf"
```

The authorization header in the request is constructed with the following parameters:

- OAuth: The keyword used to identify the type of the authorization header. It must have the value OAuth.

- realm: An identifier known to the resource server. Looking at the realm value, the resource server can decide how to authenticate the OAuth client. The value of realm here serves the same purpose as in HTTP Basic Authentication.

- oauth_consumer_key: A unique identifier issued to the OAuth client by the resource server. This key is associated with a secret key that is known to both the client and the resource server.

- oauth_signature_method: The method used to generate the oauth_signature. This can be PLAINTEXT, HMAC-SHA1, or RSA-SHA1. PLAINTEXT means no signature, HMAC-SHA1 means a shared key has been used for the signature, and RSA-SHA1 means an RSA private key has been used for the signature. The OAuth specification doesn't mandate any signature method. The resource server can enforce any signature method, based on its requirements.

- oauth_signature: The signature, which is calculated according to the method defined in oauth_signature_method.

- oauth_token: The temporary-credential identifier returned in the temporary-credential request phase.

- oauth_verifier: The verification code returned in the resource-owner authorization phase.

After the authorization server validates the access token request, it sends back the following response to the client:

```
HTTP/1.1 200 OK
Content-Type: application/x-www-form-urlencoded
oauth_token=dsdsdsdsdweoio998s&oauth_token_secret=ioui789kjhk
```

Let's examine the definition of each parameter.

- oauth_token: An identifier generated by the resource server. In future requests made by the client, this will be used to identify the value of oauth_token_secret to the authorization server. This identifier links oauth_token_secret to the oauth_consumer_key.

- oauth_token_secret: A shared secret generated by the authorization server. The client will use this in future requests to generate the oauth_signature.

To initiate the token-credential request phase, the client must have access to the oauth_token from the first phase and the oauth_verifier from the second phase. At the end of this phase, the client will have a new oauth_token and a new oauth_token_secret.

Invoking a Secured Business API with OAuth 1.0

At the end of the OAuth token dance, following tokens should be retained at the OAuth client end:

- oauth_consumer_key: An identifier generated by the authorization server to uniquely identify the client. The client gets the oauth_consumer_key at the time of registration with the authorization server. The registration process is outside the scope of the OAuth specification.

- oauth_consumer_secret: A shared secret generated by the authorization server. The client will get the oauth_consumer_secret at the time of registration, with the authorization server. The registration process is outside the scope of the OAuth specification. The oauth_consumer_secret is never sent over the wire.

- oauth_token: An identifier generated by the authorization server at the end of the token-credential request phase.

- oauth_token_secret: A shared secret generated by the authorization server at the end of the token-credential request phase.

Following is a sample HTTP request to access a secured API with OAuth 1.0. In addition to the previously described parameters, it also has oauth_timestamp and oauth_nonce. Once the the authorization server validates the authorization header, sends the corresponding response back from the invoked business service:

```
POST /student?name=pavithra HTTP/1.1
Host: server.com
Content-Type: application/x-www-form-urlencoded
Authorization: OAuth realm="simple",
oauth_consumer_key="dsdsddDdsdsds ",
oauth_token="dsdsdsdsdweoio998s",
oauth_signature_method="HMAC-SHA1",
oauth_timestamp="1474343201",
oauth_nonce="rerwerweJHKjhkdsjhkhj",
oauth_signature="bYT5CMsGcbgUdFHObYMEfcx6bsw%3D"
```

Let's examine the definition of each parameter.

- oauth_timestamp: A positive integer that is the number of seconds counted since January 1, 1970 00:00:00 GMT.

- oauth_nonce: A randomly-generated unique value added to the request by the client. It's used to avoid replay attacks. The resource server must reject any request with a nonce that has been seen before.

Demystifying oauth_signature

Of the three phases discussed in the section "The Token Dance," oauth_signature is required in two: the temporary-credential request phase and the token-credential request phase. In addition, oauth_signature is required in all client requests to the protected resource. The OAuth specification defines three kinds of signature methods: PLAINTEXT, HMAC-SHA1, and RSA-SHA1. As explained earlier, PLAINTEXT means no signature, HMAC-SHA1 means a shared key has been used for the signature, and RSA-SHA1 means a RSA private key has been used for the signature. The OAuth specification doesn't mandate any signature method. The authorization server can enforce any signature method, based on its requirements. The challenge in each signature method is how to generate the base string to sign. Let's start with the simplest case, PLAINTEXT (see Table 6-1).

Table 6-1. *Signature Calculation with the PLAINTEXT Signature Method*

Phase	oauth_signature
Temporary-credential request phase	consumer_secret&
Token-credential request phase	consumer_secret&oauth_token_secret

With the PLAINTEXT oauth_signature_method, the oauth_signature is the consumer secret followed by &. For example, if the consumer secret associated with the corresponding consumer_key is Ddedkljlj878dskjds, the value of oauth_signature is Ddedkljlj878dskjds&. In this case, transport-level security must be used to protect the secret key going over the wire. This calculation of oauth_signature with PLAINTEXT is valid only for the temporary-credential request phase. For the token-credential request phase, oauth_signature also includes the token-shared secret after the consumer secret. For example, if the consumer secret associated with the corresponding consumer_key is Ddedkljlj878dskjds and the value of the token-shared secret is ekhjkhkhrure, then the value of oauth_signature is Ddedkljlj878dskjds&ekhjkhkhrure. The token-shared secret in this case is the oauth_token_secret returned in the temporary-credential request phase.

For both HMAC-SHA1 and RSA-SHA1, first you need to generate a base string. Let's start with the temporary-credential request phase. The following is a sample OAuth request generated in this phase:

```
POST /oauth/request-token HTTP/1.1
Host: server.com
Authorization: OAuth realm="simple",
oauth_consumer_key="dsdsddDdsdsds",
oauth_signature_method="PLAINTEXT",
oauth_callback="http://client.net/client_cb",
oauth_signature="dsDSdsdsdsdddsdsdsd"
```

Step 1: Get the uppercase value of the HTTP request header (GET or POST):

```
POST
```

Step 2: Get the value of the scheme and the HTTP host header in lowercase. If the port has a nondefault value, it needs to be included as well:

```
http://server.com
```

Step 3: Get the path and the query components in the request resource URI:

```
/oauth/request-token
```

Step 4: Get all the OAuth protocol parameters, excluding oauth_signature, concatenated by & (no line breaks):

```
oauth_consumer_key="dsdsddDdsdsds"&
oauth_signature_method="PLAINTEXT"&
oauth_callback="http://client.net/client_cb"
```

Step 5: Concatenate the outputs from step 2 and step 3:

```
http://server.com/oauth/request-token
```

Step 6: Concatenate the output from step 5 and step 4 with & (no line breaks):

```
http://server.com/oauth/request-token&
oauth_consumer_key="dsdsddDdsdsds"&
oauth_signature_method="PLAINTEXT"&
oauth_callback="http://client.net/client_cb"
```

Step 7: URL-encode the output from step 6 (no line breaks):

```
http%3A%2F%2Fserver.com%2Foauth%2F
request-token%26%20oauth_consumer_key%3D%22dsdsddDdsdsds%22%26
oauth_signature_method%3D%22PLAINTEXT%22%26
oauth_callback%3D%22http%3A%2F%2Fclient.net%2Fclient_cb%22
```

Step 8: Concatenate the output from step 1 and step 7 with &. This produces the final base string to calculate the oauth_signature (no line breaks):

```
POST&http%3A%2F%2Fserver.com%2Foauth%2F
request-token%26%20oauth_consumer_key%3D%22dsdsddDdsdsds%22%26
oauth_signature_method%3D%22PLAINTEXT%22%26
oauth_callback%3D%22http%3A%2F%2Fclient.net%2Fclient_cb%22
```

Now, let's see how to calculate the base string in the token-credential request phase. Following is a sample OAuth request generated in this phase:

```
POST /access_token HTTP/1.1
Host: server.com
Authorization: OAuth realm="simple",
oauth_consumer_key="dsdsddDdsdsds",
oauth_token=" bhgdjgdds ",
oauth_signature_method="PLAINTEXT",
oauth_verifier=" dsdsdsds",
oauth_signature="fdfsdfdfdfdfsfffdf"
```

Step 1: Get the uppercase value of the HTTP request header (GET or POST):

```
POST
```

Step 2: Get the value of the scheme and the HTTP host header in lowercase. If the port has a nondefault value, it needs to be included as well:

```
http://server.com
```

Step 3: Get the path and the query components in the request resource URI:

```
/oauth/access-token
```

Step 4: Get all the OAuth protocol parameters, excluding oauth_signature, concatenated by & (no line breaks):

```
oauth_consumer_key="dsdsddDdsdsds"&
oauth_token=" bhgdjgdds"&
oauth_signature_method="PLAINTEXT"&o
auth_verifier=" dsdsdsds"
```

Step 5: Concatenate the output from step 2 and step 3:

```
http://server.com/oauth/access-token
```

Step 6: Concatenate the output from step 5 and step 4 with & (no line breaks):

```
http://server.com/oauth/access-token&
oauth_consumer_key="dsdsddDdsdsds"&
oauth_token=" bhgdjgdds"&oauth_signature_method="PLAINTEXT"&
oauth_verifier=" dsdsdsds"
```

Step 7: URL-encode the output from step 6 (no line breaks):

```
http%3A%2F%2Fserver.com%2Foauth%2F
access-token%26oauth_consumer_key%3D%22dsdsddDdsdsds%22%26
oauth_token%3D%22%20bhgdjgdds%22%26
oauth_signature_method%3D%22PLAINTEXT%22%26
oauth_verifier%3D%22%20dsdsdsds%22%20
```

Step 8: Concatenate the output from step 1 and step 7 with &. This produces the final base string to calculate the oauth_signature (no line breaks):

```
POST&http%3A%2F%2Fserver.com%2Foauth%2F
access-token%26oauth_consumer_key%3D%22dsdsddDdsdsds%22%26
oauth_token%3D%22%20bhgdjgdds%22%26
oauth_signature_method%3D%22PLAINTEXT%22%26
oauth_verifier%3D%22%20dsdsdsds%22%20
```

Once you've calculated the base string for each phase, the next step is to calculate the signature based on the signature method. For the temporary-credential request phase, if you use HMAC-SHA1 as the signature method, the signature is derived in the following manner:

```
oauth_signature= HMAC-SHA1 (key, text)
oauth_signature= HMAC-SHA1 (consumer_secret&, base-string)
```

For the token-credential request phase, the key also includes the token-shared secret after the consumer secret. For example, if the consumer secret associated with the corresponding consumer_key is Ddedkljlj878dskjds and the value of the token-shared secret is ekhjkhkhrure, then the value of the key is Ddedkljlj878dskjds&ekhjkhkhrure. The token-shared secret in this case is the oauth_token_secret returned in the temporary-credential request phase:

```
oauth_signature= HMAC-SHA1 (consumer_secret&oauth_token_secret, base-string)
```

In either phase, if you want to use RSA-SHA1 as the oauth_signature_method, the OAuth client must register an RSA public key corresponding to its consumer key, at the authorization server. For RSA-SHA1, you calculate the signature in the following manner, regardless of the phase:

```
oauth_signature= RSA-SHA1 (RSA private key, base-string)
```

In addition to the token dance, you also need to calculate the oauth_signature in each business API invocation. In the following sample request, the OAuth client invokes the student API with a query parameter. Let's see how to calculate the base string in this case:

```
POST /student?name=pavithra HTTP/1.1
Host: server.com
Content-Type: application/x-www-form-urlencoded
Authorization: OAuth realm="simple",
oauth_consumer_key="dsdsddDdsdsds ",
oauth_token="dsdsdsdsdweoio998s",
oauth_signature_method="HMAC-SHA1",
oauth_timestamp="1474343201",
oauth_nonce="rerwerweJHKjhkdsjhkhj",
oauth_signature="bYT5CMsGcbgUdFHObYMEfcx6bsw%3D"
```

Step 1: Get the uppercase value of the HTTP request header (GET or POST):

```
POST
```

Step 2: Get the value of the scheme and the HTTP host header in lowercase. If the port has a non-default value, it needs to be included as well:

```
http://server.com
```

Step 3: Get the path and the query components in the request resource URI:

```
/student?name=pavithra
```

Step 4: Get all the OAuth protocol parameters, excluding oauth_signature, concatenated by & (no line breaks):

```
oauth_consumer_key="dsdsddDdsdsds"&oauth_token="dsdsdsdsdweoio998s"&
oauth_signature_method="HMAC-SHA1"&oauth_timestamp="1474343201"&
oauth_nonce="rerwerweJHKjhkdsjhkhj"
```

Step 5: Concatenate the output from step 2 and step 3 (no line breaks):

```
http://server.com/student?name=pavithra
```

Step 6: Concatenate the output from step 5 and step 4 with & (no line breaks):

```
http://server.com/student?name=pavithra&
oauth_consumer_key="dsdsddDdsdsds"&
oauth_token="dsdsdsdsdweoio998s"&
oauth_signature_method="HMAC-SHA1"&
oauth_timestamp="1474343201"&oauth_nonce="rerwerweJHKjhkdsjhkhj"
```

Step 7: URL-encode the output from step 6 (no line breaks):

```
http%3A%2F%2Fserver.com%2Fstudent%3Fname%3Dpavithra%26
oauth_consumer_key%3D%22dsdsddDdsdsds%20%22%26
oauth_token%3D%22dsdsdsdsdweoio998s%22%26
oauth_signature_method%3D%22HMAC-SHA1%22%26
oauth_timestamp%3D%221474343201%22%26
oauth_nonce%3D%22rerwerweJHKjhkdsjhkhj%22
```

Step 8: Concatenate the output from step 1 and step 7 with &. This produces the final base string to calculate the oauth_signature (no line breaks):

```
POST& http%3A%2F%2Fserver.com%2Fstudent%3Fname%3Dpavithra%26
oauth_consumer_key%3D%22dsdsddDdsdsds%20%22%26
oauth_token%3D%22dsdsdsdsdweoio998s%22%26
oauth_signature_method%3D%22HMAC-SHA1%22%26
oauth_timestamp%3D%221474343201%22%26
oauth_nonce%3D%22rerwerweJHKjhkdsjhkhj%22
```

Once you have the base string, the OAuth signature is calculated in the following manner with the HMAC-SHA1 and RSA-SHA1 signature methods. The value of oauth_token_secret is from the token-credential request phase:

```
oauth_signature= HMAC-SHA1 (consumer_secret&oauth_token_secret, base-string)
```

```
oauth_signature= RSA-SHA1 (RSA private key, base-string)
```

OAUTH 1.0 WITH TWITTER APIS

Before invoking any of the Twitter APIs, first you need to generate OAuth keys:

1. To generate OAuth keys, you need to create a Twitter App. Go to https://dev.twitter.com/apps, and click Create New App.

2. Once the app is created, go to https://dev.twitter.com/apps and click the link to the app you just created.

3. Go to Permissions, check Read and Write, and click Update Settings at the bottom of the page. Allow some time for the changes to update.

4. Go to API Keys, and copy the values of API Key and API Secret. API Key here is the oauth_consumer_key, and the API Secret is the consumer_secret.

5. Download gdata-core-1.0.0.jar and google-collect-1.0.0.jar from https://svn.wso2.org/repos/wso2/people/prabath/api-security/twitter/lib and add them to your Java classpath.

6. The following Java code shows how to get temporary credentials from Twitter in the OAuth temporary-credential request phase. You need to invoke this method by passing your own consumer key and consumer secret and the callback URL corresponding to your Twitter application:

```
public void getRequestToken(String consumerKey, String consumerSecret, String
callbackUrl) throws Exception {

        Service.GDataRequest request;
        GoogleOAuthParameters oauthParameters = new GoogleOAuthParameters();
        oauthParameters.setOAuthConsumerKey(consumerKey);
        oauthParameters.setOAuthConsumerSecret(consumerSecret);
        OAuthHmacSha1Signer signer = new OAuthHmacSha1Signer();
        GoogleService service = new GoogleService("api_security_book_sample",
                "api_security_book_sample");
        service.setOAuthCredentials(oauthParameters, signer);
        String baseString = "https://api.twitter.com/oauth/request_token";

        URL feedUrl = new URL(baseString);
        request = service.createFeedRequest(feedUrl);
        request.execute();
        System.out.println(convertStreamToString(request.getResponseStream()));
}
```

7. The helper method convertStreamToString() takes a byte stream and converts it into a string:

```
private static String convertStreamToString(InputStream is) throws IOException {
        if (is != null) {
            StringBuilder sb = new StringBuilder();
            String line;
            BufferedReader reader
            try {
            reader = new BufferedReader(new InputStreamReader(is, "UTF-8"));
                while ((line = reader.readLine()) != null) {
                    sb.append(line).append("\n");
                }
            } finally {
                is.close();
            }
            return sb.toString();
        } else {
            return "";
        }
}
```

8. The getRequestToken() method, with the proper parameters, prints the following response:

```
oauth_token=bOjTGcb4Ul5g9ecumlhaNqaGF1DDOs1xzFJEfO7dNTY&
oauth_token_secret=7w1rqff46MCxlcbLlGsc84ZLLnE2XgGqXVmMz7TKk&
oauth_callback_confirmed=true
```

9. You need to get the returned token authorized by the user in the resource-owner authorization phase. Copy and paste the following URL into the browser. Make sure you replace the value of the oauth_token query parameter with the value you got in the previous step:

```
https://api.twitter.com/oauth/authorize?
oauth_token=bOjTGcb4Ul5g9ecumlhaNqaGF1DDOs1xzFJEfO7dNTY
```

10. The end user or the resource owner must log in to his or her Twitter account and approve the authorization grant.

11. Once approved, the user is redirected back to the registered callback URL. Copy the values of oauth_token and oauth_verifier:

```
https://client.net/client_cb ?
oauth_token=bOjTGcb4Ul5g9ecumlhaNqaGF1DDOs1xzFJEfO7dNTY&
oauth_verifier=h4BdfOOtNQfXJFyq9DoXs1gGbe5l9XY4TbEPrIcTU
```

12. Next is the token-credential request phase: the client must get an access token from Twitter. You need to invoke this method by passing your own consumer key, consumer secret, and oauth_token from the temporary-credential request phase; the oauth_token_secret from the temporary-credential request phase; and the oauth_verifier from the resource-owner authorization phase:

```
public void getAccessToken(String consumerKey, String consumerSecret, String
oauthToken, String tokenSecret, String tokenVerifier) throws Exception {

        Service.GDataRequest request ;
        GoogleOAuthParameters oauthParameters = new GoogleOAuthParameters();
        oauthParameters.setOAuthConsumerKey(consumerKey);
        oauthParameters.setOAuthConsumerSecret(consumerSecret);
        oauthParameters.setOAuthToken(oauthToken);
        oauthParameters.setOAuthTokenSecret(tokenSecret);
        oauthParameters.setOAuthVerifier(tokenVerifier);
        OAuthHmacSha1Signer signer = new OAuthHmacSha1Signer();
        GoogleService service = new GoogleService("api_security_book_sample",
                "api_security_book_sample");
        service.setOAuthCredentials(oauthParameters, signer);
        String baseString = "https://api.twitter.com/oauth/access_token";
        URL feedUrl = new URL(baseString);
        request = service.createFeedRequest(feedUrl);
        request.execute();
        System.out.println(convertStreamToString(request.getResponseStream()));
}
```

13. The getAccessToken() method, with the proper parameters, prints the following response:

```
oauth_token=10963912-Jwg57V31CxWlq3aJtVBipjZ5m5OcIXb7tAioX8WRL&
oauth_token_secret=UtNRYryECuSqy5rTvcNokUCo8lXXjftQMyGOb3pQtcI7H&
user_id=10963912&screen_name=prabath
```

That's the end of the token dance. Now you can directly call the Twitter APIs with the tokens obtained in the token-credential request phase.

The following Java code shows how to invoke the Twitter API https://api.twitter.com/1.1/statuses/update.json to publish tweets on behalf of the end user. You need to invoke this method by passing your own consumer key, consumer secret, oauth_token from the token-credential request phase and the oauth_token_secret from the same phase:

```java
public void callTwitterAPI(String consumerKey, String consumerSecret, String oauthToken,
            String tokenSecret) throws Exception {

    Service.GDataRequest request ;
    GoogleOAuthParameters oauthParameters = new GoogleOAuthParameters();
    oauthParameters.setOAuthConsumerKey(consumerKey);
    oauthParameters.setOAuthConsumerSecret(consumerSecret);
    oauthParameters.setOAuthToken(oauthToken);
    oauthParameters.setOAuthTokenSecret(tokenSecret);
    OAuthHmacSha1Signer signer = new OAuthHmacSha1Signer();
    GoogleService service = new GoogleService("api_security_book_sample",
            "api_security_book_sample");
    service.setOAuthCredentials(oauthParameters, signer);
    String baseString = "https://api.twitter.com/1.1/statuses/update.json?
                    status=%27Having+fun+with+Twitter+API%27";
    URL feedUrl = new URL(baseString);
    request = service.createRequest(RequestType.INSERT, feedUrl, ContentType.ANY);
    request.execute();
    System.out.println(convertStreamToString(request.getResponseStream()));

}
```

Three-Legged OAuth vs. Two-Legged OAuth

The OAuth flow discussed so far involves three parties: the resource owner, the client, and the resource server (also known as the authorization server). The client accesses a resource hosted in the resource server on behalf of the user. This is the most common pattern in OAuth, and it's also known as *three-legged OAuth* (three parties involved). In two-legged OAuth, you have only two parties: the client becomes the resource owner. There is no access delegation in two-legged OAuth.

■ **Note** Two-legged OAuth never made it to the IETF. The initial draft specification is available at http://oauth.googlecode.com/svn/spec/ext/consumer_request/1.0/drafts/2/spec.html.

If the same student API discussed earlier is secured with two-legged OAuth, the request from the client looks like following. The value of oauth_token is an empty string. There is no token dance in two-legged OAuth. You only need oauth_consumer_key and consumer_secret. The HMAC-SHA1 signature is generated using consumer_secret& as the key:

```
POST /student?name=pavithra HTTP/1.1
Host: server.com
Content-Type: application/x-www-form-urlencoded
Authorization: OAuth realm="simple",
oauth_consumer_key="dsdsddDdsdsds ",
oauth_token="",
oauth_signature_method="HMAC-SHA1",
oauth_timestamp="1474343201",
oauth_nonce="rerwerweJHKjhkdsjhkhj",
oauth_signature="bYT5CMsGcbgUdFHObYMEfcx6bsw%3D"
```

■ **Note** In both HTTP Basic Authentication and two-legged OAuth, the resource owner acts as the client and directly invokes the API. With HTTP Basic Authentication, you pass the credentials over the wire; this must be over TLS. With two-legged OAuth, you never pass the consumer_secret over the wire, so it need not be on TLS.

HTTP Digest Authentication looks very similar to two-legged OAuth. In both cases, you never pass credentials over the wire. The difference is that HTTP Digest Authentication authenticates the user, whereas two-legged OAuth authenticates the application on behalf of the resource owner. A given resource owner can own multiple applications, and each application can have its own consumer key and consumer secret.

OAuth WRAP

As discussed in the last section of Chapter 5, in November 2009, a new draft specification for access delegation called Web Resource Authorization Profiles (WRAP) was proposed, built on top of the OAuth 1.0 model. WRAP was later deprecated in favor of OAuth 2.0.

■ **Note** The initial draft of the WRAP profile submitted to the IETF is available at http://tools.ietf.org/html/draft-hardt-oauth-01.

Unlike OAuth 1.0, WRAP didn't depend on a signature scheme. At a high level, the user experience was the same as in OAuth 1.0. The client first redirects the user to the authorization server with its consumer key and the callback URL. Once the user authorized the access rights to the client, the user is redirected back to the callback URL with a verification code. Then the client has to do a direct call to the access-token endpoint of the authorization server with the verification code, to get the access token. Thereafter, the client only needs to include the access token in all API calls (all API calls must be on TLS):

```
https://friendfeed-api.com/v2/feed/home?wrap_access_token=dsdsdrwerwr
```

▨ **Note**   In November 2009, Facebook joined the Open Web Foundation, together with Microsoft, Google, Yahoo!, and many others, with a commitment to support open standards for web authentication. Keeping that promise, in December 2009, Facebook added OAuth WRAP support to FriendFeed, which it had acquired a few months earlier.

Summary

This chapter introduced OAuth 1.0, which was the first IETF standard for delegated access control. Prior to OAuth 2.0, 1.0 dominated the Web; and Twitter still uses OAuth 1.0. The chapter explained how OAuth 1.0 works by using an example that showed how to talk to Twitter OAuth endpoints.

In the next chapter, we will delve deeper into OAuth 2.0.

CHAPTER 7

■ ■ ■

OAuth 2.0

OAuth 2.0 is a major breakthrough in identity delegation. It has its roots in OAuth 1.0, but OAuth WRAP primarily influenced it. The main difference between OAuth 1.0 and 2.0 is that OAuth 1.0 is a standard protocol for identity delegation, whereas 2.0 is a highly extensible framework. OAuth 2.0 is already the de facto standard for API security and is widely used across leading web sites including Facebook, Google, LinkedIn, Microsoft (MSN, Live), PayPal, Instagram, Foursquare, GitHub, Yammer, Meetup, and many more. There is one popular exception: Twitter still uses OAuth 1.0.

OAuth WRAP

In November 2009, during the Internet Identity Workshop (IIW), Dick Hardt of Microsoft, Brian Eaton of Google, and Allen Tom of Yahoo! presented a new draft specification for access delegation. It was called Web Resource Authorization Profiles (WRAP) and it was built on top of the OAuth 1.0 model. WRAP addressed some of the limitations found in OAuth 1.0. Later in 2010, WRAP was deprecated in favor of OAuth 2.0.

■ **Note**   The initial draft of the OAuth WRAP specification submitted to the IETF is available at `http://tools.ietf.org/html/draft-hardt-oauth-01`.

OAuth WRAP was one of the initial steps toward OAuth 2.0. Unlike OAuth 1.0, WRAP doesn't depend on a signature scheme. At a high level, the user experience is the same as in OAuth 1.0. The client first redirects the user to the resource server with its consumer key and the callback URL. Once the user has authorized the access rights for the client, the user is redirected back to the callback URL with a verification code. Then the client must do a direct call to the access-token endpoint of the resource server with the verification code to get the access token. Thereafter, the client only needs to include the access token in all API calls. All these API calls must be on TLS.

WRAP introduced two types of profiles for acquiring an access token: autonomous client profiles and user delegation profiles. In autonomous client profiles, the client becomes the resource owner, or the client is acting on behalf of itself. In other words, the resource owner is the one who accesses the resource. This is equivalent to the two-legged OAuth model discussed regarding OAuth 1.0 in Chapter 6. In user delegation profiles, the client acts on behalf of the resource owner. OAuth 1.0 didn't have this profile concept, which is limited to a single flow. This extensibility introduced by OAuth WRAP later became a key part of OAuth 2.0.

Client Account and Password Profile

The OAuth WRAP specification introduced two autonomous client profiles: the Client Account and Password Profile and the Assertion Profile. The Client Account and Password Profile uses the client's or the resource owner's credentials at the authorization server to obtain an access token. This pattern is mostly used for server-to-server authentication where no end user is involved. The following cURL command does an HTTP POST to the WRAP token endpoint of the authorization server, with three attributes. wrap_name is the username, wrap_password is the password corresponding to the username, and wrap_scope is the expected level of access required by the client. wrap_scope is an optional parameter:

```
curl -v -X POST -H "Content-Type:application/x-www-form-urlencoded;
                            charset=UTF-8" -k
                -d "wrap_name=admin&
                    wrap_password=admin&
                    wrap_scope=read_profile" https://authorization-server/wrap/token
```

This returns wrap_access_token, wrap_refresh_token, and wrap_access_token_expires_in parameters. wrap_access_token_expires_in is an optional parameter that indicates the lifetime of wrap_access_token in seconds. When wrap_access_token expires, wrap_refresh_token can be used to get a new access token. OAuth WRAP introduced for the first time this token-refreshing functionality. The access-token refresh request only needs wrap_refresh_token as a parameter, as shown next, and it returns a new wrap_access_token. It doesn't return a new wrap_refresh_token. The same token obtained in the first access-token request can be used to refresh subsequent access tokens:

```
curl -v -X POST -H "Content-Type:application/x-www-form-urlencoded;
                            charset=UTF-8" -k
                -d "wrap_refresh_token=Xkjk78iuiuh876jhhkwkjhewew"
                    https://authorization-server/wrap/token
```

Assertion Profile

The other profile that falls under the autonomous client profiles is the Assertion Profile. This assumes that the client somehow obtains an assertion—say, for example, a SAML token—and uses it to acquire a wrap-access token. The following example cURL command does an HTTP POST to the WRAP token endpoint of the authorization server, with three attributes: wrap_assertion_format is the type of the assertion included in the request in a way known to the authorization server; wrap_assertion is the encoded assertion, and wrap_scope is the expected level of access required by the client. wrap_scope is an optional parameter:

```
curl -v -X POST -H "Content-Type:application/x-www-form-urlencoded;
                            charset=UTF-8" -k
                -d "wrap_assertion_format=saml20&
                    wrap_assertion=encoded-assertion&
                    wrap_scope=read_profile"
                    https://authorization-server/wrap/token
```

The response is the same as in the Client Account and Password Profile, except that in the Assertion Profile, there is no wrap_refresh_token.

Username and Password Profile

The WRAP user delegation profiles introduced three profiles: the Username and Password Profile, the Web App Profile, and the Rich App Profile. The Username and Password Profile is mostly recommended for installed trusted applications. The application is the client, and the end user or the resource owner must provide their username and password to the application. Then the application exchanges the username and password for an access token and stores it in the application. This is a better approach than storing the user's username and password—especially for mobile applications, which, to provide a better user experience, don't want users to have to enter their credentials repeatedly.

The following cURL command does an HTTP POST to the WRAP token endpoint of the authorization server, with four attributes: wrap_client_id is an identifier for the application, wrap_username is the username of the end user, wrap_password is the password corresponding to the username, and wrap_scope is the expected level of access required by the client (wrap_scope is an optional parameter):

```
curl -v -X POST -H "Content-Type:application/x-www-form-urlencoded;
                              charset=UTF-8" -k
          -d "wrap_client_id=app1&
              wrap_username=admin&
              wrap_password=admin&
              wrap_scope=read_profile"
              https://authorization-server/wrap/token
```

This returns wrap_access_token and wrap_access_token_expires_in parameters. wrap_access_token_expires_in is an optional parameter that indicates the lifetime of wrap_access_token in seconds. If the authorization server detects any malicious access patterns, then instead of sending wrap_access_token to the client application, it returns a wrap_verification_url. It's the responsibility of the client application to load this URL into the user's browser or advise them to visit that URL. Once the user has completed that step, the user must indicate to the client application that verification is complete. Then the client application can initiate the token request once again. Instead of sending a verification URL, the authorization server can also enforce a CAPTCHA verification through the client application. There the authorization server sends back a wrap_captcha_url, which points to the location where the client application can load the CAPTCHA. Once it's loaded and has the response from the end user, the client application must POST it back to the authorization server along with the token request:

```
curl -v -X POST -H "Content-Type:application/x-www-form-urlencoded;
                              charset=UTF-8" -k
          -d "wrap_captcha_url=url-encoded-captcha-url&
              wrap_captch_solution-solution&
              wrap_client_id=app1&
              wrap_username=admin&
              wrap_password=admin&
              wrap_scope=read_profile"
              https://authorization-server/wrap/token
```

Web App Profile

The Web App Profile defined under the WRAP user delegation profiles is mostly recommended for web applications, where the web application must access a resource belonging to the end user on their behalf. The web application follows a two-step process to acquire an access token: it gets a verification code from the authorization server and then exchanges that for an access token. The end user must initiate the first step by visiting the client web application. Then the user is redirected to the authorization server. The following example shows how the user is redirected to the authorization server with appropriate WRAP parameters:

```
https://authorization-server/wrap/authorize?
                              wrap_client_id=OrhQErXIX49svVYoXJGtODWBuFca&
                              wrap_callback=https%3A%2F%2Fmycallback&
                              wrap_client_state=client-state&
                              wrap_scope=read_profile
```

`wrap_client_id` is an identifier for the client web application. `wrap_callback` is the URL where the user is redirected after successful authentication at the authorization server. Both `wrap_client_state` and `wrap_scope` are optional parameters. Any value in `wrap_client_state` must be returned back to the client web application. After the end user's approval, a `wrap_verification_code` and other related parameters are returned to the callback URL associated with the client web application as query parameters.

The next step is to exchange this verification code to an access token:

```
curl -v -X POST -H "Content-Type:application/x-www-form-urlencoded;
                              charset=UTF-8" -k
              -d "wrap_client_id=OrhQErXIX49svVYoXJGtODWBuFca &
                  wrap_client_secret=weqeKJHjhkhkihjk&
                  wrap_verification_code=dsadkjljljrrer&
                  wrap_callback=https://mycallback"
                  https://authorization-server/wrap/token
```

This cURL command does an HTTP POST to the WRAP token endpoint of the authorization server, with four attributes: `wrap_client_id` is an identifier for the application, `wrap_client_secret` is the password corresponding to `wrap_client_id`, `wrap_verification_code` is the verification code returned in the previous step, and `wrap_callback` is the callback URL where the verification code was sent. This returns `wrap_access_token`, `wrap_refresh_token`, and `wrap_access_token_expires_in` parameters. `wrap_access_token_expires_in` is an optional parameter that indicates the lifetime of `wrap_access_token` in seconds. When `wrap_access_token` expires, `wrap_refresh_token` can be used to get a new access token.

Rich App Profile

The Rich App Profile defined under the WRAP user delegation profiles is most commonly used in scenarios where the OAuth client application is an installed application that can also work with a browser. Hybrid mobile apps are the best example. The protocol flow is very similar to that of the Web App Profile. The rich client application follows a two-step process to acquire an access token: it gets a verification code from the authorization server and then exchanges that for an access token. The end user must initiate the first step by visiting the rich client application. Then the application spawns a browser and redirects the user to the authorization server:

```
https://authorization-server/wrap/authorize?
                              wrap_client_id=OrhQErXIX49svVYoXJGtODWBuFca&
                              wrap_callback=https%3A%2F%2Fmycallback&
                              wrap_client_state=client-state&
                              wrap_scope=read_profile
```

`wrap_client_id` is an identifier for the rich client application. `wrap_callback` is the URL where the user is redirected after successful authentication at the authorization server. Both `wrap_client_state` and `wrap_scope` are optional parameters. Any value in `wrap_client_state` is returned back to the callback URL. After the end user's approval, a `wrap_verification_code` is returned to the rich client application.

The next step is to exchange this verification code for an access token:

```
curl -v -X POST -H "Content-Type:application/x-www-form-urlencoded;
                          charset=UTF-8" -k
          -d "wrap_client_id=OrhQErXIX49svVYoXJGtODWBuFca&
              wrap_verification_code=dsadkjljljrrer&
              wrap_callback=https://mycallback"
              https://authorization-server/wrap/token
```

This cURL command does an HTTP POST to the WRAP token endpoint of the authorization server, with three attributes: `wrap_client_id` is an identifier for the application, `wrap_verification_code` is the verification code returned in the previous step, and `wrap_callback` is the callback URL where the verification code was sent. This returns `wrap_access_token`, `wrap_refresh_token`, and `wrap_access_token_expires_in` parameters. `wrap_access_token_expires_in` is an optional parameter that indicates the lifetime of `wrap_access_token` in seconds. When `wrap_access_token` expires, `wrap_refresh_token` can be used to get a new access token. Unlike in the Web App Profile, the Rich App Profile doesn't need to send `wrap_client_secret` in the access-token request.

Accessing a WRAP-Protected API

All the previous profiles talk about how to get an access token. Once you have the access token, the rest of the flow is independent of the WRAP profile. The following cURL command shows how to access a WRAP protected resource:

```
curl -H "Authorization:WRAP
                access_token=cac93e1d29e45bf6d84073dbfb460"
                http://localhost:8080/recipe
```

WRAP to OAuth 2.0

OAuth WRAP was able to sort out many of the limitations and drawbacks found in OAuth 1.0: primarily extensibility. OAuth 1.0 is a concrete protocol for identity delegation that has its roots in Flickr Authentication, Google AuthSub, and Yahoo! BBAuth. Another key difference between OAuth 1.0 and WRAP is the dependency on signatures: OAuth WRAP eliminated the need for signatures and mandated using TLS for all types of communications.

OAuth 2.0 is a big step forward from OAuth WRAP. It further improved the extensibility features introduced in OAuth WRAP and introduced two major extension points: grant types and token types.

OAuth 2.0 Grant Types

A grant type defines how a client can obtain an authorization grant from a resource owner to access a resource on their behalf. The grant types in OAuth 2.0 are very similar to the OAuth profiles in WRAP. The OAuth 2.0 core specification introduces four core grant types: the Authorization Code grant type, the Implicit grant type, the Resource Owner Password Credentials grant type, and the Client Credentials grant type.

Authorization Code Grant Type

The Authorization Code grant type in OAuth 2.0 is very similar to the Web App Profile in WRAP. It's mostly recommended for applications—either web applications or native mobile applications—that have the capability to spawn a web browser (see Figure 7-1). The resource owner that visits the application initiates the Authorization Code grant type. The client, which must be a registered application at the authorization server, must redirect the resource owner to the authorization server to get approval:

```
https://localhost:9443/oauth2/authorize?
                        response_type=code&
                        client_id=OrhQErXIX49svVYoXJGtODWBuFca&
                        redirect_uri=https%3A%2F%2Fmycallback
```

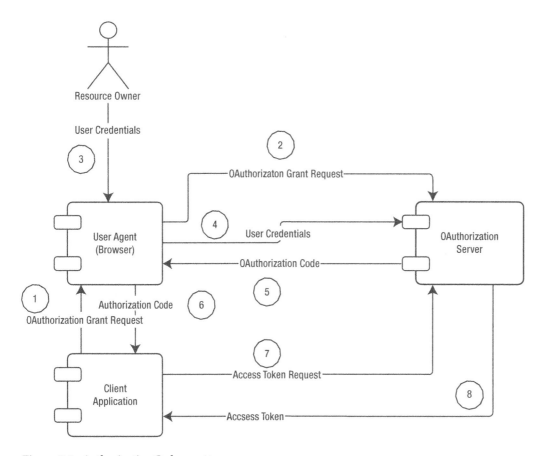

Figure 7-1. *Authorization Code grant type*

The value of response_type must be code. This indicates to the authorization server that the request is for an authorization code. client_id is an identifier for the client application. Once the client application is registered with the authorization server, the client gets a client_id and a client_secret. The value of redirect_uri should be equivalent to the one registered with the authorization server. During the client-registration phase, the client application must provide a URL under its control as the redirect_uri. The URL-encoded value of the callback URL is added to the request as the redirect_uri parameter. In addition to these parameters, a client application can also include a scope parameter. The value of the scope parameter is shown to the resource owner on the approval screen: it indicates to the authorization server the level of access the client needs on the target resource/API. The previous application returns the requested code to the registered callback URL:

```
https://mycallback/?code=9142d4cad58c66d0a5edfad8952192
```

■ **Note**   Each authorization code should have a lifetime. A lifetime longer than 10 minutes isn't recommended.

The value of the authorization code is delivered to the client application via an HTTP redirect and is visible to the resource owner. In the next step, the client must exchange the authorization code for an OAuth access token by talking to the OAuth token endpoint exposed by the authorization server. This must be an authenticated request where the client_id and the client_secret of the client application are in the HTTP Authorization header. The token endpoint must be secured with HTTP Basic Authentication. The value of the grant_type parameter must be the authorization_code, and the value of the code should be the one returned from the previous step. If the client application sent a value to the redirect_uri parameter in the previous request, then it must include the same value in the token request:

■ **Note**   The authorization code returned from the authorization server acts as an intermediate code. This code is used to map the end user or resource owner to the OAuth client. The OAuth client must authenticate itself to the token endpoint of the authorization server. The authorization server should check whether the code is issued to the authenticated OAuth client prior to exchanging it for an access token.

```
curl -v -X POST --basic
            -u OrhQErXIX49svVYoXJGtODWBuFca:eYOFkL756W8usQaVNgCNkz9C2DOa
            -H "Content-Type:application/x-www-form-urlencoded;charset=UTF-8" -k
            -d "grant_type=authorization_code&
                code=9142d4cad58c66d0a5edfad8952192&
                redirect_uri=https://mycallback" https://localhost:9443/oauth2/token
```

■ **Note**   The authorization code should be used only once by the client. If the authorization server detects that it's been used more than once, it must revoke all the tokens issued for that particular authorization code.

The previous cURL command returns the following response from the authorization server. The `token_type` parameter in the response indicates the type of the token. (The section "OAuth 2.0 Token Types" talks more about token types.) In addition to the access token, the authorization server also returns a refresh token, which is optional. The refresh token can be used by the client application to obtain a new access token before the refresh token expires. The `expires_in` parameter indicates the lifetime of the access token in seconds:

```
{
        "token_type":"bearer",
        "expires_in":3600,
        "refresh_token":"22b157546b26c2d6c0165c4ef6b3f736",
        "access_token":"cac93e1d29e45bf6d84073dbfb460"
}
```

■ **Note** Each refresh token has its own lifetime. Compared to the lifetime of the access token, the refresh token's is longer: the lifetime of an access token is in minutes, whereas the lifetime of a refresh token is in days.

Implicit Grant Type

The Implicit grant type to acquire an access token is mostly used by JavaScript clients running in the web browser (see Figure 7-2). Unlike the Authorization Code grant type, the Implicit type doesn't have any equivalent profiles in OAuth WRAP. The JavaScript client initiates the authorization grant by redirecting the user to the authorization server. The `response_type` parameter in the request indicates to the authorization server that the client expects a token, not a code. The Implicit grant type doesn't require to authenticate the JavaScript client; it only has to send the `client_id` in the request. This is for logging and auditing purposes and also to find out the corresponding `redirect_uri`. The `redirect_uri` in the request is optional; if it's present, it must match what is provided at the client registration:

```
https://localhost:9443/oauth2/authorize?
                        response_type=token&
                        client_id=OrhQErXIX49svVYoXJGtoDWBuFca&
                        redirect_uri=https%3A%2F%2Fmycallback
```

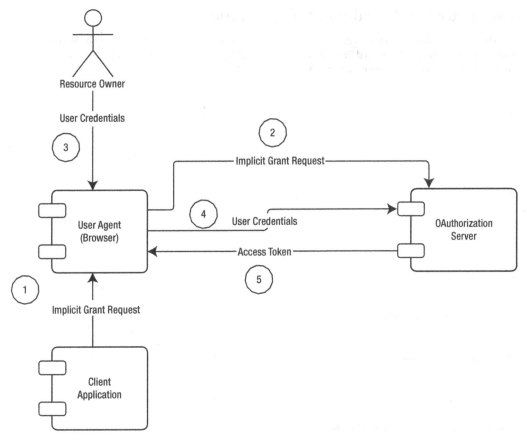

Figure 7-2. *Implicit grant type*

This returns the following response. The Implicit grant type sends the access token as a URI fragment and doesn't provide any refreshing mechanism:

```
https://mycallback/#access_token=cac93e1d29e45bf6d84073dbfb460&expires_in=3600
```

Unlike the Authorization Code grant type, the Implicit grant type client receives the access token in the grant request.

■ **Note**   The authorization server must treat the authorization code, the access token, the refresh token, and the client secret key all as extremely confidential data. They should be never sent over HTTP—the authorization server must use TLS. These tokens should be stored securely, possibly by encrypting or hashing them.

Resource Owner Password Credentials Grant Type

Under the Resource Owner Password Credentials grant type, the resource owner must trust the client application. This is equivalent to the Username and Password Profile in OAuth WRAP. The resource owner has to give its credentials directly to the client application (see Figure 7-3).

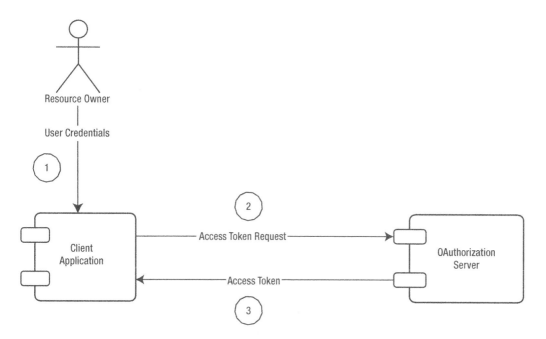

Figure 7-3. *Resource Owner Password Credentials grant type*

The following cURL command talks to the token endpoint of the authorization server, passing the resource owner's username and the password as parameters. In addition, the client application must prove its identity. The token endpoint must be secured with HTTP Basic Authentication, and the client application passes its client key and the client secret in the HTTP `Authorization` header. The value of the `grant_type` parameter must be set to `password`:

```
curl -v -X POST --basic
            -u OrhQErXIX49svVYoXJGtODWBuFca:eYOFkL756W8usQaVNgCNkz9C2DOa
            -H "Content-Type:application/x-www-form-urlencoded;charset=UTF-8" -k
            -d "grant_type=password&
                username=admin&password=admin"
                https://localhost:9443/oauth2/token
```

This returns the following response, which includes an access token along with a refresh token:

```
{
        "token_type":"bearer",
        "expires_in":685,
        "refresh_token":"22b157546b26c2d6c0165c4ef6b3f736",
        "access_token":"cac93e1d29e45bf6d84073dbfb460"
}
```

> ■ **Note** If using the Authorization Code grant type is an option, it should be used over the Resource Owner Password Credentials grant type. The Resource Owner Password Credentials grant type was introduced to aid migration from HTTP Basic Authentication and Digest Authentication to OAuth 2.0.

Client Credentials Grant Type

The Client Credentials grant type is equivalent to the Client Account and Password Profile in OAuth WRAP, and to two-legged OAuth in OAuth 1.0. With this grant type, the client itself becomes the resource owner (see Figure 7-4):

```
curl -v -X POST --basic
      -u OrhQErXIX49svVYoXJGtODWBuFca:eYOFkL756W8usQaVNgCNkz9C2DOa
      -H "Content-Type:application/x-www-form-urlencoded;
                      charset=UTF-8" -k
      -d "grant_type=client_credentials" https://localhost:9443/oauth2/token
```

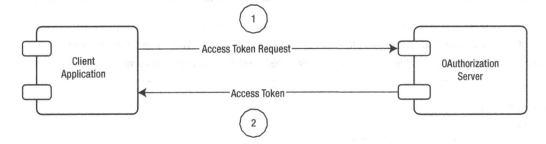

Figure 7-4. *Client Credentials grant type*

This returns the following response, which includes an access token. Unlike the Resource Owner Password Credentials grant type, the Client Credentials grant type doesn't return a refresh token:

```
{
      "token_type":"bearer",
      "expires_in":3600,
      "access_token":"4c9a9ae7463ff9bb93ae7f169bd6a"
}
```

Table 7-1 lists out the key differences between OAuth 2.0 and OAuth WRAP.

Table 7-1. *OAuth 2.0 Grant Types vs. OAuth WRAP Profiles*

OAuth 2.0	OAuth WRAP
Authorization Code grant type	Web App Profile / Rich App Profile
Implicit grant type	–
Resource Owner Password Credentials grant type	Username and Password Profile
Client Credentials grant type	Client Account and Password Profile

OAuth 2.0 Token Types

Neither OAuth 1.0 nor WRAP could support custom token types. OAuth 1.0 always used signature-based tokens, and OAuth WRAP always used bearer tokens over TLS. OAuth 2.0 isn't coupled into any token type. In OAuth 2.0, you can introduce your own token type if needed. Regardless of the token type returned in the OAuth token response from the authorization server, the client must understand it before using it. Based on the token type, the authorization server can add additional attributes/parameters to the response.

OAuth 2.0 has two main token profiles: OAuth 2.0 Bearer Token Profile, and OAuth 2.0 MAC Token Profile. The most popular OAuth token profile is Bearer; almost all OAuth 2.0 deployments today are based on the OAuth 2.0 Bearer Token Profile. The next section talks about the Bearer Token Profile in detail, and Chapter 8 discusses the MAC Token Profile.

OAuth 2.0 Bearer Token Profile

The OAuth 2.0 Bearer Token Profile was influenced by OAuth WRAP, which only supported bearer tokens. As its name implies, anyone who bears the token can use it—don't lose it! Bearer tokens must always be used over TLS to avoid losing them in transit. Once the bearer access token is obtained from the authorization server, the client can use it in three ways to talk to the resource server. The most popular way is to include it in the HTTP Authorization header:

■ **Note** An OAuth 2.0 bearer token is an arbitrary string. An attacker can carry out a brute-force attack to guess the token. The authorization server must pick the right length and use other possible measures to prevent brute forcing.

```
GET /resource HTTP/1.1
Host:resourceserver.com
Authorization:Bearer JGjhgyuyibGGjgjkjdlsjkjdsd
```

It can also be included as a query parameter. This approach is mostly used with the Implicit grant type, when a JavaScript client gets the access token from the authorization server:

```
GET /resource?access_token=JGjhgyuyibGGjgjkjdlsjkjdsd
Host:resourceserver.com
```

■ **Note** When the value of the OAuth access token is sent as a query parameter, the name of the parameter must be access_token. Both Facebook and Google use the correct parameter name, but LinkedIn uses oauth2_access_token and Salesforce uses oauth_token.

It's also possible to send the access token as a form-encoded body parameter. An authorization server supporting the Bearer Token Profile should be able to handle any of these patterns:

```
POST /resource HTTP/1.1
Host:server.example.com
Content-Type:application/x-www-form-urlencoded

access_token=JGjhgyuyibGGjgjkjdlsjkjdsd
```

> ■ **Note** The value of the OAuth bearer token is only meaningful to the authorization server. Neither the client nor the resource server should try to interpret what it says. To make the processing logic efficient, the authorization server may include some meaningful but non-confidential data in the access token. For example, if the authorization server supports multiple domains with multi-tenancy, it may include the tenant domain in the access token and then Base64-encode it.

OAuth 2.0 Client Types

OAuth 2.0 identifies two types of clients: confidential clients and public clients. Confidential clients are capable of protecting their own credentials (the client key and the client secret), whereas public clients can't. The OAuth 2.0 specification is built around three types of client profiles: web applications, user-agent-based applications, and native applications. Web applications are considered to be confidential clients, running on a web server: end users or resource owners access such applications via a web browser. User-agent-based applications are considered to be public clients: they download the code from a web server and run it on the user agent, such as JavaScript running in the browser. These clients are incapable of protecting their credentials—the end user can see anything in the JavaScript. Native applications are also considered as public clients: these clients are under the control of the end user, and any confidential data stored in them can be extracted. Android and iOS native applications are a couple of examples.

> ■ **Note** All four grant types defined in the OAuth 2.0 core specification require the client to preregister with the authorization server and in return get a client identifier. Under the Implicit grant type, the client doesn't get a client secret.

Table 7-2 lists the key differences between OAuth 1.0 and OAuth 2.0 bearer token profile.

Table 7-2. *OAuth 1.0 vs. OAuth 2.0*

OAuth 1.0	OAuth 2.0 Bearer Token Profile
An access-delegation protocol	An authorization framework for access delegation
Signature based: HMAC-SHA256/RSA-SHA256	Non-signature-based, Bearer Token Profile
Less extensibility	Highly extensible via grant types and token types
Less developer friendly	More developer friendly
TLS required only during the initial handshake	Bearer Token Profile mandates using TLS during the entire flow
Secret key never passed on the wire	Secret key goes on the wire (Bearer Token Profile)

> ■ **Note** OAuth 2.0 introduces a clear separation between the client, the resource owner, the authorization server, and the resource server. But the core OAuth specification doesn't talk about how the resource server validates an access token. Most OAuth implementations do this by talking to a proprietary API exposed by the authorization server. Chapter 9 talks more about this.

SECURING THE CUTE CUPCAKE FACTORY RECIPE API WITH OAUTH 2.0

In this exercise, you see how to secure an API deployed in Apache Tomcat with OAuth 2.0. According to OAuth terminology, the Recipe API is the resource and Apache Tomcat is the resource server. In addition to the resource server, you need an authorization server, which issues tokens to client applications. To validate the issued tokens, which come with the API invocation request, the resource server must call an API exposed by the authorization server.

■ **Note** WSO2 Identity Server is a free, open source identity and entitlement management server released under the Apache 2.0 license.

Follow these steps:

1. Download WSO2 Identity Server 5.0.0 from `http://wso2.com/products/identity-server/`, set up the `JAVA_HOME` environment variable, and start the server from `wso2server.sh/wso2server.bat` in `WSO2_IS_HOME/bin`. If WSO2 Identity Server 5.0.0 isn't available from the main download page, you can find it at `http://wso2.com/more-downloads/identity-server/`.

2. Download `recipe.war` from `https://svn.wso2.org/repos/wso2/people/prabath/api-security/recipe/`, and copy it to `CATALINA_HOME/webapps`.

3. Download all the jars at `https://svn.wso2.org/repos/wso2/people/prabath/api-security/oauth-filter/`, and copy them to `CATALINA_HOME/lib`.

4. Import WSO2 Identity Server's certificate authority (CA) certificate to `JAVA_HOME/lib/security/cacerts` as a trusted CA. Download Identity Server's CA certificate from `https://svn.wso2.org/repos/wso2/people/prabath/api-security/wso2is.cert`, and use the following `keytool` command to import it to the `cacerts` Java keystore. The default keystore password for `cacerts` is `changeit`:

   ```
   cd JAVA_HOME/lib/security
   keytool -import  -file wso2is.cert -keystore cacerts -alias wso2is -storepass changeit
   ```

5. Start Apache Tomcat server, and then shut it down. That will make `recipe.war` explode. Open `CATALINA_HOME/webapps/recipe/WEB-INF/web.xml`, and add the following under the root element. This will engage the OAuth filter with the Recipe API. All requests directed to the Recipe API are intercepted by the OAuth filter and calls WSO2 Identity Server (OAuth authorization server) to validate the token. The username/password `init-params` for `OAuthFilter` should be changed accordingly. It should use the credentials of a user from WSO2 Identity Server who has access to the OAuth token validation service. By default, the credentials are `admin/admin`. The `serverURL` `init-param` should point to the host/port where WSO2 Identity Server is running:

   ```
   <filter>
           <filter-name>OAuthFilter</filter-name>
           <filter-class>org.wso2.is.oauth.OAuthFilter</filter-class>
           <init-param>
               <param-name>username</param-name>
   ```

```
            <param-value>admin</param-value>
        </init-param>
        <init-param>
            <param-name>password</param-name>
            <param-value>admin</param-value>
        </init-param>
        <init-param>
            <param-name>serverUrl</param-name>
            <param-value>https://localhost:9443/services</param-value>
        </init-param>
    </filter>
    <filter-mapping>
        <filter-name>OAuthFilter</filter-name>
        <url-pattern>/*</url-pattern>
    </filter-mapping>
```

6. That's all you need to do. Now your API is secured with OAuth. If you invoke the following cURL command, it will fail with a 401:

```
curl http://localhost:8080/recipe
```

GETTING AN ACCESS TOKEN WITH THE OAUTH 2.0 AUTHORIZATION CODE GRANT TYPE

In the previous exercise, you deployed the Recipe API in an Apache Tomcat server and secured it with OAuth 2.0. To access the Recipe API, you need to have a client application. The client application first must be registered at the OAuth authorization server to get a client key and a client secret. Follow these steps:

1. Start WSO2 Identity Server from `wso2server.sh/wso2server.bat` in `WSO2_IS_HOME/bin`.

2. Go to `https://localhost:9443`, and log in using `admin/admin`.

3. Go to Main ➤ Identity ➤ Service Providers ➤ Add. Give an appropriate service provider name, and choose Register.

4. Choose Inbound Authentication Configuration ➤ OAuth/OpenID Connect Configuration ➤ Configure.

5. Give an appropriate value for Callback Url. It should point to a URL under your application's domain. For example, here you use `https://mycallback`.

6. Make sure all allowed grant types are selected.

7. Click Add to create the application, and click Update.

8. Under the OAuth/OpenID Connect Configuration of the corresponding service provider, you can find the client ID and the client secret of the application you just created:

```
Client Id        OrhQErXIX49svVYoXJGtoDWBuFca
Client Secret    eYOFkL756W8usQaVNgCNkz9C2DOa
Access Token Url https://localhost:9443/oauth2/token
Authorize Url    https://localhost:9443/oauth2/authorize
```

Now your client application is registered and you have a client key and a client secret corresponding to it. The next step is to obtain a code from the OAuth authorization server. Because you aren't using a web application in this example, you can simply copy the following URL and paste it in the browser. This request should go to the `Authorize Url` of the authorization server. The value of `redirect_uri` should be the URL-encoded value of the `Callback Url` you used at the time of application registration:

```
https://localhost:9443/oauth2/authorize?
                        response_type=code&
                        client_id=OrhQErXIX49svVYoXJGtODWBuFca&
                        redirect_uri=https%3A%2F%2Fmycallback
```

You need to authenticate to WSO2 Identity Server and then approve the authorization grant. Then, you're redirected to the provided callback URL with the code. Copy the value of the code—you'll need it in the future:

```
https://mycallback/?code=9142d4cad58c66d0a5edfad8952192
```

Once you have the authorization code, the next step is to exchange it for an access token:

```
curl -v -X POST --basic
                -u OrhQErXIX49svVYoXJGtODWBuFca:eYOFkL756W8usQaVNgCNkz9C2DOa
                -H "Content-Type:application/x-www-form-urlencoded;
                               charset=UTF-8" -k
                -d "grant_type=authorization_code&
                   code=9142d4cad58c66d0a5edfad8952192&
                   redirect_uri=https://mycallback" https://localhost:9443/oauth2/token
```

This returns the following response:

```
{
    "token_type":"bearer",
    "expires_in":3600,
    "refresh_token":"22b157546b26c2d6c0165c4ef6b3f736",
    "access_token":"cac93e1d29e45bf6d84073dbfb460"
}
```

Now you can access the Recipe API with the following cURL command, with the access token obtained in the previous step:

```
curl -H "Authorization:Bearer cac93e1d29e45bf6d84073dbfb460" http://localhost:8080/recipe
```

▪ **Note** Accessing a protected API secured with the OAuth 2.0 bearer token profile MUST be over TLS. Some examples in this book may use HTTP to access protected APIs solely for the demonstration purpose. But this is not recommended in a production setup. Enabling TLS for APIs deployed in Tomcat is discussed in the section "Enabling TLS in Apache Tomcat" in Chapter 3.

GETTING AN ACCESS TOKEN WITH THE OAUTH 2.0 IMPLICIT CODE GRANT TYPE

This exercise extends the previous one to show how to obtain an access token from the authorization server using the Implicit grant type and use it to invoke the Recipe API. By now your client application should be registered with WSO2 Identity Server (authorization server), and you should have obtained a client key and a secret.

To get an access token with the Implicit grant type, copy the following URL and paste it in the browser. The value of the response_type parameter must be set to token:

```
https://localhost:9443/oauth2/authorize?
                       response_type=token&
                       client_id=OrhQErXIX49svVYoXJGtoDWBuFca&
                       redirect_uri=https%3A%2F%2Fmycallback
```

You need to authenticate to WSO2 Identity Server and then approve the authorization grant. Then, you're redirected to the provided callback URL with the access token. This comes as a URI fragment that can be accessed by a JavaScript running in the browser:

```
https://mycallback/#access_token=cac93e1d29e45bf6d84073dbfb460&expires_in=3600
```

Now you can access the Recipe API with the following cURL command, with the access token obtained in the previous step:

```
curl -H "Authorization:Bearer cac93e1d29e45bf6d84073dbfb460" http://localhost:8080/recipe
```

GETTING AN ACCESS TOKEN WITH THE OAUTH 2.0 RESOURCE OWNER PASSWORD CREDENTIALS GRANT TYPE

In this exercise, you see how to get an access token with the Resource Owner Password Credentials grant type. By now you should have registered your client application with WSO2 Identity Server (authorization server), and you should have obtained a client key and a secret. To get an access token with the Resource Owner Password Credentials grant type, use the following cURL command. The values of the username and password should be from a valid user in the user store behind the authorization server:

```
curl -v -X POST --basic
             -u OrhQErXIX49svVYoXJGtoDWBuFca:eYOFkL756W8usQaVNgCNkz9C2D0a
             -H "Content-Type:application/x-www-form-urlencoded;
                        charset=UTF-8" -k
             -d "grant_type=password&
                 username=admin&
                 password=admin" https://localhost:9443/oauth2/token
```

This returns the following response:

```
{
    "token_type":"bearer",
    "expires_in":685,
    "refresh_token":"22b157546b26c2d6c0165c4ef6b3f736",
    "access_token":"cac93e1d29e45bf6d84073dbfb460"
}
```

Now you can access the Recipe API with the following cURL command, with the access token obtained in the previous step:

```
curl –H "Authorization:Bearer cac93e1d29e45bf6d84073dbfb460" http://localhost:8080/recipe
```

GETTING AN ACCESS TOKEN WITH THE OAUTH 2.0 CLIENT CREDENTIALS GRANT TYPE

In this exercise, you see how to get an access token with the Client Credentials grant type. By now you should have registered your client application with WSO2 Identity Server (authorization server), and you should have obtained a client key and a secret. To get an access token with the Client Credentials grant type, use the following cURL command:

```
curl -v -X POST --basic
                -u OrhQErXIX49svVYoXJGtODWBuFca:eYOFkL756W8usQaVNgCNkz9C2DOa
                -H "Content-Type:application/x-www-form-urlencoded;
                            charset=UTF-8" -k
                -d "grant_type=client_credentials" https://localhost:9443/oauth2/token
```

This returns the following response:

```
{
    "token_type":"bearer",
    "expires_in":3600,
    "access_token":"4c9a9ae7463ff9bb93ae7f169bd6a"
}
```

Now you can access the Recipe API with the following cURL command, with the access token obtained in the previous step:

```
curl –H "Authorization:Bearer 4c9a9ae7463ff9bb93ae7f169bd6a" http://localhost:8080/recipe
```

OAUTH 2.0 REFRESH TOKENS

Although it's not the case with the Implicit grant type and the Client Credentials grant type, with the other two grant types the OAuth access token comes with a refresh token. This refresh token can be used to extend the validity of the access token without the involvement of the resource owner. The following cURL command shows how to get a new access token from the refresh token:

```
curl -v -X POST --basic
             -u OrhQErXIX49svVYoXJGtoDWBuFca:eYOFkL756W8usQaVNgCNkz9C2DOa
             -H "Content-Type:application/x-www-form-urlencoded;
                         charset=UTF-8" -k
             -d "grant_type=refresh_token&
                 refresh_token=22b157546b26c2d6c0165c4ef6b3f736"
                 https://localhost:9443/oauth2/token
```

This returns the following response:

```
{
    "token_type":"bearer",
    "expires_in":3600,
    "refresh_token":"9ecc381836fa5e3baf5a9e86081",
    "access_token":"b574d1ba554c26148f5fca3cceb05e2"
}
```

■ **Note** The refresh token has a much longer lifetime than the access token. If the lifetime of the refresh token expires, then the client must initiate the OAuth token flow from the start and get a new access token and refresh token. The authorization server also has the option to return a new refresh token each time the client refreshes the access token. In such cases, the client has to discard the previously obtained refresh token and begin using the new one.

OAuth 2.0 and Facebook

Facebook opened its login functionality to the rest of the Internet in December 2008. It was the time of OAuth 1.0, but Facebook was reluctant to follow that path. Facebook came up with its own protocol called Facebook Connect to give third parties access to Facebook users' profiles. Facebook Connect was first announced during the F8 conference in July 2008. TechCrunch, CNN, Govit, Howcast, and vLane took part in the initial launch of Facebook Connect by implementing login with Facebook.

■ **Note** The following is from the official announcement of Facebook Connect (www.facebook.com/notes/facebook/platform-one-yearish-later/24577977130): "Facebook Connect is a new way to use applications, on the open web and not just on Facebook. Soon, you'll be able to use your Facebook account to login and connect on websites throughout the web. Imagine never filling out another profile at a new site, or having to find your friends all over again. Facebook Connect will help make this a reality and allow you to use Facebook to share information from all over the web with your friends."

A few reasons kept Facebook from using OAuth 1.0. Performance was a key concern. OAuth 1.0 took four HTTP requests to create a user login session and make an API call, whereas Facebook Connect took only two.

■ **Note**   In OAuth 1.0, the first HTTP request is made to acquire a request token from the authorization server. The second request is to get it authorized by the resource owner. The third is to exchange the authorized request token to an access token. The fourth is to make an API call using the access token.

In November 2009, Facebook joined the Open Web Foundation with Microsoft, Google, Yahoo!, and many others with a commitment to support open standards for web authentication. Keeping this promise, in December 2009, Facebook added OAuth WRAP support to FriendFeed, which it had acquired a few months earlier. In May 2010, Facebook brought OAuth 2.0 into the mainstream authentication flow. By October 2010, all Facebook applications were expected to migrate from the older Facebook Connect to OAuth 2.0. Of the four core grant types supported by OAuth 2.0, Facebook initially added support for the Authorization Code grant type (also known as server-side) and the Implicit grant type (also known as client-side).

■ **Note**   The blog post by David Recordon that introduced Facebook FriendFeed support for OAuth WRAP is at `https://developers.facebook.com/blog/post/350/`. The blog post "Facebook Developer Roadmap Update: Moving to OAuth 2.0 + HTTPS," by Naitik Shah, is at `https://developers.facebook.com/blog/post/497/`.

Facebook supports three types of access tokens: user access tokens, app access tokens, and page access tokens. The user access token is the most commonly used type, when an application wants to access a Facebook API on behalf of another user. The application has to use either the Authorization Code grant type or the Implicit grant type to get the access token. The application owner uses the app access token to update application settings through the Facebook API. App access tokens are generated using the OAuth Client Credentials grant type. The page access token is very similar to the user access token, except it has an additional manage_pages permission. Once you have the user access token, it can be exchanged for a page access token via the Facebook Graph API.

REGISTERING A CLIENT APPLICATION WITH FACEBOOK

In this exercise, you see how to register an OAuth client application with Facebook:

1.   Log in to Facebook, and go to `https://developers.facebook.com/`.

2.   Click Apps ➤ Create New, fill in the required details, and complete the app-creation process.

3.   The app you just created is accessible through the Apps menu at any time. Click the name of your app, and you see that an app ID and an app secret have been generated for your application. The app ID is the OAuth client key, and the app key is the OAuth client secret. Copy the values of App ID and App Key—these are used in the following exercises.

4.   Click Settings ➤ Advanced. Make sure Client OAuth Login is set to Yes.

■ **Note**   Only the owner can use an application registered in Facebook until it's been promoted to the general public. To promote the application, you need to submit it for review via the Status & Review menu item under the application you created.

GETTING AN OAUTH APP ACCESS TOKEN FROM FACEBOOK

In this exercise, you see how to get an app access token from Facebook. This assumes you've already registered your client application with Facebook and are in possession of an app ID and an app key.

The following cURL command shows how to get an app access token from Facebook with the Client Credentials grant type:

```
curl -v -X POST --basic
              -u 588997174524690:d5cc4d8e01c9bd7ac14b4d5e91006b5b
              -H "Content-Type:application/x-www-form-urlencoded;
                          charset=UTF-8" -k
              -d "client_id=588997174524690&
                  grant_type=client_credentials"
                  https://graph.facebook.com/oauth/access_token
```

This returns the following response. The returned access token can be used to manage your application:

```
access_token=588997174524690|jYDqtJ-F4M_kVvYCjeW5fwtvmL8
```

The following cURL command talks to the Facebook Graph API with the app access token to get more details about the application. 588997174524690 is the app ID, in the URL:

```
curl https://graph.facebook.com/588997174524690?
              access_token="588997174524690|jYDqtJ-F4M_kVvYCjeW5fwtvmL8"
```

The following is the JSON response:

```
{
    "id":"588997174524690",
    "name":"apress-security-app",
    "category":"Education",
    "link":"http://www.facebook.com/apps/application.php?id=588997174524690",
    "icon_url":"http://static.ak.fbcdn.net/rsrc.php/v2/yT/r/4QVMqOjUhcd.gif",
    "logo_url":"http://photos-c.ak.fbcdn.net/hphotos-ak-prn1/
                    t39.2081-0/p75x75/
                    851578_455087414601994_1601110696_n.png",
    "daily_active_users":"1",
    "weekly_active_users":"1",
    "monthly_active_users":"1",
    "daily_active_users_rank":"453809",
    "monthly_active_users_rank":"1615461"
}
```

GETTING AN OAUTH USER ACCESS TOKEN FROM FACEBOOK

In this exercise, you see how to get a user access token from Facebook (see Figure 7-5). This assumes you've already registered your client application with Facebook and are in possession of an app ID and an app key. Copy the following URL, replace the value of `client_id` with the one corresponding to your application, and paste it in a browser. Prior to that, make sure you've set `https://www.facebook.com/connect/login_success.html` as the redirect URI of your registered client application:

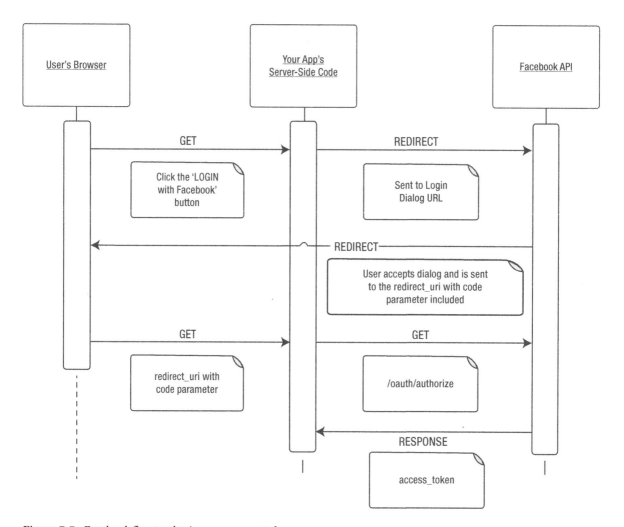

Figure 7-5. *Facebook flow to obtain a user access token*

■ **Note** To set a redirect URI for your client application, log in to Facebook and go to `https://developers.facebook.com/`. From the Apps menu, click the name of your app, and choose Settings ➤ Advanced. Enter `https://www.facebook.com/connect/login_success.html` in the Valid OAuth Redirect URIs text box, and click Save Changes.

```
https://www.facebook.com/dialog/oauth?
                            client_id=588997174524690&
                            redirect_uri=https://www.facebook.com/connect/login_success.html&
                            scope=publish_actions
```

■ **Note**   Even though `response_type` is a required parameter in OAuth 2.0 RFC, Facebook doesn't mandate it. It assumes the value of `response_type` is `code`, although in case it's not present. The value of `scope` should be a valid permission defined in the Facebook Graph API. More details about Facebook permissions are at `https://developers.facebook.com/docs/facebook-login/permissions`.

This returns the following response. Make sure you quickly copy the value from the browser address bar—otherwise it could disappear. In an ideal scenario, you need a redirect URI that is under your control; the authorization code is returned there. In the authorization grant request, you set the value of `scope` to `publish_actions`. That means your client application is able to post messages to the user's Facebook wall:

```
https://www.facebook.com/connect/login_success.html?
          code=AQDQoRlLf5xHIMA--vR1CsMeu-HONBPyfMOX2JTVXN_
                OqH8z1NkQQRu7r19_vYfSu-L6WzA71ffr75LoUqlLT_wLy
                sHGqjcoJZpryH3geF7_cOvxWjTNTYwvsYTpErbK2P1nw5
                qRSeo8qJnLO57MahNgsTb8MtTZB4l7tLB4IBWTccJG8w
                vsnGTzx4vQ_Sp6iWOafq2O7dLMwzGyKZkD9HMQ8sW4
                WSqnXm95QAsZRZeWmRp7MmtPGReltHIO75f4KDoALO
                R81Jx7qfruNeF4wizh4OFc-SoXpMASxagVRQUBYdRwSn
                rQVzsDON1G4_1qHZE#_=_
```

Copy the value of `code` from this response, and add it to the access-token request. Copy the following URL; replace the values of the appropriate parameters (`client_id`, `client_secret`, and `code`), and paste it in the browser. Make sure the value of `redirect_uri` is same as in the previous authorization grant request. This returns the access token:

```
https://graph.facebook.com/oauth/access_token?
          client_id=588997174524690&
          redirect_uri=https://www.facebook.com/connect/login_success.html&
          client_secret=d5cc4d8e01c9bd7ac14b4d5e91006b5b&
          code=AQDQoRlLf5xHIMA--vR1CsMeu-HONBPyfMOX2JTVXN_
                OqH8z1NkQQRu7r19_vYfSu-L6WzA71ffr75LoUqlLT_wLy
                sHGqjcoJZpryH3geF7_cOvxWjTNTYwvsYTpErbK2P1nw5
                qRSeo8qJnLO57MahNgsTb8MtTZB4l7tLB4IBWTccJG8w
                vsnGTzx4vQ_Sp6iWOafq2O7dLMwzGyKZkD9HMQ8sW4
                WSqnXm95QAsZRZeWmRp7MmtPGReltHIO75f4KDoALO
                R81Jx7qfruNeF4wizh4OFc-SoXpMASxagVRQUBYdRwSn
                rQVzsDON1G4_1qHZE#_=_
```

Copy the value of access_token from the following response:

```
access_token=CAAIXsJdcexIBANoR7sRFbQMAlBTuVtZATUdKypc5m6
             dURLqTOirQ2hQ7oXcOqxeXzec2ylPOUHWnSFw6fZAcTG
             CJgzhNxZBtHr7q0jZCZBwGL3gzfPrUSUGHtBntNtIzDWd
             8KeYZC3WYKcmljxeTNRZAaa9ZCzHZC7oVFWWckra7z
             JCbplTHG9ElW&
expires=5179012
```

The following cURL command posts a message to the user's Facebook wall, with the previous access token:

```
curl -v -X POST -d "message=test" https://graph.facebook.com/me/feed?
                 access_token="CAAIXsJdcexIBANoR7sRFbQMAlBT
                               uVtZATUdKypc5m6dURLqTOirQ2hQ7oXcOqxeXzec2ylPOUH
                               WnSFw6fZAcTGCJgzhNxZBtHr7q0jZCZBwGL3gzfPrUSUGHt
                               BntNtIzDWd8KeYZC3WYKcmljxeTNRZAaa9ZCzHZC7oVFWW
                               ckra7zJCbplTHG9ElW"
```

If the message posted successfully, the Facebook Graph API returns the following response:

```
{"id":"787236966_10152305588201967"}
```

■ **Note**   A complete reference for Facebook Graph API is available at
https://developers.facebook.com/docs/graph-api/reference/.

GETTING AN OAUTH PAGE ACCESS TOKEN FROM FACEBOOK

In this exercise, you see how to get a page access token from Facebook. This assumes you've already registered your client application with Facebook and are in possession of an app ID and an app key. Copy the following URL, replacing the value of client_id with the one corresponding to your application, and paste it in a browser. Prior to that, make sure you've set https://www.facebook.com/connect/login_success.html as the redirect URI of your registered client application. The page access token is very similar to the user access token, except it needs to have the additional manage_pages permission:

```
https://www.facebook.com/dialog/oauth?
           client_id=588997174524690&
           redirect_uri=https://www.facebook.com/connect/login_success.html&
           scope=manage_pages
```

This returns the following response. Make sure you quickly copy the value from the browser address bar—otherwise it could disappear. In an ideal scenario, you need a redirect URI that is under your control; the authorization code is returned there. In the authorization grant request, you set the value of scope to `manage_permission`. That means your client application is able to exchange the access token for a page access token later:

```
https://www.facebook.com/connect/login_success.html?
          code=AQAkuqOXstUuEmCgMcOz9zBCUBUquTareD3Ezfx
              vOydJd8EqglHeLYuMvg2-lNWOTb78JRvHFHH-XjWo
              Sj3PvIaTyMDk1OiLGvgCpA89NOt3O_QQaC1TMGib
              bY6v4CCWVgh2rsoEqXTOtwNFlR4GhUPFzzivYVIah
              ZF6wUpnm5jwX-OyxD4WFyGoNQ6vltoEkUWBl3Pdfr
              S1ZQaa4Xprr_lnfHGgMlOKTW-ECPNKA6fUeG-GmK
              ylqCsmbp_SOWDatpmhwASIDER-NXv2xLUOrxEN6n
              uRR5zGP_-2-V5PfKYbDMIzKzcRaHjjTMRSGlOf8VM#_=_
```

Copy the value of `code` from this response, and add it to the access token request. Copy the following URL; replacing the values of the appropriate parameters (`client_id`, `client_secret`, and `code`), and paste it in the browser. Make sure the value of `redirect_uri` is same as in the authorization grant request. This returns the access token:

```
https://graph.facebook.com/oauth/access_token?
          client_id=588997174524690&
          redirect_uri=https://www.facebook.com/connect/login_success.html&
          client_secret=d5cc4d8e01c9bd7ac14b4d5e91006b5b&
          code=AQAkuqOXstUuEmCgMcOz9zBCUBUquTareD3Ezfx
              vOydJd8EqglHeLYuMvg2-lNWOTb78JRvHFHH-XjWo
              Sj3PvIaTyMDk1OiLGvgCpA89NOt3O_QQaC1TMGib
              bY6v4CCWVgh2rsoEqXTOtwNFlR4GhUPFzzivYVIah
              ZF6wUpnm5jwX-OyxD4WFyGoNQ6vltoEkUWBl3Pdfr
              S1ZQaa4Xprr_lnfHGgMlOKTW-ECPNKA6fUeG-GmK
              ylqCsmbp_SOWDatpmhwASIDER-NXv2xLUOrxEN6n
              uRR5zGP_-2-V5PfKYbDMIzKzcRaHjjTMRSGlOf8VM#_=_
```

Copy the value of `access_token` from the following response:

```
access_token=CAAIXsJdcexIBAGpiefGkNX9FfdCLnxExEwvZBIk5WiQZAIavHL
              mD4gU9pjT3O5Wr4OeT586xtOogg9R9xKXsTvZB4CvzyZAiJTG2
              GGsHQuTxZBVoaAiPhMgBLOP58Kg62ZCH55wU5bzVQ8xHxsb
              4xc1egZA5TkGihshgiiJVIwZBDAoihphaaKAchgrq4f9PYcMZD&
expires=5177015
```

The following cURL command exchanges the user access token for a set of page access tokens:

```
curl -v https://graph.facebook.com/me/accounts?
          access_token="CAAIXsJdcexIBAGpiefGkNX9FfdCLnxExEwvZBIk5WiQZAIavHL
                  mD4gU9pjT3O5Wr4OeT586xtOogg9R9xKXsTvZB4CvzyZAiJTG2
                  GGsHQuTxZBVoaAiPhMgBLOP58Kg62ZCH55wU5bzVQ8xHxsb
                  4xc1egZA5TkGihshgiiJVIwZBDAoihphaaKAchgrq4f9PYcMZD"
```

This returns all the pages the user has access to, with the corresponding page-access tokens:

```
{
"data":[
                {
                        "category":"Community",
                        "name":"JAVA Colombo",
                        "access_token":"CAAIXsJdcexIBACYQEcdw4nOyTlQXqwxHaTm
                                        Fsx2OKAiTMvg7N5CtZBUVLwZAm3WKKVgO9e
                                        9qTYB2xMe4ZBiB2QDVZBfvnDOZBhuROv2UNL
                                        ffxF8SxDJ5KHZAid9vTzMxFAGujA9YZC1O6Qgp
                                        pTSdZBbvyCfBHw4jeldZAICJru5SOFk4Dk2qzRAHc",
                        "perms":["ADMINISTER","EDIT_PROFILE",
                                  "CREATE_CONTENT","MODERATE_CONTENT",
                                  "CREATE_ADS","BASIC_ADMIN"],
                        "id":"348163825217082"
                }
        ]
}
```

The following cURL command posts a message to the Java Colombo page with the corresponding access token:

```
curl -v -X POST -d "message=test"
                https://graph.facebook.com/348163825217082/feed?
                access_token="CAAIXsJdcexIBACYQEcdw4nOyTlQXqwxHaTmFsx2OKAiT
                              Mvg7N5CtZBUVLwZAm3WKKVgO9e9qTYB2xMe4ZBiB2QD
                              VZBfvnDOZBhuROv2UNLffxF8SxDJ5KHZAid9vTzMxFAGujA
                              9YZC1O6QgppTSdZBbvyCfBHw4jeldZAICJru5SOFk4Dk2qzRAHc"
```

OAuth 2.0 and LinkedIn

LinkedIn added OAuth 2.0 support in February 2013. Prior to that, LinkedIn APIs were secured with OAuth 1.0. Like many others that migrated from OAuth 1.0 to OAuth 2.0, LinkedIn found it much easier and simpler to implement than OAuth 1.0. But it continues to support both OAuth 1.0 and 2.0.

▪ **Note** The forum post by Kamyar Mohager that introduced OAuth 2.0 support for LinkedIn is available at https://developer.linkedin.com/forum/authentication-oauth-20.

REGISTERING A CLIENT APPLICATION WITH LINKEDIN

In this exercise, you see how to register an OAuth client application with LinkedIn:

1. Go to `https://www.linkedin.com/secure/developer`.

2. Click Add New Application, complete the registration form, click Add Application, and click Done. Keep `r_basicProfile` as the default scope. When you set a value for OAuth 2.0 Redirect URLs, make sure it ends with a top-level domain name (such as `https://mycallback.com`).

3. Go to `https://www.linkedin.com/secure/developer`, and click the client application you just created.

4. In the OAuth Keys section, the page displays four values: API Key, Secret Key, OAuth User Token, and OAuth User Secret. Copy the values and keep them for future use.

ACCESSING LINKEDIN APIS WITH AN OAUTH CLIENT

In this exercise, you see how to acquire an access token from LinkedIn and use it to access LinkedIn APIs. Copy the following URL, and paste it in the browser. Replace the values of `client_id` and `redirect_uri` appropriately. The value of `client_id` is the API key from the previous exercise. Here you set `scope` to `r_fullprofile`:

```
https://www.linkedin.com/uas/oauth2/authorization?
        response_type=code&
        client_id=75dq25a43vewbx&
        scope=r_fullprofile&
        redirect_uri=https://mycallback.com&
        state=mystate
```

■ **Note** According to the OAuth 2.0 RFC, `state` and `redirect_uri` aren't mandatory parameters in the authorization grant request, but LinkedIn has made them mandatory. Whatever value you set in `state` is returned to the `redirect_uri` with the authorization code. Even though `state` isn't a mandatory parameter, the OAuth specification recommends using it as a protective measure against a cross-site request forgery (CSRF).

This returns the authorization code to the `redirect_uri`. Copy the value of the `code` parameter:

```
https://mycallback.com/?
        code=AQTeOQ7sM1BdnRFFISpjTzeYBJ76nEu9xBO--
            WQeZ5cO1JFRoFfDY752cxBcjg6Kui33x8wxEJnRUtnYBROX
            XwqlqXdN3FhgRHqHJaj5JPKnxmrRno4&
        state=mystate
```

■ **Note** The authorization code generated here has a very short lifetime—around 20 seconds. You need to be very quick when you proceed to the next step. If you aren't, you'll see the error "AppId or redirect uri does not match authorization code or authorization code expired."

Once you have the authorization code, you need to exchange it for an access token. Run the following cURL command with appropriate values for code, redirect_uri, client_id, and client_secret. The value of redirect_uri should match the value used in the previous step:

```
curl -v -X POST -d "grant_type=authorization_code&
                    code=AQT-5KdfZO-bIbaflEOgXolOvRlOiVLmbYsB483
                        UZLSjnxDQnNDhw-806mKZmPIm24yR3-x4YNK
                        MAxK-8dBU4SELcefotOcpWBThkDsiaRWORu8-Dqk&
                    redirect_uri=https://mycallback.com&
                    client_id=75dq25a43vewbx&
                    client_secret=nEnFqKjB4aMYh9fV"
                    https://www.linkedin.com/uas/oauth2/accessToken
```

This returns an access token, which has a lifetime of 20 days:

```
{
    "expires_in":5183999,
    "access_token":"AQVKwPCyJoTDl9CZl5ID9S9hig9qdOPYJdAvks
                    6oyLeBp9J59lxhyQrXcHzJ_VrJ6a-FL-1diqHs_MK
                    l_kHTKOslCXXk7cnjj1pnFM8-oZeI3TI33HMsUrk
                    WZkkC3vAnavvJHJUMZIlIWX3eWcOytJ6SMNH4
                    3iPKetXOEr7PJwVQPy6UNiA"
}
```

Once you have the access token, you can invoke LinkedIn APIs. The following API call with this access token gets the user's basic profile information:

```
curl https://api.linkedin.com/v1/people/~?
             oauth2_access_token=AQVKwPCyJoTDl9CZl5ID9S9hig9qdOP
                                 YJdAvks6oyLeBp9J59lxhyQrXcHzJ_VrJ
                                 6a-FL-1diqHs_MKl_kHTKOslCXXk7cnjj1
                                 pnFM8-oZeI3TI33HMsUrkWZkkC3vAnav
                                 vJHJUMZIlIWX3eWcOytJ6SMNH43iPKet
                                 XOEr7PJwVQPy6UNiA
```

■ **Note** According to the OAuth 2.0 Bearer Token Profile, when accessing a resource protected with OAuth 2.0, the bearer token can go in the HTTP Authorization header or be a form-encoded body parameter or a query parameter. If it's a query parameter, its value *must* be access_token. But here, LinkedIn deviates from the OAuth 2.0 Bearer Token Profile.

The response is returned as an XML payload:

```
<?xml version="1.0" encoding="UTF-8" standalone="yes"?>
<person>
  <first-name>Prabath</first-name>
  <last-name>Siriwardena</last-name>
  <headline>Director of Security Architecture at WSO2</headline>
  <site-standard-profile-request>
```

```
        <url>http://www.linkedin.com/profile/view?id=18817210&amp;
                                 authType=name&amp;
                                 authToken=Zd8V&amp;
                                 trk=api*a3681071*s3751911*</url>

    </site-standard-profile-request>
</person>
```

OAuth 2.0 and Salesforce

Salesforce introduced OAuth 2.0 support with its winter 2011 platform release. Currently it supports the OAuth 2.0 Authorization Code grant type, Implicit grant type, and Resource Owner Password Credentials grant type.

▓ **Note**   The announcement of Salesforce support for OAuth 2.0 is available at:
https://developer.salesforce.com/releases/release/related/OAuth+2+Support.

REGISTERING A CLIENT APPLICATION WITH SALESFORCE

In this exercise, you see how to set up a Salesforce account and register a client application to consume Salesforce APIs secured with OAuth 2.0:

1. Create a Salesforce account if you don't have one. You can create a free developer account at http://developer.force.com.

2. After you log in to your Salesforce developer account, you need to create an application to represent the application you're going to develop to consume Salesforce APIs. To do so, click Setup in the drop-down menu under your Salesforce logged-in name. Under App Setup, click Create and then Apps. Under Connected Apps, click New. Fill in the required details, and then select Enable OAuth Settings.

3. Type an HTTPS URL as the Callback URL. For the moment, this can be anything—even something that doesn't exist will work. In this example, you aren't using it; this is needed only if you try to authenticate via a browser. Also select Full Access as the OAuth scope. Then save the changes. You see the OAuth consumer key and consumer secret generated for your application. Copy them for future use.

4. Salesforce enforces more security controls over API access. To access an API using the previous keys, you need to whitelist the IP addresses where you're going to run your application. This is extremely useful in cases where you need to make sure the APIs are accessed only from your corporate domain/network. Then again, keep in mind that IP addresses can be spoofed.

5. If you want your Salesforce APIs to be accessible from anywhere, you need to create a security token. To do so, under My Settings/Personal/Reset My Security Token, click Reset Security Token. You receive the security token to your registered e-mail account. Keep it; you'll need it in future steps.

GETTING AN ACCESS TOKEN FROM THE SALESFORCE WEB SERVER AUTHENTICATION FLOW

In this exercise, you see how to get an access token from Salesforce using the OAuth 2.0 Authorization Code grant type, also known as the web server authentication flow. This assumes you've already registered your OAuth application with Salesforce and have the corresponding consumer key and consumer secret. Copy the following URL, replacing the values of client_id and redirect_uri appropriately, and paste it in the browser:

```
https://login.salesforce.com/services/oauth2/authorize?
                              response_type=code&
                              client_id=3MVG9Y6d_Btp4xp5jz7MvysvlXtY44T2PFwadEeJT
                                      B6EC1wyOuakCU3rNvRx7vNVNbT4OveMfjVDoz569_nlK&
                              redirect_uri=https://mycallback.info&
                              state=mystate
```

This returns the authorization code to the redirect_uri, with the provided state value:

```
https://mycallback.info/?
        code=aPrxaSyVmC8fBbeOjjmyHoNhPTKehpnyzQU8WUGyIS.14C7CxLh7
              lOrAh3shDDOLHyC9om_P6w%3D%3D&
        state=mystate
```

Once you have the authorization code, you need to exchange it for an access token. Run the following cURL command with the appropriate values for code, redirect_uri, client_id, and client_secret. The value of redirect_uri should match the value used in the previous step:

```
curl -v -X POST -d "grant_type=authorization_code&
                    code=aPrxaSyVmC8fBbeOjjmyHoNhPTKehpnyzQU8WUGyIS.
                          14C7CxLh7lOrAh3shDDOLHyC9om_P6w%3D%3D&
                    client_id=3MVG9Y6d_Btp4xp5jz7MvysvlXtY44T2PFwadEeJTB6
                          EC1wyOuakCU3rNvRx7vNVNbT4OveMfjVDoz569_nlK&
                    client_secret=3623940361107861841&
                    redirect_uri=https://mycallback.info"
                    https://login.salesforce.com/services/oauth2/token
```

This returns the access token with an URI for the authenticated user (represented by the id attribute):

```
{
        "id":"https://login.salesforce.com/id/00D90000000mOZiEAI/00590000001QHFEAA4",
        "issued_at":"1395343085296",
        "scope":"id",
        "instance_url":"https://ap1.salesforce.com",
        "signature":"roZJ1pUyAJfOhS4TeJYpq1yKKapptHpilDeSrRED9AE=",
        "access_token":"00D90000000mOZi!ARsAQJtHnsDU.hiMpaOsrkDhiDROjdZMj1P
                        _J6qVJZ_OGYRzxzxuP4ppHzDNhQz8vK2RCRhFi4IAdb1ouSrZc
                        EH_jbzM21K3"
}
```

To get the user details, you need to talk to the specified URI, corresponding to the authenticated user (from the previous response), with the access token:

```
curl https://ap1.salesforce.com/id/00D90000000mOZiEAI/00590000001QHFEAA4?
          oauth_token='00D90000000mOZi!ARsAQH9G7bNVqya4A5Qsn3Rziq
                      Aybt.xfOoDJrHr_28M6G3RHV6mcVi_OT367AjorudSe_
                      YkSeVsycgOyDQNH_7djHaxeNOk'
```

> ■ **Note** According to the OAuth 2.0 Bearer Token Profile, when accessing a resource protected with OAuth 2.0, the bearer token can go in the HTTP Authorization header or be a form-encoded body parameter or a query parameter. If it's a query parameter, its value must be access_token. But here, Salesforce deviates from the OAuth 2.0 Bearer Token Profile.

This returns the following JSON response:

```
{
    "id":"https://login.salesforce.com/id/00D90000000mOZiEAI/00590000001QHFEAA4",
    "asserted_user":true,
    "user_id":"00590000001QHFEAA4",
    "organization_id":"00D90000000mOZiEAI",
    "username":"prabath@wso2.com",
    "nick_name":"prabath1.3686094247092776E12",
    "display_name":"Prabath Siriwardena",
    "email":"prabath@wso2.com",
    "first_name":"Prabath",
    "last_name":"Siriwardena",
    "status":{
        "created_date":null,
        "body":null
    },
    "photos":{
        "picture":"https://c.ap1.content.force.com/profilephoto/005/F",
        "thumbnail":"https://c.ap1.content.force.com/profilephoto/005/T"
    },
    "urls":{
        "enterprise":"https://ap1.salesforce.com/services/Soap/c/{version}/00D90000000mOZi",
        "metadata":"https://ap1.salesforce.com/services/Soap/m/{version}/00D90000000mOZi",
        "partner":"https://ap1.salesforce.com/services/Soap/u/{version}/00D90000000mOZi",
        "rest":"https://ap1.salesforce.com/services/data/v{version}/",
        "sobjects":"https://ap1.salesforce.com/services/data/v{version}/sobjects/",
        "search":"https://ap1.salesforce.com/services/data/v{version}/search/",
        "query":"https://ap1.salesforce.com/services/data/v{version}/query/",
        "recent":"https://ap1.salesforce.com/services/data/v{version}/recent/",
        "profile":"https://ap1.salesforce.com/00590000001QHFEAA4",
        "feeds":"https://ap1.salesforce.com/services/data/v{version}/chatter/feeds",
        "groups":"https://ap1.salesforce.com/services/data/v{version}/chatter/groups",
        "users":"https://ap1.salesforce.com/services/data/v{version}/chatter/users",
        "feed_items":"https://ap1.salesforce.com/services/data/v{version}/chatter/feed-items",
        "custom_domain":"https://wso2-dev-ed.my.salesforce.com"
    },
```

```
        "active":true,
        "user_type":"STANDARD",
        "language":"en_US",
        "locale":"en_US",
        "utcOffset":-28800000,
        "last_modified_date":"2013-08-20T02:15:22.000+0000"
}
```

GETTING AN ACCESS TOKEN FROM THE SALESFORCE USER AGENT AUTHENTICATION FLOW

In this exercise, you see how to get an access token from Salesforce using the OAuth 2.0 Implicit grant type, also known as the user agent authentication flow. This assumes you've already registered your OAuth application with Salesforce and have the corresponding consumer key and consumer secret. Copy the following URL, replacing the values of client_id and redirect_uri appropriately, and paste it in the browser. The value of response_type here is set to token:

```
https://login.salesforce.com/services/oauth2/authorize?
        response_type=token&
        client_id=3MVG9Y6d_Btp4xp5jz7MvysvlXtY44T2PFwadEeJTB6
                EC1wyOuakCU3rNvRx7vNVNbT4OveMfjVDoz569_nlK&
        redirect_uri=https://mycallback.info&
        state=mystate
```

This returns the access token to the redirect_uri, with the provided state value:

```
https://mycallback.info/#
        access_token=00D90000000mOZi%21ARsAQPbh5eOqaGnm8X
                PUkb1H1sKvEiNqYxX6fgVi4Iray_tF5.gb.nxYJNItT
                MM7GD8Zam22TN7YyAwLIUadrjeuS24R5VKY&
        instance_url=https%3A%2F%2Fap1.salesforce.com&
        id=https%3A%2F%2Flogin.salesforce.com%2Fid%2F00D90000000mOZiEAI%2F
            00590000001QHFEAA4&
        issued_at=1395347773975&
        signature=X26nqmRmKMoml6OdsCdtrqyStOtD4qn6H96v%2BFq3Qy0%3D&
        state=mystate&scope=id
```

■ **Note** The access token response from Salesforce includes a set of Salesforce-specific parameters. The value of signature is the Base64 value of HMAC-SHA256(id+issued_at), signed with the client secret.

To get the user details, you need to talk to the specified URI, corresponding to the authenticated user (from the previous response in the parameter id), with the access token:

```
curl https://ap1.salesforce.com/id/00D90000000mOZiEAI/00590000001QHFEAA4?
        oauth_token='00D9000000NqYxX6fgVi4Iray_tF5.gb.nxYJNItTMM7GD8Zam
                22TN7YyAwLIUadrjeuS24R5VKY'
```

GETTING AN ACCESS TOKEN FROM THE SALESFORCE
USERNAME-PASSWORD AUTHENTICATION FLOW

In this exercise, you see how to get an access token from Salesforce using the OAuth 2.0 Resource Owner Password Credentials grant type, also known as the username-password authentication flow. This assumes you've already registered your OAuth application with Salesforce and have the corresponding consumer key and consumer secret. Run the following cURL command after replacing the values of client_id and client_secret appropriately. The value of username is your Salesforce username, and the value of password is constructed by concatenating your Salesforce password with your security token. For example, if the Salesforce password is mypassword and the security token is XXXXYYYY, then the password is mypasswordXXXXYYYY:

■ **Note**   To create a security token, under My Settings/Personal/Reset My Security Token, click Reset Security Token. You receive the security token to your registered e-mail account.

```
curl -v -k --form client_id=3MVG9Y6d_Btp4xp5jz7MvysvlXtY44T2PFwadEeJT
                      B6EC1wyOuakCU3rNvRx7vNVNbT4OveMfjVDoz569_nlK
          --form client_secret=3623940361107861841
          --form grant_type=password
          --form username=prabath@wso2.com
          --form password='myPasswordvWtDk1CrPhKgzQkDPma5S2W4'
          https://login.salesforce.com/services/oauth2/token
```

This returns the following response with the access token:

```
{
        "id":"https://login.salesforce.com/id/00D90000000mOZiEAI/00590000001QHFEAA4",
        "issued_at":"1395351938998",
        "instance_url":"https://ap1.salesforce.com",
        "signature":"IsKKlf2ejVSfHaBxXawJ6Lxo+NeyRBld6xJ9Ru8P3rs=",
        "access_token":"00D90000000mOZi!ARsAQMNVC5Ltk_UXzlxQmG
                      5F3hY9y12B5dKX6B12U8wI_BTOULPstqayGojkw
                      goBoXlQcfCT6nkNk6Vt6_4Tbn1J5ESDxf.6"
}
```

To get the user details, you need to talk to the specified URI, corresponding to the authenticated user (from the previous response under the parameter id), with the access token:

```
curl https://ap1.salesforce.com/id/00D90000000mOZiEAI/00590000001QHFEAA4?
    oauth_token='00D90000000mOZi!ARsAQMNVC5Ltk_UXzlxQmG5F3
                hY9y12B5dKX6B12U8wI_BTOULPstqayGojkwgoBoXlQcfCT
                6nkNk6Vt6_4Tbn1J5ESDxf.6'
```

OAuth 2.0 and Google

Google began with its own identity delegation protocols, Google ClientLogin and Google AuthSub. Then, in 2008, Google announced its support for OAuth 1.0. In March 2011, Google introduced OAuth 2.0 support for its APIs.

▪ **Note**   The blog post that introduced OAuth 2.0 support for Google APIs is available at
`http://googledevelopers.blogspot.com/2011/03/making-auth-easier-oauth-20-for-google.html`.

REGISTERING A CLIENT APPLICATION WITH GOOGLE

In this exercise, you register an OAuth client application with Google and then access the Google Calendar API:

1. Go to `https://console.developers.google.com`, click Create Project, provide an appropriate name, and complete the registration.

2. Go to `https://console.developers.google.com`, where you see the project you just created listed. Click your project name.

3. Click APIs and Auth.

4. Click the Off button next to Calendar API to switch it On.

5. Click APIs and Auth ➤ Credentials.

6. Click OAuth ➤ Create New Client ID, and select Web Application as the Application Type. Provide a valid redirect URI, such as `https://mycallback.com`, and click Create Client ID.

7. Copy the values of Client ID and Client Secret.

8. Click OAuth ➤ Create New Client ID, and select Installed Application as the Application Type. Click Create Client ID.

9. Copy the values of Client ID and Client Secret.

GETTING AN ACCESS TOKEN FROM THE GOOGLE WEB SERVER APPLICATION AUTHENTICATION FLOW

In this exercise, you see how to get an access token from Google using the OAuth 2.0 Authorization Code grant type, also known as the web server application authentication flow. This assumes you've already registered your OAuth application as a web application with Google and have the corresponding client key and client secret. Copy the following URL, replacing the values of `client_id` and `redirect_uri` appropriately, and paste it in the browser:

```
https://accounts.google.com/o/oauth2/auth?
        scope=email&
        state=mystate&
        redirect_uri=https://mycallback.com&
        response_type=code&
```

```
client_id=825249835659-te8qgl701kgonnomnp
            4sqv7erhu1211s.apps.googleusercontent.com&
approval_prompt=force
```

■ **Note**   A list of Google authorization scopes is available at `https://developers.google.com/+/api/oauth`. The parameter `approval_prompt` in the authorization grant request indicates to the authorization server whether to prompt for user consent. If the value is `force`, then no matter what, the authorization server should prompt the end user with the user consent page.

This returns the access token to the `redirect_uri`, with the provided state value:

```
https://mycallback.com/?
        state=mystate&
        code=4/dlfuPEHWG8QU9MaJN8vCSEpTzuYo.YlcCVmKswV4SXE-sT2ZLcbQrzK7PiQI
```

Once you have the authorization code, you need to exchange it for an access token. Run the following cURL command with the appropriate values for `code`, `redirect_uri`, `client_id`, and `client_secret`. The value of `redirect_uri` should match the value used in the previous step:

```
curl -v -X POST -d "grant_type=authorization_code&
                code=4/dlfuPEHWG8QU9MaJN8vCSEpTzuYo.
                    YlcCVmKswV4SXE-sT2ZLcbQrzK7PiQI&
                client_id=825249835659-te8qgl701kgonnomnp4sqv7erhu1211s.
                        apps.googleusercontent.com&
                client_secret=jNjXEOD922mmcFopsjJJXNJc&
                redirect_uri=https://mycallback.com"
                https://accounts.google.com/o/oauth2/token
```

This returns the access token in the following JSON response:

```
{
  "access_token":"ya29.1.AADtN_WY1SHPAYomlwrcutZZnw
                    WToBds-DbrYvqIsUUStWKodxdf4YwKBKOd1BradEvh",
  "token_type":"Bearer",
  "expires_in":3600,
  "id_token":""
}
```

To get the user details, you need to talk to the Google `userinfo` endpoint with the access token obtained in the previous step:

```
curl https://www.googleapis.com/oauth2/v1/userinfo?
    access_token=ya29.1.AADtN_WY1SHPAYomlwrcutZZnw
                    WToBds-DbrYvqIsUUStWKodxdf4YwKBKOd1BradEvh
```

This returns the following JSON response:

```
{
 "id":"104063262378861625904",
 "email":"siriwardena.prabath@gmail.com",
 "verified_email":true,
 "name":"Prabath Siriwardena",
 "given_name":"Prabath",
 "family_name":"Siriwardena",
 "link":"https://plus.google.com/104063262378861625904",
 "picture":"https://lh3.googleusercontent.com/-nA7Ndz8oYF8/AAAAAAAAAAI/
                   AAAAAAAABCO/2vY1M8egglA/photo.jpg",
 "gender":"male",
 "locale":"en"
}
```

▪ **Note**   Detailed documentation for the Google web server application authentication flow is available at https://developers.google.com/accounts/docs/OAuth2WebServer.

GETTING AN ACCESS TOKEN FROM THE GOOGLE INSTALLED APPLICATION AUTHENTICATION FLOW

In this exercise, you see how to get an access token from Google using the installed application authentication flow. This assumes you've already registered your OAuth application as an installed application with Google and have the corresponding client key and client secret. Copy the following URL, replacing the values of client_id and redirect_ uri appropriately, and paste it in the browser. The value of redirect_uri should be urn:ietf:wg:oauth:2.0:oob:

```
https://accounts.google.com/o/oauth2/auth?
        scope=email&
        redirect_uri=urn:ietf:wg:oauth:2.0:oob&
        response_type=code&
        client_id=825249835659-a2d01b6j8ogcn3Oms3rm2lcj
                  mijrdsds.apps.googleusercontent.com
```

▪ **Note**   The Google installed application flow is better suited for installed applications on a mobile device, a tablet, or a computer that have access to a browser.

This redirects you to the following URL, with the authorization code:

```
https://accounts.google.com/o/oauth2/approval?
        as=-4923a7231af76cc2&hl=en&
        pageId=none&
        xsrfsign=APsBz4gAAAAAUyOfNKFyCD_AiOdZuMuYtouMWNpYSsjJ
```

The authorization code is in the browser title bar:

```
4/3nnHXjncHJMyd2rOKrOsf6pahkTc.Mkpg7y3BBgoWXE-sT2ZLcbSrolDQiQI
```

■ **Note** The Google installed application flow still uses the OAuth Authorization Code grant type, like the web server application flow, with a couple of exceptions. In the installed application flow, the `redirect_uri` must be either `urn:ietf:wg:oauth:2.0:oob` or `http://localhost`. The value `urn:ietf:wg:oauth:2.0:oob` instructs the authorization server to send the authorization code to the browser's title bar. If it's `http://localhost`, then the authorization server sends the authorization code as a query parameter.

Once you have the authorization code, you need to exchange it for an access token. Run the following cURL command with the appropriate values for `code`, `redirect_uri`, `client_id`, and `client_secret`. The value of `redirect_uri` should match the value used in the previous step:

```
curl -v -X POST -d "grant_type=authorization_code&
                    code=4/3nnHXjncHJMyd2rOKrOsf6pahkTc.
                        Mkpg7y3BBgoWXE-sT2ZLcbSrolDQiQI&
                    client_id=825249835659-a2d01b6j8ogcn30ms3rm2lcjmijrdsds.
                            apps.googleusercontent.com&
                    client_secret=Nd4Ql9dbqTxnuvjvri2hrzhJ&
                    redirect_uri=urn:ietf:wg:oauth:2.0:oob"
                    https://accounts.google.com/o/oauth2/token
```

This returns the access token in the following JSON response:

```
{
    "access_token":"ya29.1.AADtN_VMrQRuZh7HpL5ZawpM1c8sBOVZ5
                    PpkqBDemHp25l_tiRUroKKIyyxdXqOtxl1WDQ",
    "token_type":"Bearer",
    "expires_in":3600,
    "id_token":"",
    "refresh_token":"1/C86hKGezzDWb4myzFgYpMuorTgRlIJse-pfbmJgG3b4"
}
```

To get the user details, you need to talk to the Google `userinfo` endpoint with the access token obtained in the previous step:

```
curl https://www.googleapis.com/oauth2/v1/userinfo?
            access_token=ya29.1.AADtN_VMrQRuZh7HpL5ZawpM1c8s
                        BOVZ5PpkqBDemHp25l_tiRUroKKIyyxdXqOtxl1WDQ
```

■ **Note** Detailed documentation for the Google installed application authentication flow is available at `https://developers.google.com/accounts/docs/OAuth2InstalledApp`.

> # GETTING AN ACCESS TOKEN FROM THE GOOGLE CLIENT-SIDE APPLICATION AUTHENTICATION FLOW

In this exercise, you see how to get an access token from Google using the OAuth 2.0 Implicit grant type, also known as the client-side application authentication flow. This assumes you've already registered your OAuth application as a web application with Google and have the corresponding client key and client secret. Copy the following URL, replacing the values of `client_id` and `redirect_uri` appropriately, and paste it in the browser. The value of `response_type` should be set to `token`:

```
https://accounts.google.com/o/oauth2/auth?
        scope=email&
        state=mystate&
        redirect_uri=https://mycallback.com&
        response_type=token&
        client_id=825249835659-te8qgl701kgonnomnp4sqv7erhu1211s.
                  apps.googleusercontent.com&
        approval_prompt=force
```

This returns the access token as a query parameter to the registered callback URL:

```
https://mycallback.com/#
        state=mystate&
        access_token=ya29.1.AADtN_UBJudPXr8aGUgHVhVCcksLe
                     Fx2zMS7ngADpSqShUf8RPEFTu1N-T8HM4iQRgdyNA&
        token_type=Bearer&
        expires_in=3600
```

Unlike in other cases, the Google client-side application flow requires you to validate the access token returned in the previous step by talking to the Google `tokeninfo` endpoint:

```
curl https://www.googleapis.com/oauth2/v1/tokeninfo?
     access_token=ya29.1.AADtN_UBJudPXr8aGUgHVhVCcksLe
                  Fx2zMS7ngADpSqShUf8RPEFTu1N-T8HM4iQRgdyNA
```

This returns the following JSON response:

```
{
 "issued_to":"825249835659-te8qgl701kgonnomnp4sqv7erhu1211s.apps.googleusercontent.com",
 "audience":"825249835659-te8qgl701kgonnomnp4sqv7erhu1211s.apps.googleusercontent.com",
 "user_id":"104063262378861625904",
 "scope":"https://www.googleapis.com/auth/userinfo.email
          https://www.googleapis.com/auth/plus.me",
 "expires_in":3240,
 "email":"siriwardena.prabath@gmail.com",
 "verified_email":true,
 "access_type":"online"
}
```

To get the user details, you need to talk to the Google `userinfo` endpoint with the access token obtained in the previous step:

```
curl https://www.googleapis.com/oauth2/v1/userinfo?
    access_token=ya29.1.AADtN_UBJudPXr8aGUgHVhV
                 CcksLeFx2zMS7ngADpSqShUf8RPEFTu1N-T8HM4iQRgdyNA
```

> ■ **Note** Detailed documentation for the Google client-side application authentication flow is available at https://developers.google.com/accounts/docs/OAuth2UserAgent.

GETTING AN ACCESS TOKEN FROM THE GOOGLE DEVICE AUTHENTICATION FLOW

In this exercise, you see how to get an access token from Google using the device authentication flow. The device authentication flow targets applications running on devices with limited input capabilities. Google has gone beyond the standard OAuth grant types and introduced its own custom grant type to cater to this requirement, identified by `http://oauth.net/grant_type/device/1.0`. This expects users to first interact with the application running on the device, get a user code and a URL, and then go to a device having access to a browser, enter the code, and grant access to the device. The device can use its device code to acquire an access token.

This assumes you've already registered your OAuth application as an installed application with Google and have the corresponding client key and client secret. Run the following cURL command, replacing the value of `client_id`:

```
curl -v -X POST
    -d "client_id=825249835659-a2d01b6j8ogcn30ms3rm2lcjmijrdsds.
                apps.googleusercontent.com&
        scope=email"
        https://accounts.google.com/o/oauth2/device/code
```

This returns the following JSON response. It includes a `device_code`, a `user_code`, and a `verification_url`. You need to copy the value of `verification_url` and paste it in a browser, and then paste the value of `user_code` and grant access to the device:

```
{
  "device_code":"4/Ny8hHFSUzLEKVp67GWaxsRV020rs",
  "user_code":"47bkr67a",
  "verification_url":"http://www.google.com/device",
  "expires_in":1800,
  "interval":5
}
```

After verifying the code, you can return to the device. The device application can acquire an access token by executing the following cURL command:

```
curl -v -X POST
     -d "client_id=825249835659-a2d01b6j8ogcn30ms3rm2lcj
                  mijrdsds.apps.googleusercontent.com&
         client_secret=Nd4Ql9dbqTxnuvjvri2hrzhJ&
         code=4/Ny8hHFSUzLEKVp67GWaxsRVO20rs&
         grant_type=http://oauth.net/grant_type/device/1.0"
         https://accounts.google.com/o/oauth2/token
```

This returns an access token in the following JSON response:

```
{
  "access_token":"ya29.1.AADtN_Vzh1jZ85XMAXvlY88k2FYFgz5VIZWqh5RiigKnov5htKR1fis_
                  A5WaiMxgGJhyEA",
  "token_type":"Bearer",
  "expires_in":3600,
  "id_token":"",
  "refresh_token":"1/lbaTPeOzgfzoPLJwHqCcZ8ii3mwqoNT8zEiInPPjuNw"
}
```

To get the user details, you need to talk to the Google `userinfo` endpoint with the access token obtained in the previous step:

```
curl https://www.googleapis.com/oauth2/v1/userinfo?
           access_token=ya29.1.AADtN_Vzh1jZ85XMAXvlY88k2
                        FYFgz5VIZWqh5RiigKnov5htKR1fis_A5WaiMxgGJhyEA
```

■ **Note**   Detailed documentation for the Google Device authentication flow is available at https://developers.google.com/accounts/docs/OAuth2ForDevices.

SUMMARY OF OAUTH 2.0 VENDOR IMPLEMENTATIONS

OAuth 2.0 Authorization Endpoints

- *Facebook:* https://www.facebook.com/dialog/oauth

- *LinkedIn:* https://www.linkedin.com/uas/oauth2/authorization

- *Salesforce:* https://login.salesforce.com/services/oauth2/authorize

- *Google:* https://accounts.google.com/o/oauth2/auth

OAuth 2.0 Token Endpoints

- *Facebook:* https://graph.facebook.com/oauth/access_token

- *LinkedIn:* https://www.linkedin.com/uas/oauth2/accessToken

- *Salesforce:* https://login.salesforce.com/services/oauth2/token

- *Google:* https://accounts.google.com/o/oauth2/token

User Info Endpoints

- *Facebook:* https://graph.facebook.com/me

- *LinkedIn:* https://api.linkedin.com/v1/people/~

- *Salesforce:* https://login.salesforce.com/id/{domain_id}/{use_id}

- *Google:* https://www.googleapis.com/oauth2/v1/userinfo

Authentication vs. Authorization

In the simplest terms, *authentication* is the act of proving who you are, whereas *authorization* is the act of determining what you can do. OAuth 2.0 is about delegated authorization, not about authentication. This may be somewhat confusing, because there are many instances in which you use OAuth 2.0 to log in to client web applications. If you use OAuth 2.0 for login, isn't it about authentication? If you secure an API with OAuth 2.0, isn't it all about authentication? Not really. An authentication process must end by figuring out and validating the identity of the end user. OAuth doesn't do that. OAuth only provides a temporary token, which can be used to access a resource on behalf of the end user—but it doesn't provide any identity information about the user.

Let's look at a few examples. The following is the response you get from the Facebook token endpoint; it doesn't include any user information. If you use this token against an API, the API only checks whether this is a valid token and whether it's authorized to invoke the given API:

```
access_token=CAAIXsJdcexIBANoR7sRFbQMAlBTuVtZATUdK
            ypc5m6dURLqTOirQ2hQ7oXcOqxeXzec2ylPOUH
            WnSFw6f ZAcTGCJgzhNxZBtHr7q0jZCZBwGL3g
            zfPrUSUGHtBntNtIzDWd8KeYZC3WYKcmljxeTN
            RZAaa9ZCzHZC7oVFWWckra7zJCbplTHG9ElW&
expires=5179012
```

If the API wants to find out more about the user, it has to talk to Facebook's user endpoint. That is what completes the authentication, and that is how most applications use Facebook Login. The following cURL command returns the logged-in user's information:

```
curl https://graph.facebook.com/me/feed?
    access_token="CAAIXsJdcexIBANoR7sRFbQMAlBTuVtZAT
                 UdKypc5m6dURLqTOirQ2hQ7oXcOqxeXzec
                 2ylPOUHWnSFw6fZAcTGCJgzhNxZBtHr7q0
                 jZCZBwGL3gzfPrUSUGHtBntNtIzDWd8KeY
                 ZC3WYKcmljxeTNRZAaa9ZCzHZC7oVFWW
                 ckra7zJCbplTHG9ElW"
```

■ **Note** OpenID Connect is an OAuth profile that talks about authentication. Chapter 12 takes an in-depth look at OpenID Connect.

Summary

OAuth 2.0 is the de facto standard for API security. This chapter explored OAuth 2.0 and also discussed its immediate predecessor, OAuth WRAP. OAuth 2.0 concepts were demonstrated using real-world examples with Facebook, LinkedIn, Salesforce, and Google. One of the extensions in OAuth 2.0 is the token type. The OAuth 2.0 core specification doesn't bind to a specific token type. All the examples used in this chapter assumed the use of the OAuth 2.0 Bearer Token Profile.

The next chapter looks at the MAC Token Profile for OAuth 2.0.

■ ■ ■

CHAPTER 8

OAuth 2.0 MAC Token Profile

The OAuth 2.0 core specification doesn't mandate any specific token type. It's one of the extension points introduced in OAuth 2.0. Almost all public implementations use the OAuth 2.0 Bearer Token Profile. This came up with the OAuth 2.0 core specification, but as an independent profile, documented under RFC 6750. Eran Hammer, who was the lead editor of the OAuth 2.0 specification by that time, introduced the MAC Token Profile for OAuth 2.0. (Hammer also led the OAuth 1.0 specification.) Since its introduction to the OAuth 2.0 IETF working group in November 2011, the MAC Token Profile has made a slow progress. The slow progress was mostly due to the fact that the working group was interested in building a complete stack around bearer tokens before moving into another token type. In this chapter, we will take a deeper look into the OAuth 2.0 MAC token profile and its applications.

OAUTH 2.0 AND THE ROAD TO HELL

One of the defining moments of OAuth 2.0 history was the resignation of OAuth 2.0 specification lead editor Eran Hammer. On July 26, 2012, he wrote a famous blog post titled "OAuth 2.0 and the Road to Hell"[1] after announcing his resignation from the OAuth 2.0 IETF working group. As highlighted in the blog post, Hammer thinks OAuth 2.0 is a bad protocol, just like any WS-* (web services) standard. In his comparison, OAuth 1.0 is much better than OAuth 2.0 in terms of complexity, interoperability, usefulness, completeness, and security. Hammer was worried about the direction in which OAuth 2.0 was heading, because it was not that intended by the web community that initially formed the OAuth 2.0 working group.

According to Hammer, the following were the initial objectives of the OAuth 2.0 working group:

- Build a protocol very similar to OAuth 1.0.

- Simplify the signing process.

- Add a light identity layer.

- Address native applications.

- Add more flows to accommodate more client types.

- Improve security.

---

[1]Available at http://hueniverse.com/2012/07/oauth-2-0-and-the-road-to-hell/.

In his blog post, Hammer highlighted the following architectural changes from OAuth 1.0 to 2.0 (extracted from http://hueniverse.com/2012/07/oauth-2-0-and-the-road-to-hell/):

- *Unbounded Tokens*: In 1.0, the client has to present two sets of credentials on each protected resource request, the token credentials and the client credentials. In 2.0, the client credentials are no longer used. This means that tokens are no longer bound to any particular client type or instance. This has introduced limits on the usefulness of access tokens as a form of authentication and increased the likelihood of security issues.

- *Bearer Tokens*: 2.0 got rid of all signatures and cryptography at the protocol level. Instead it relies solely on TLS. This means that 2.0 tokens are inherently less secure as specified. Any improvement in token security requires additional specifications and as the current proposals demonstrate, the group is solely focused on enterprise use cases.

- *Expiring Tokens*: 2.0 tokens can expire and must be refreshed. This is the most significant change for client developers from 1.0, as they now need to implement token state management. The reason for token expiration is to accommodate self-encoded tokens – encrypted tokens, which can be authenticated by the server without a database look-up. Because such tokens are self-encoded, they cannot be revoked and therefore must be short-lived to reduce their exposure. Whatever is gained from the removal of the signature is lost twice in the introduction of the token state management requirement.

- *Grant Types*: In 2.0, authorization grants are exchanged for access tokens. Grant is an abstract concept representing the end-user approval. It can be a code received after the user clicks 'Approve' on an access request, or the user's actual username and password. The original idea behind grants was to enable multiple flows. 1.0 provides a single flow, which aims to accommodate multiple client types. 2.0 adds significant amount of specialization for different client type.

Most of all, Hammer wasn't in favor of the authorization framework built by OAuth 2.0 and the extensibility introduced. His argument was that the Web doesn't need another security framework: what it needs is a simple, well-defined security protocol. Regardless of these arguments, over the years OAuth 2.0 has become the de facto standard for API security—and the extensibility introduced by OAuth 2.0 is paying off.

Bearer Token vs. MAC Token

Bearer tokens are just like cash. Whoever owns one can use it. At the time you use it, you don't need to prove you're the legitimate owner. It's similar to the way you could use stolen cash with no problem; what matters is the validity of the cash, not the owner.

MAC tokens, on the other hand, are like credit cards. Whenever you use a credit card, you have to authorize the payment with your signature. If someone steals your card, the thief can't use it unless they know how to sign exactly like you. That's the main advantage of MAC tokens.

With bearer tokens, you always have to pass the token secret over the wire. But with MAC tokens, you never pass the token secret over the wire. The key difference between bearer tokens and MAC tokens is very similar to the difference between HTTP Basic Authentication and HTTP Digest Authentication.

■ **Note** Draft 5 of the OAuth 2.0 MAC Token Profile is available at `http://tools.ietf.org/html/draft-ietf-oauth-v2-http-mac-05`. This chapter is based on draft 5, but this is an evolving specification. The objective of this chapter is to introduce the MAC Token Profile as an extension of OAuth token types. The request/response parameters discussed in this chapter may change as the specification evolves, but the basic concepts will remain the same. It's recommended that you keep an eye on `https://datatracker.ietf.org/doc/draft-ietf-oauth-v2-http-mac/` to find out the latest changes taking place.

Obtaining a MAC Token

The OAuth 2.0 core specification isn't coupled with any of the token profiles. The OAuth flow discussed under the bearer token flow in Chapter 7 applies in the same way for MAC tokens. OAuth grant types don't have any dependency on the token type. A client can obtain a MAC token by using any grant type. Under the Authorization Code grant type, the resource owner that visits the application initiates the flow. The client, which must be a registered application at the authorization server, redirects the resource owner to the authorization server to get approval. The following is a sample HTTP redirect, which takes the resource owner to the OAuth authorization server:

```
https://localhost:9443/oauth2/authorize?response_type=code&
client_id=OrhQErXIX49svVYoXJGtODWBuFca&
redirect_uri=https%3A%2F%2Fmycallback
```

The value of `response_type` must be code. This indicates to the authorization server that the request is for an authorization code. `client_id` is an identifier for the client application. Once the client application is registered with the authorization server, the client gets a `client_id` and a `client_secret`. The value of `redirect_uri` should be equivalent to the value registered with the authorization server. During the client-registration phase, the client application must provide a URL under its control as the `redirect_uri`. The URL-encoded value of the callback URL is added to the request as the `redirect_uri` parameter. In addition to these parameters, a client application can also include a `scope` parameter. The value of the `scope` parameter is shown to the resource owner on the approval screen. It indicates to the authorization server the level of access the client needs on the target resource/API. The previous HTTP redirect returns the requested code to the registered callback URL:

```
https://mycallback/?code=9142d4cad58c66d0a5edfad8952192
```

The value of the authorization code is delivered to the client application via an HTTP redirect and is visible to the resource owner. In the next step, the client must exchange the authorization code for an oauth access token by talking to the OAuth token endpoint exposed by the authorization server. This must be an authenticated request with the `client_id` and the `client_secret` of the client application in the HTTP authorization header. The token endpoint must be secured with HTTP Basic Authentication. The value of the `grant_type` parameter must be the `authorization_code`, and the value of the code should be the one returned from the previous step. If the client application set a value for the `redirect_uri` parameter in the previous request, then it must include the same value in the token request. The client can't suggest to the authorization server the type of the token it expects: it's entirely up to the authorization server to decide, or it can be based on a pre-agreement between the client and the authorization server at the time of client registration, which is outside the scope of OAuth.

The following cURL command to exchange the authorization code for a MAC token is very similar to what you saw for the Bearer Token Profile. The only difference is that this introduces a new parameter called audience, which is a *must* for a MAC token request:

```
curl -v -X POST --basic
    -u OrhQErXIX49svVYoXJGtODWBuFca:eYOFkL756W8usQaVNgCNkz9C2DOa
    -H "Content-Type: application/x-www-form-urlencoded;charset=UTF-8" -k
    -d "grant_type=authorization_code&
        code=9142d4cad58c66d0a5edfad8952192&
        redirect_uri=https://mycallback&
        audience=https://resource-server-URI"
    https://localhost:9443/oauth2/token
```

▪ **Note**   The audience parameter is defined in the OAuth 2.0: Audience Information Internet draft available at http://tools.ietf.org/html/draft-tschofenig-oauth-audience-00. This is a new parameter introduced into the OAuth token request flow and is independent of the token type. Once it's approved as an IETF proposed standard, the Bearer Token Profile also will be updated to include this in the access token request.

OAUTH 2.0: AUDIENCE INFORMATION

The objective of the audience parameter introduced by the OAuth 2.0: Audience Information Internet draft is to identify the audience of an issued access token. With this, the access token issued by the authorization server is for a specific client, to be used against a specific resource server or a specific set of resource servers. All resource servers should validate the audience of the access token before considering it valid.

After completing the authorization-granting phase, the client must decide which resource server to access and should find the corresponding audience URI. That must be included in the access-token request to the token endpoint. Then the authorization server must check whether it has any associated resource servers that can be identified by the provided audience URI. If not, it must send back the error code invalid_request. If all validations pass at the authorization server, the new Internet draft suggests including the allowed audience in the access token. While invoking an API hosted in the resource server, it can decode the access token and find out whether the allowed audience matches its own.

The previous cURL command returns the following response:

```
HTTP/1.1 200 OK
Content-Type: application/json
Cache-Control: no-store
 {
        "access_token": "eyJhbGciOiJSUOExXzUiLCJlbmMiOiJBM ",
        "token_type":"mac",
        "expires_in":3600,
        "refresh_token":"8xLOxBtZp8",
        "kid":"22BIjxU93h/IgwEb4zCRu5WF37s=",
        "mac_key":"adijq39jdlaska9asud",
        "mac_algorithm":"hmac-sha-256"
}
```

Let's examine the definition of each parameter.

access_token: The OAuth 2.0 access token, which binds the client, the resource owner, and the authorization server together. With the introduction of the audience parameter, this now binds all of those with the resource server, as well. Under the MAC Token Profile, by decoding the access token, you should be able to find the audience of the access token. If someone tampers with the access token to change the audience, that will make the token validation fail automatically at the authorization server.

token_type: Type of the token returned from the authorization server. The client should first try to understand the value of this parameter and begin processing accordingly. The processing rules differ from one token type to another. Under the MAC Token Profile, the value of the token type must be mac.

expires_in: The lifetime of the access token in seconds.

refresh_token: The refresh token associated with the access token. The refresh token can be used to acquire a new access token.

kid: Stands for *key identifier*. This is an identifier generated by the authorization server. It's recommended that you generate the key identifier by Base64-encoding the hashed access token: kid = base64encode (sha-1 (access_token)). This identifier uniquely identifies the mac_key used later to generate the MAC while invoking the resource APIs.

mac_key: A session key generated by the authorization server, having the same lifetime as the access token. The mac_key is a shared secret used later to generate the MAC while invoking the resource APIs. The authorization server should never reissue the same mac_key or the same kid.

mac_algorithm: The algorithm to generate the MAC during API invocation. The value of the mac_algorithm should be well understood by the client, authorization server, and resource server.

■ **Note**   The OAuth 2.0 access token is opaque to anyone outside the authorization server. It may or may not carry meaningful data, but no one outside the authorization server should try to interpret it. The OAuth 2.0 MAC Token Profile defines a more meaningful structure for the access token; it's no longer an arbitrary string. The resource server should understand the structure of the access token generated by the authorization server. Still, the client should not try to interpret it.

The access token returned from the authorization server to the client is encoded with the audience, key identifier, and encrypted value of the mac_key. The mac_key must be encrypted with the public key of the resource server or with a shared key established between the resource server and the authorization server via a prior agreement outside the scope of OAuth. When accessing a protected API, the client must send the access token along with the request. The resource server can decode the access token and get the encrypted mac_key, which it can later decrypt from its own private key or the shared key.

Invoking an API Protected with the OAuth 2.0 MAC Token Profile

Following any of the grant types, you can obtain a MAC token from the authorization server. Unlike with the Bearer Token Profile, this needs more processing at the client end before you invoke an API protected with the MAC Token Profile. Prior to invoking the protected API, the client must construct an `authenticator`. The value of the `authenticator` is then added to the HTTP authorization header of the outgoing request. The `authenticator` is constructed from the following parameters:

> `kid`: The key identifier from the authorization grant response.

> `ts`: Timestamp, in milliseconds, since January 1, 1970.

> `seq-nr`: Indicates the initial sequence number to be used during the message exchange between the client and the resource server, from client to server.

> `access_token`: The value of the access token from the authorization grant response.

> `mac`: The value of the MAC for the request message. Later, this chapter discusses how to calculate the MAC.

> `h`: Colon-separated header fields, used to calculate the MAC.

> `cb`: Specifies the channel binding. Channel bindings are defined in "Channel Bindings for TLS," RFC 5929, available at `http://tools.ietf.org/html/rfc5929`.

■ **Note**   The "Channel Bindings for TLS" RFC defines three bindings: `tls-unique`, `tls-server-end-point`, and `tls-unique-for-telnet`.

The following is a sample request to access an API secured with an OAuth 2.0 MAC token profile.

```
GET /patient?name=peter&id=10909HTTP/1.1
Host: medicare.com
Authorization: MAC kid="22BIjxU93h/IgwEb4zCRu5WF37s=",
                   ts="1336363200",
                   seq-nr="12323",
                   access_token="eyJhbGciOiJSUOExXzUiLCJlbmMiOiJBM",
                   mac="bhCQXTVyfj5cmA9uKkPFx1zeOXM=",
                   h="host",
                   cb="tls-unique:9382c93673d814579ed1610d3"
```

Calculating the MAC

The OAuth 2.0 MAC Token Profile defines two algorithms to calculate the MAC: `HMAC-SHA1` and `HMAC-SHA256`. It also provides an extension for additional algorithms.

■ **Note**   The message authentication code (MAC) provides integrity and authenticity assurance for the associated message. The MAC algorithm accepts a message and a secret key to produce the associated MAC. To verify the MAC, the receiving party should have the same key and calculate the MAC of the received message. If the calculated MAC is equal to the MAC in the message, that guarantees integrity and authenticity.

A *hash-based Message Authentication Code (HMAC)* is a specific way of calculating the MAC using a hashing algorithm. If the hashing algorithm is SHA-1, it's called HMAC-SHA1. If the hashing algorithm is SHA-256, then it's called HMAC-SHA256. More information about HMAC is available at `http://tools.ietf.org/html/rfc2104`. The HMAC-SHA1 and HMAC-SHA256 functions need to be implemented in the corresponding programming language.

Here's the calculation with `HMAC-SHA1`:

```
mac = HMAC-SHA1(mac_key, input-string)
```

And here it is with `HMAC-SHA256`:

```
mac = HMAC-SHA256(mac_key, input-string)
```

For an API invocation request, the value of `input-string` is the `Request-Line` from the HTTP request, the timestamp, the value of `seq-nr`, and the concatenated values of the headers specified under the parameter `h`.

HTTP REQUEST-LINE

The HTTP `Request-Line` is defined in section 5 of the HTTP RFC, available at `http://www.w3.org/Protocols/rfc2616/rfc2616-sec5.html`. The request line is defined as follows:

```
Request-Line = Method SP Request-URI SP HTTP-Version CRLF
```

The value of `Method` can be OPTIONS, GET, HEAD, POST, PUT, DELETE, TRACE, CONNECT, or any extension method. SP stands for space—to be technically accurate, it's ASCII code 32. `Request-URI` identifies the representation of the resource where the request is sent. According to the HTTP specification, there are four ways to construct a `Request-URI`:

```
Request-URI = "*" | absoluteURI | abs_path | authority
```

```
The asterisk (*) means the request targets not a specific resource but the server it self.
For example, OPTIONS * HTTP/1.1.
```

The absolute URI must be used when the request is made through a proxy. For example, GET `https://resource-server/myresource HTTP/1.1`.

abs_path is the most common form of a `Request-URI`. In this case, the absolute path with respect to the host server is used. The URI or the network location of the server is transmitted in the HTTP Host header. For example:

```
GET /myresource HTTP/1.1
Host: resource-server
```

The authority form of the Request-URI is only used with HTTP CONNECT method. This method is used to make a connection through a proxy with tunneling, as in the case of SSL tunneling.

After the Request-URI must be a space and then the HTTP version, followed by a carriage return and a line feed.

Let's take the following example:

```
POST /patient?name=peter&id=10909&blodgroup=bpositive HTTP/1.1
Host: medicare.com
```

The value of the input-string is

```
POST /patient?name=peter&id=10909&blodgroup=bpositive HTTP/1.1 \n
1336363200 \n
12323 \n
medicare.com \n
```

1336363200 is the timestamp, 12323 is the sequence number, and medicare.com is the value of the Host header. The value of the Host header is included here because it is set in the h parameter of the API request under the HTTP Authorization header. All of these entries should be separated by newline separator characters, denoted by \n in the example. Once the input string is derived, the MAC is calculated on it using the mac_key and the MAC algorithm specified under mac_algorithm.

MAC Validation by the Resource Server

To access any API secured with the OAuth 2.0 MAC Token Profile, the client should send the relevant parameters with the API invocation request. If any of the parameters are lacking in the request or the provided values are invalid, the resource server will respond with an HTTP 401 status code. The value of the WWW-Authenticate header should be set to MAC, and the value of the error parameter should explain the nature of the error:

```
HTTP/1.1 401 Unauthorized
WWW-Authenticate: MAC error="Invalid credentials"
```

Let's consider the following valid API request, which comes with a MAC header:

```
GET /patient?name=peter&id=10909HTTP/1.1
Host: medicare.com
Authorization: MAC kid="22BIjxU93h/IgwEb4zCRu5WF37s=",
                   ts="1336363200",
                   seq-nr="12323",
                   access_token="eyJhbGciOiJSUOExXzUiLCJlbmMiOiJBM",
                   mac="bhCQXTVyfj5cmA9uKkPFx1zeOXM=",
                   h="host",
                   cb="tls-unique:9382c93673d814579ed1610d3"
```

To validate the MAC of the request, the resource server has to know the mac_key. The client must pass the mac_key to the resource server, encoded in the access_token. The first step in validation is to extract the mac_key from the access_token in the request. Once the access_token is decoded, the resource server has to verify its audience. The authorization server encodes the audience of the access_token is into the access_token.

Once the access token is verified and the scopes associated with it are validated, the resource server can cache the mac_key by the kid. The cached mac_key can be used in future message exchanges.

▪ **Note** According to the MAC Token Profile, the access_token needs to be included only in the first request from the client to the resource server. The resource server must use the cached mac_key (against the kid) to validate subsequent messages in the message exchange. If the initial access_token doesn't have enough privileges to invoke a later API, the resource server can request a new access_token or a complete authenticator by responding with an HTTP WWW-Authenticate header.

The resource server must calculate the MAC of the message the same way the client did before and compare the calculated MAC with the value included in the request. If the two match, the request can be considered a valid, legitimate one. But you still need to make sure there are no replay attacks. To do that, the resource server must verify the timestamp in the message by comparing it with its local timestamp.

▪ **Note** An attacker that can eavesdrop on the communication channel between the client and the resource server can record messages and replay them at a different time to gain access to the protected resource. The OAuth 2.0 MAC Token Profile uses timestamps as a way of detecting and mitigating replay attacks.

OAuth Grant Types and the MAC Token Profile

OAuth grant types and token types are two independent extension points introduced in the OAuth 2.0 core specification. They don't have any direct dependency between each other. This chapter only talks about the Authorization Code grant type, but all the other grant types work in the same manner: the structure of the access token returning from the Implicit grant type, the Resource Owner Password Credentials grant type, and the Client Credentials grant type is the same.

OAuth 1.0 vs. OAuth 2.0 MAC Token Profile

Eran Hammer (who at that point was the lead editor of the OAuth 2.0 specification) submitted the initial OAuth 2.0 MAC Token Profile draft to the OAuth working group in May 2011, and the first draft (also submitted by Hammer) followed with some improvements in February 2012. Both drafts were greatly influenced by the OAuth 1.0 architecture. After a long break, and after Hammer's resignation from the OAuth working group, Internet draft 4 of the MAC Token Profile introduced a revamped architecture. This architecture, which was discussed in this chapter, has many architectural differences from OAuth 1.0 (see Table 8-1).

Table 8-1. *OAuth 1.0 vs. OAuth 2.0 MAC Token Profile*

OAuth 1.0	OAuth 2.0 MAC Token Profile
Requires a signature both during the initial handshake and during the business API invocation.	Requires a signature only for the business API invocation.
The resource server must know the secret key used to sign the message beforehand.	The encrypted shared secret used to sign the message is passed to the resource server, embedded in the `access_token`.
The shared secret doesn't have an associated lifetime.	A lifetime is associated with the `mac_key`, which is used as the key to sign.
Doesn't have any audience restrictions. Tokens can be used against any resource server.	The authorization server enforces an audience restriction on the issued `access_tokens`, so that those access tokens can't be used against any resource server.

Summary

The OAuth 2.0 MAC Token Profile is an extension of the OAuth 2.0 core specification that provides a way of accessing a protected API without passing credentials over the wire. This chapter discussed the internals of the MAC Token Profile and where it stands with respect to OAuth 1.0 and the OAuth 2.0 Bearer Token Profile.

In the next chapter, we will take a deeper look at four key OAuth 2.0 profiles: Token Introspection profile, Chain Grant Type profile, Dynamic Client Registration profile, and Token Revocation profile.

CHAPTER 9

OAuth 2.0 Profiles

OAuth 2.0 is a framework for delegated authorization. It doesn't address all specific enterprise API security use cases. The OAuth 2.0 profiles built on top of the core framework work to build a security ecosystem to make OAuth 2.0 ready for enterprise grade deployments. OAuth 2.0 introduced two extension points via grant types and token types. The profiles for OAuth 2.0 are built on top of this extensibility. This chapter talks about four key OAuth 2.0 profiles for token introspection, chained API invocation, dynamic client registration, and token revocation.

Token Introspection Profile

OAuth 2.0 doesn't define a standard API for communication between the resource server and the authorization server. As a result, vendor-specific, proprietary APIs have crept in to couple the resource server to the authorization server. The Token Introspection profile for OAuth 2.0 fills this gap by proposing a standard API to be exposed by the authorization server, allowing the resource server to talk to it and retrieve token metadata.

Note OAuth 2.0 Token Introspection Internet draft is available at
`https://datatracker.ietf.org/doc/draft-richer-oauth-introspection/`.

Any party in possession of the access token can generate a token-introspection request. The introspection endpoint must be secured with HTTP Basic Authentication:

```
POST /introspection HTTP/1.1
Accept: application/x-www-form-urlencoded
Host: authz.server.com
Authorization: Basic czZCaGRSa3FOMzo3RmpmcDBaQnIxS3REUmJuZlZkbUl3
token=X3241Affw.4233-99JXJ&
token_type_hint=access_token&
resource_id=http://my-resource
```

Let's examine the definition of each parameter.

- token: The value of the access_token or the refresh_token
- token_type_hint: The type of the token (either the access_token or the refresh_token)
- resource_id: An identifier that represents the corresponding resource for introspection

This request returns the following JSON response:

```
HTTP/1.1 200 OK
Content-Type: application/json
Cache-Control: no-store
{
        "active": true,
        "client_id":"s6BhdRkqt3",
        "scope": "read write dolphin",
        "sub": "2309fj32kl",
        "aud": "http://my-resource/*"
}
```

Let's examine the definition of each parameter.

- active: Indicates whether the token is active. To be active, the token should not be expired or revoked. The authorization server can define its own criteria for how to define active.

- client_id: The identifier of the client to which the token was issued.

- scope: Approved scopes associated with the token.

- sub: The subject identifier of the user who approved the authorization grant.

- aud: The allowed audience for the token.

Note The audience (aud) parameter is defined in the OAuth 2.0: Audience Information Internet draft available at http://tools.ietf.org/html/draft-tschofenig-oauth-audience-00. This is a new parameter introduced into the OAuth token-request flow and is independent of the token type.

While validating the response from the introspection endpoint, the resource server should first check whether the value of active is set to true. Then it should check whether the value of aud in the response matches the aud URI associated with the resource server or the resource. Finally, it can validate the scope. The required scope to access the resource should be a subset of the scope values returned in the introspection response. If the resource server wants to do further access control based on the client or the resource owner, it can do so with respect to the values of sub and client_id.

FINE-GRAINED ACCESS CONTROL WITH XACML

eXtensible Access Control Markup Language (XACML) is a standard developed by the OASIS XACML technical committee. Over the years, it has become the de facto standard for fine-grained access control. In February 2003, the first XACML specification (1.0) was released, followed in July 2003 by 1.1. The XACML 2.0 specification released in February 2005 was a major breakthrough and is the most popular specification so far. XACML 3.0, released in January 2013, is the latest.

Note You can learn more about XACML 1.0 vs. 2.0 at http://xml.coverpages.org/JoslinXACMLDiffs1-2.html. You can learn more about XACML 2.0 vs. 3.0 at https://wiki.oasis-open.org/xacml/DifferencesBetweenXACML2.0AndXACML3.0.

As discussed in Chapter 2, XACML provides a reference architecture (see Figure 9-1), a request response protocol, and a policy language. The reference architecture includes a Policy Administration Point (PAP), a Policy Decision Point (PDP), a Policy Enforcement Point (PEP), and a Policy Information Point (PIP). This is a highly distributed architecture in which none of these components are tightly coupled with each other. The PAP is where you author policies and the PDP is where policies are evaluated. While evaluating policies, if any information is missing and can't be derived from the XACML request, the PDP calls the PIP. The role of the PIP is to feed the PDP any missing information, which can be user attributes or any other required details. The policy is enforced through the PEP, which sits between the client and the service and intercepts all requests. From the client request, it extracts certain attributes like the subject, the resource, and the action, after which it builds a standard XACML request and calls the PDP. It gets a XACML response back from the PDP; this is defined under XACML request/response model. The XACML policy language defines a schema to create XACML policies for access control.

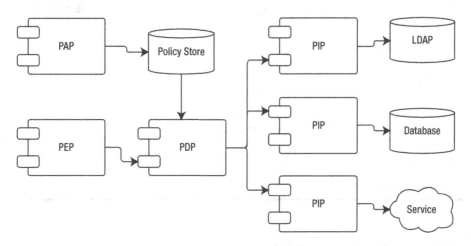

Figure 9-1. XACML reference architecture

Figure 9-2 shows the XACML runtime policy execution flow.

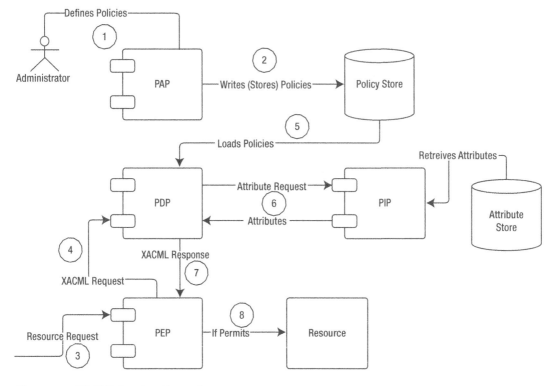

Figure 9-2. *XACML Runtime Execuction*

XACML and OAuth Token Introspection

The token-introspection endpoint only returns metadata about the token. It isn't supposed to do any sort of access control other than checking the token's status. Access control needs to happen at the resource-server end. The resource server can build a XACML request from the introspection response and talk to a XACML policy decision point. If it returns PERMIT, the API gateway can route the request to the resource server. The API gateway, as shown in Figure 9-3, acts as a security gateway that does all authentication and authorization centrally.

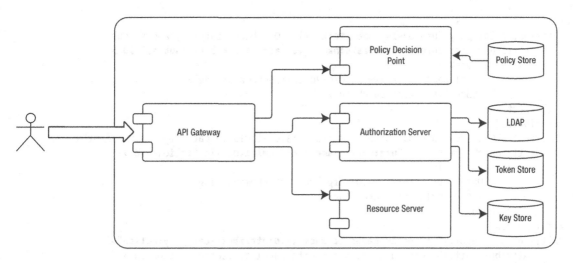

Figure 9-3. *XACML and OAuth token introspection*

Let's take the following token-introspection response as an example. This is returned from the introspection endpoint of the OAuth authorization server to the API gateway:

```
HTTP/1.1 200 OK
Content-Type: application/json
Cache-Control: no-store
{
        "active": true,
        "client_id":"s6BhdRkqt3",
        "scope": "read write dolphin",
        "sub": "2309fj32kl",
        "aud": "http://my-resource/*"
}
```

With this response, you can generate the following XACML request. Table 9-1 shows the relationship between the introspection response and the XACML request attributes. In addition to the introspection response, the API gateway takes other attributes from the API request. The HTTP method from the request is `urn:oasis:names:tc:xacml:1.0:action:action-id`, and the context of the API is `urn:oasis:names:tc:xacml:1.0:resource:resource-id` in the XACML request:

Table 9-1. *Attribute Mapping between the OAuth Introspection-Token Response and the XACML Request*

Token Introspection Response	XACML Request
client_id	urn:oasis:names:tc:xacml:1.0:client:client-id
scope	urn:oasis:names:tc:xacml:1.0:scope:scope-id
sub	urn:oasis:names:tc:xacml:1.0:subject:subject-id

```
<Request>
      <Attributes Category="urn:oasis:names:tc:xacml:1.0:subject-category:access-subject">
            <Attribute AttributeId="urn:oasis:names:tc:xacml:1.0:subject:subject-id">
                <AttributeValue
                    DataType="http://www.w3.org/2001/XMLSchema#string">
                    s6BhdRkqt3</AttributeValue>
            </Attribute>
      <Attributes>
      <Attributes Category="urn:oasis:names:tc:xacml:3.0:attribute-category:oauth-client">
            <Attribute AttributeId="urn:oasis:names:tc:xacml:1.0:client:client-id">
                <AttributeValue
                    DataType="http://www.w3.org/2001/XMLSchema#string">
                    2309fj32kl</AttributeValue>
            </Attribute>
      <Attributes>
      <Attributes Category="urn:oasis:names:tc:xacml:3.0:attribute-category:action">
            <Attribute AttributeId="urn:oasis:names:tc:xacml:1.0:action:action-id">
                <AttributeValue
                    DataType="http://www.w3.org/2001/XMLSchema#string">GET</AttributeValue>
            </Attribute>
      </Attributes>
      <Attributes Category="urn:oasis:names:tc:xacml:3.0:attribute-category:scope">
            <Attribute AttributeId="urn:oasis:names:tc:xacml:1.0:scope:scope-id">
                <AttributeValue
                    DataType="http://www.w3.org/2001/XMLSchema#string">
                    read write dolphin</AttributeValue>
            </Attribute>
      </Attributes>
      <Attributes Category="urn:oasis:names:tc:xacml:3.0:attribute-category:resource">
            <Attribute AttributeId="urn:oasis:names:tc:xacml:1.0:resource:resource-id">
                <AttributeValue
                    DataType="http://www.w3.org/2001/XMLSchema#string">
                    http://my-resource/accounts</AttributeValue>
            </Attribute>
      </Attributes>
</Request>
```

Once the XACML PDP receives the request, it evau-lates the request against all matching policies. The XACML engine picks the matching policies by comparing the request with the `Target` element of each policy. In the following policy, the `Target` element looks for any XACML request that has an attribute with attribute ID `urn:oasis:names:tc:xacml:1.0:resource:resource-id` and an attribute value that matches the regular expression `http://my-resource/*`. Once the engine chooses a policy, it goes through each matching rule in the policy. Each rule also can have its own `Target` element. In the Rule element, there can be a `Condition` element that defines the criteria for access control. For example, you can check whether the subject (or the end user) belongs to a particular role:

```
<Policy>
      <Target>
          <AnyOf>
                <AllOf>
                      <Match MatchId="urn:oasis:names:tc:xacml:1.0:function:string-regexp-match">
                          <AttributeValue
```

```
                         DataType="http://www.w3.org/2001/XMLSchema#string">
                         http://my-resource/*</AttributeValue>
                  <AttributeDesignator MustBePresent="false"
                         Category="urn:oasis:names:tc:xacml:3.0:attribute-category:resource"
                         AttributeId="urn:oasis:names:tc:xacml:1.0:resource:resource-id"
                         DataType="http://www.w3.org/2001/XMLSchema#string">
                  </AttributeDesignator>
               </Match>
            </AllOf>
        </AnyOf>
    </Target>
    <Rule RuleId="permit_rule" Effect="Permit">
    </Rule>
    <Rule RuleId="deny_rule" Effect="Deny">
    </Rule>
</Policy>
```

Chain Grant Type Profile

Once the audience restriction is enforced on OAuth tokens, they can only be used against the intended audience. You can access an API with an access token that has an audience restriction corresponding to that API. If this API wants to talk to another protected API to form the response to the client, the first API must authenticate to the second API. When it does so, the first API can't just pass the access token it received initially from the client. That will fail the audience-restriction validation at the second API. The Chain Grant Type OAuth 2.0 profile defines a standard way to address this concern.

As shown in Figure 9-4, according to the OAuth Chain Grant Type profile, the API hosted in the first resource server must talk to the authorization server and exchange the OAuth access token it received from the client for a new one that can be used to talk to the other API hosted in the second resource server.

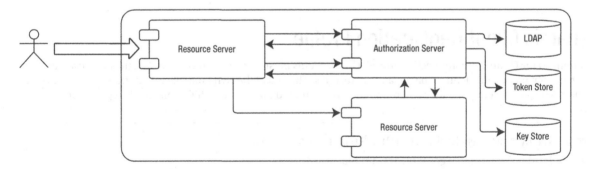

Figure 9-4. *OAuth 2.0 Chain Grant Type profile*

■ **Note**   The Chain Grant Type for OAuth 2.0 profile is available at
https://datatracker.ietf.org/doc/draft-hunt-oauth-chain.

The chain grant type request must be generated from the first resource server to the authorization server. The value of the grant type must be set to `http://oauth.net/grant_type/chain` and should include the OAuth access token received from the client. The `scope` parameter should express the required scopes for the second resource in space-delimited strings. Ideally, the scope should be the same as or a subset of the scopes associated with original access token. If there is any difference, then the authorization server can decide whether to issue an access token. This decision can be based on an out-of-band agreement with the resource owner:

```
POST /token HTTP/1.1
Host: authz.server.net
Content-Type: application/x-www-form-urlencoded
grant_type= http://oauth.net/grant_type/chain
oauth_token=dsddDLJkuiiuieqjhk238khjh
scope=read
```

This returns the following JSON response. The response includes an access token with a limited lifetime, but it should not have a refresh token. To get a new access token, the first resource server once again must present the original access token:

```
HTTP/1.1 200 OK
Content-Type: application/json;charset=UTF-8
Cache-Control: no-store
Pragma: no-cache
{
        "access_token":"2YotnFZFEjr1zCsicMWpAA",
        "token_type"  :"Bearer",
        "expires_in"  :1800,
}
```

The first resource server can use the access token from this response to talk to the second resource server. Then the second resource server talks to the authorization server to validate the access token.

Dynamic Client Registration Profile

According to the OAuth 2.0 core specification, all OAuth clients must be registered with the OAuth authorization server and obtain a client identifier before any interactions. The aim of the Dynamic Client Registration OAuth 2.0 profile is to expose an endpoint for client registration in a standard manner to facilitate on-the-fly registrations.

■ **Note** The Dynamic Client Registration OAuth 2.0 profile is available at
`https://datatracker.ietf.org/doc/draft-ietf-oauth-dyn-reg`.

The dynamic-registration endpoint exposed by the authorization server can be secured or not. If it's secured, it can be secured with OAuth, HTTP Basic Authentication, Mutual TLS, or any other security protocol as desired by the authorization server. The Dynamic Client Registration profile doesn't enforce any authentication protocols over the registration endpoint, but it must be secured with TLS. If the authorization server decides that it should allow the endpoint to be public and let anyone be registered, it can do so. To register a client, it must pass all its metadata to the registration endpoint:

```
POST /register HTTP/1.1
Content-Type: application/json
Accept: application/json
Host: authz.server.com
{
    "redirect_uris":["https://client.org/callback","https://client.org/callback2"],
    "token_endpoint_auth_method":"client_secret_basic",
    "grant_types": ["authorization_code" , "implicit"],
    "response_types": ["code" , "token"],
}
```

Let's examine the definition of each parameter.

- redirect_uris: An array of URIs under the control of the client. The user is redirected to one of these redirect_uris after the authorization grant.

- token_endpoint_auth_method: The supported authentication scheme when talking to the token endpoint. If the value is client_secret_basic, the client sends its client ID and the client secret in the HTTP Basic Authorization header. If it's client_secret_post, the client ID and the client secret are in the HTTP POST body. If the value is none, the client doesn't want to authenticate, which means it's a public client (as in the case of the OAuth Implicit grant type).

- grant_types: An array of grant types supported by the client.

- response_types: An array of expected response types from the authorization server.

Based on the policies of the authorization server, it can decide whether it should proceed with the registration. Even if it decides to go ahead with the registration, the authorization server need not accept all the suggested parameters from the client. For example, the client may suggest using both authorization_code and implicit as grant types, but the authorization server can decide what to allow. The same is true for the token_endpoint_ auth_method: the authorization server can decide what to support. The following is a sample response from the authorization server:

```
HTTP/1.1 200 OK
Content-Type: application/json
Cache-Control: no-store
Pragma: no-cache
{
        "client_id":"iuyiSgfgfhffgfh",
        "client_secret": "hkjhkiiu89hknhkjhuyjhk",
        "client_id_issued_at":2343276600,
        "client_secret_expires_at":2503286900,
        "redirect_uris":["https://client.org/callback", "https://client.org/callback2"],
        "grant_types": "authorization_code",
        "token_endpoint_auth_method": "client_secret_basic",
}
```

Let's examine the definition of each parameter.

- `client_id`: A generated unique identifier for the client.

- `client_secret`: The generated client secret corresponding to the `client_id`. This is optional. For the Implicit grant type, `client_secret` isn't required.

- `client_id_issued_at`: The number of seconds since January 1, 1970.

- `client_secret_expires_at`: The number of seconds since January 1, 1970.

- `redirect_uris`: Accepted `redirect_uris`.

- `token_endpoint_auth_method`: The accepted authentication method for the token endpoint.

■ **Note**   The Dynamic Client Registration OAuth 2.0 profile is extremely useful in mobile applications. Mobile client applications secured with OAuth have the client ID and the client secret baked into the application. These are the same for all installations for a given application. If a given client secret is compromised, that will affect all installations, and rogue client applications can be developed using the stolen keys. These rogue client applications can generate more traffic on the server and exceed the legitimate throttling limit, hence causing a denial of service attack. With dynamic client registration, you need not set the same client ID and client secret for all installations. During the installation process, the application can talk to the authorization server's registration endpoint and generate a client ID and a client secret per installation.

Token Revocation Profile

Two parties can perform OAuth token revocation. The resource owner should be able to revoke an access token issued to a client, and the client should be able to revoke an access token or a refresh token it has acquired. The Token Revocation OAuth 2.0 profile addresses the latter. It introduces a standard token-revoke endpoint at the authorization server end. To revoke an access token or a refresh token, the client must notify the revoke endpoint.

■ **Note**   In October 2013, there was an attack against Buffer (a social media management service that can be used to cross-post between Facebook, Twitter, and others). Buffer was using OAuth to access user profiles in Facebook and Twitter. Once Buffer detected that it was under attack, it revoked all its access keys from Facebook, Twitter, and other social media sites, which prevented attackers from getting access to users' Facebook and Twitter accounts.

The cient must initiate the token-revocation request. The client must authenticate to the authorization server via HTTP Basic Authentication (with its client ID and client secret) and then talk to the revoke endpoint. The request should consist of either the access token or the refresh token and then a `token_type_hint` that informs the authorization server about the type of the token (access token or refresh token). This parameter may not be required, but the authorization server can optimize its search criteria using it.

■ **Note**   The OAuth 2.0 Token Revocation profile is defined under RFC 7009 and is available at `https://tools.ietf.org/html/rfc7009`.

Here is an sample request:

```
POST /revoke HTTP/1.1
Host: server.example.com
Content-Type: application/x-www-form-urlencoded
Authorization: Basic czZCaGRSdadsdI9iuiaHk99kjkh
token=dsdOlkjkkljkkllkdsdds&token_type_hint=access_token
```

In response to this request, the authorization server first must validate the client credentials and then proceed with the token revocation. If the token is a refresh token, the authorization server must invalidate all the access tokens issued for the authorization grant associated with the refresh token. If it's an access token, it's up to the authorization server to decide whether to revoke the refresh token. In most cases, it's ideal to revoke the refresh token, too. Once the token revocation is completed successfully, the authorization server must send an HTTP 200 status code back to the client.

REVOKING A SALESFORCE ACCESS TOKEN

Salesforce has support for the OAuth 2.0 Token Revocation profile. In this exercise, you see how to revoke an access token issued by Salesforce. This assumes you already have a client ID, a client secret, and an access token.

■ **Note**   To register an application with Salesforce and obtain a client ID and a client secret, follow the steps in the exercise "Registering a Client Application with Salesforce" in Chapter 7. To get an access token from Salesforce, follow the steps in the exercise "Getting an Access Token from the Salesforce Web Server Authentication Flow," also in Chapter 7.

Say your client ID is
3MVG9Y6d_Btp4xp5jz7MvysvlXtY44T2PFwadEeJTB6EC1wyOuakCU3rNvRx7vNVNbT4OveMfjVDoz569_nlK,
your client secret is 3623940361107861841, and the access token is
OOD90000000mOZi!ARsAQMhPVU5k8tqz926Nyo2MCU1ZmfYgvsNPk31xGPBfmfRYdG8DvRKsgP4
Eld1gFuel59sjYTMRh262Udj6KVl5wTeo4RMT. The following cURL command revokes the access token:

```
curl https://login.salesforce.com/services/oauth2/revoke?
token='OOD90000000mOZi!ARsAQMhPVU5k8tqz926Nyo
       2MCU1ZmfYgvsNPk31xGPBfmfRYdG8DvRKsgP
       4Eld1gFuel59sjYTMRh262Udj6KVl5wTeo4RMT'
```

■ **Note**   The Salesforce token-revocation endpoint isn't protected. Anyone who has access to the access token can revoke the token.

Summary

OAuth profiles help to build the ecosystem around OAuth 2.0. This chapter focused on four key OAuth 2.0 profiles: the Token Introspection profile, the Chain Grant Type profile, the Dynamic Client Registration profile, and the Token Revocation profile.

In the next chapter, we will take a deeper look at the User Managed Access (UMA) OAuth 2.0 profile.

■ ■ ■

CHAPTER 10

User Managed Access (UMA)

User Managed Access (UMA, pronounced "OOH-mah") is an OAuth 2.0 profile. OAuth 2.0 decouples the resource server from the authorization server. UMA takes one step forward: it lets you control a distributed set of resource servers from a centralized authorization server. It also enables the resource owner to define a set of policies at the authorization server, which can be evaluated at the time a client is granted access to a protected resource. This eliminates the need for the resource owner's presence to approve access requests from arbitrary clients or requesting parties. The authorization server can make the decision based on the policies defined by the resource owner.

■ **Note** The historic blog post "ProtectServe News: User-Managed Access Group," by Eve Maler, announcing the launch of the UMA working group under the Kantara Initiative, is available at www.xmlgrrl.com/blog/2009/07/20/protectserve-news-user-managed-access-group/.

ProtectServe

UMA has its roots in the Kantara Initiative. The Kantara Initiative is a non-profit professional association focused on building digital identity management standards. The first meeting of the UMA working group was held on August 6, 2009. There were two driving forces behind UMA: ProtectServe and vendor relationship management (VRM). ProtectServe is a standard that was heavily influenced by VRM. The goal of ProtectServe was to build a permissioned data-sharing model that was simple, secure, efficient, RESTful, powerful, OAuth-based, and system-identity agnostic. ProtectServe defines four parties in its protocol flow: the user, the authorization manager, the service provider, and the consumer.

The *service provider* (SP) manages the user's resources and exposes them to the rest of the world. The *authorization manager* (AM) keeps track of all service providers associated with a given user. The *user* is the resource owner, who introduces all their service providers to the authorization manager and builds access-control policies that define the basis on which to share resources with others. The *consumer* consumes the user's resources via the SP. Before consuming any services or resources, the consumer must request an access grant from the AM. The requested access grant is evaluated against the policies defined on the associated service by its owner, at the AM. ProtectServe uses OAuth 1.0 as the protocol for access delegation.

The steps in the ProtectServe protocol flow are as follows:

1. The user or the resource owner introduces the SP to the AM (see Figure 10-1):

    a. The user provides the metadata URL of the AM to the SP.

    b. The SP talks to the metadata endpoint of the AM and gets details related to the consumer-key issuer, the request-token issuer, the access-token issuer, and the associated policies.

c. The SP initiates an OAuth 1.0 flow by requesting an OAuth request token from the request-token issuer (which could be the same AM).

d. The AM generates an authorization-request token and sends it back to the SP.

e. The SP redirects the user to the AM with a token reference, to get it authorized.

f. Once authorized by the user, the authorization manager returns the authorized request token to the SP.

g. To complete the OAuth 1.0 flow, the SP exchanges the authorized request token for an access token, with the AM.

h. Once the OAuth flow is completed, the SP talks to the AM endpoint (which is secured with OAuth 1.0) to get a SP handle.

i. The AM validates the OAuth signature and, once verified, issues a SP handle to the SP. A SP handle is a unique identifier generated by the AM to identify the SP in future communications.

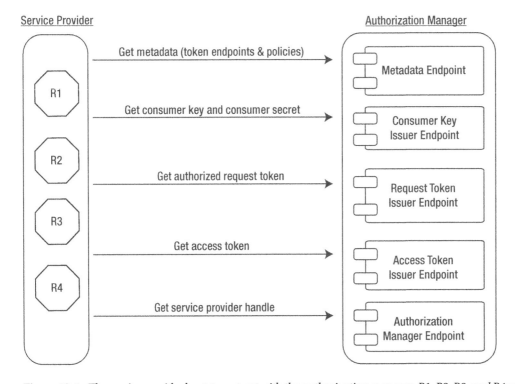

Figure 10-1. *The service provider bootstraps trust with the authorization manager. R1, R2, R3, and R4 represent resources*

That completes the initial step in the ProtectServe protocol flow.

■ **Note**   The service provider handle is a key that uniquely identifies the service provider at the authorization manager. This information is publicly available. A given service provider can have multiple service provider handles—one per each associated authorization manager.

2.   Each consumer who wants to get access to protected resources must be provisioned with corresponding consumer keys:

    a.   The consumer tries to access a protected resource hosted in a SP.

    b.   The SP detects the unauthenticated access attempt and returns an HTTP 401 status code with required details to get the SP metadata (see Figure 10-2).

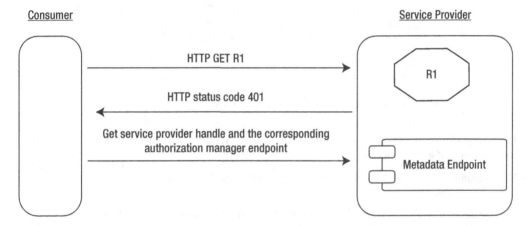

Figure 10-2.   *The consumer is rejected by the service provider with a 401 response. R1 represents a resource*

    c.   With the details in the 401 response, the consumer talks to the SP's metadata endpoint (see Figure 10-3).

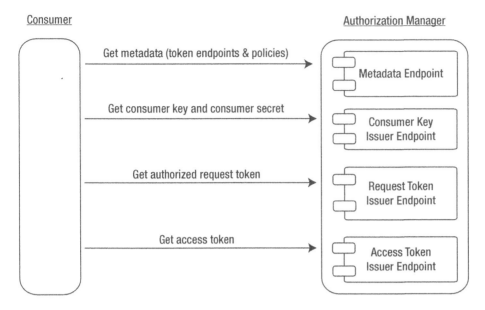

Figure 10-3. *The consumer gets an access token from the authorization manager*

> d. The SP metadata endpoint returns the SP handle (which is registered at the AM) and the corresponding AM endpoint.
>
> e. The consumer talks to the AM endpoint to obtain a consumer key and a consumer secret.
>
> f. The consumer requests an access token from the AM, with its consumer key and the SP handle. The request must be digitally signed by the corresponding consumer secret.
>
> g. The AM validates the parameters in the access-token request and issues an access token and a token secret to the consumer.

3. A consumer with a valid access token can access the protected resource hosted in the SP (see Figure 10-4):

> a. The consumer tries to access the protected resource in the SP with its access token, signed with the access-token secret.
>
> b. The SP talks to the AM and gets the secret key corresponding to the consumer's access token. If required, the SP can store it locally.
>
> c. The SP validates the signature of the request using the access-token secret.
>
> d. If the signature is valid, the SP talks to the policy-decision endpoint of the AM, passing the access token and the SP handle. The request must be digitally signed by the corresponding access-token secret.
>
> e. The AM first validates the request, next evaluates the corresponding policies set by the user or the resource owner, and then sends the decision to the SP.
>
> f. If the decision is a Deny, the location of the terms is returned to the SP, and the SP returns the location to the consumer with a 403 HTTP status code.

g. The consumer requests the terms by talking to the terms endpoint hosted in the AM. The request includes the consumer key, signed with the consumer secret.

h. When the consumer receives the terms, it evaluates them and talks to the AM with additional information to prove its legitimacy. This request includes the consumer key and is signed with the consumer secret.

i. The AM evaluates the additional information and claims provided by the consumer. If those meet the required criteria, the AM creates an agreement resource and sends the location of the agreement resource to the consumer.

j. If this requires the user's consent, the AM must send it for the user's approval before sending the location of the agreement resource.

k. Once the consumer receives the location of the agreement resource, it can talk to the corresponding endpoint hosted in the AM and get the agreement resource to see the status.

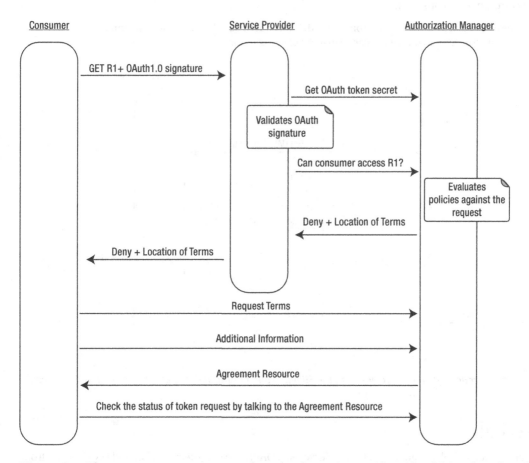

Figure 10-4. *The consumer accesses a resource hosted at the service provider with valid OAuth credentials, but with limited privileges*

4. Once approved by the authorization manager, the consumer can access the protected resource with its access token and the corresponding secret key (see Figure 10-5):

   a. The consumer tries to access the protected resource at the SP with its access token, signed with the access-token secret.

   b. The SP talks to the AM and gets the secret key corresponding to the consumer's access token. If required, the SP can store it locally.

   c. The SP validates the signature of the request using the access-token secret.

   d. If the signature is valid, the SP talks to the policy-decision endpoint of the AM, passing the access token and SP handle, signed with the corresponding access-token secret.

   e. The AM first validates the request, next evaluates the corresponding policies set by the user or the resource owner, and then sends the decision to the SP.

   f. If the decision is an Allow from the AM, the SP returns the requested resource to the corresponding consumer.

   g. The SP can cache the decision from the AM. Subsequent calls by the same consumer for the resource can utilize the cache instead of going to the AM.

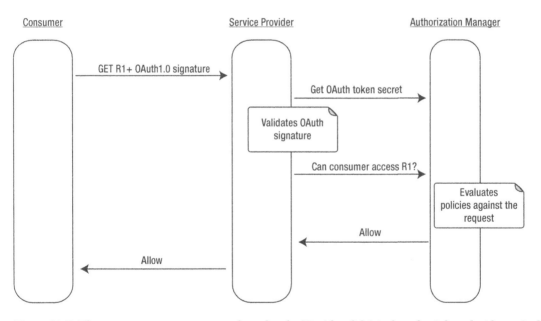

Figure 10-5. *The consumer accesses a resource hosted at the SP with valid OAuth credentials and with required privileges*

UMA and OAuth

Over the years, ProtectServe evolved into UMA. ProtectServe used OAuth 1.0 to protect its APIs, and UMA moved from OAuth 1.0 to OAuth WRAP to OAuth 2.0. The UMA specification, which was developed under the Kantara Initiative for almost three years, was submitted to the IETF OAuth working group on July 9, 2011 as a draft recommendation for a user-managed data access protocol.

UMA Architecture

The UMA architecture has five main components (see Figure 10-6): the *resource owner* (analogous to the user in ProtectServe), the *resource server* (analogous to the service provider in ProtectServe), the *authorization server* (analogous to the authorization manager in ProtectServe), the *client* (analogous to the consumer in ProtectServe), and the *requesting party*. These five components interact with each other during the three phases as defined in the UMA core specification.

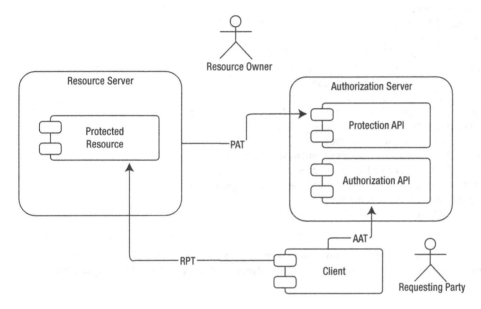

Figure 10-6. *UMA high-level architecture*

UMA Phases

The first phase of UMA is to protect the resource. The resource owner initiates this phase by introducing the resource servers associated with him or her to a centralized authorization server.

The client initiates the second phase when it wants to access a protected resource. The client talks to the authorization server and obtains the required level of authorization to access the protected resource that's hosted in the resource server. Finally, in the third phase, the client directly accesses the protected resource.

■ **Note** The latest draft of the UMA core specification is available at
http://tools.ietf.org/html/draft-hardjono-oauth-umacore-09.

UMA Phase 1: Protecting a Resource

Resources are owned by the resource owner and may be at different resource servers. Let's look at an example. Suppose my photos are with Flickr, my calendar is with Google, and my friend list is with Facebook. How can I protect all these resources, which are distributed across different resource servers, with a centralized authorization server? The first step is to introduce the centralized authorization server to Flickr, Google, and Facebook—to all the resource servers. The resource owner must do this. The resource owner can log in to each resource server and provide the authorization-server configuration endpoint to each of them. The authorization server must provide its configuration data in JSON format.

The following is a set of sample configuration data. The data in this JSON format should be understood by any of the resource servers that support UMA. This section digs into the details of each configuration element as you proceed:

```
{
    "version":"1.0",
    "issuer":"https://auth.server.com",
    "pat_profiles_supported":["bearer"],
    "aat_profiles_supported":["bearer"],
    "rpt_profiles_supported":["bearer"],
    "pat_grant_types_supported":["authorization_code"],
    "aat_grant_types_supported":["authorization_code"],
    "claim_profiles_supported":["openid"],
    "dynamic_client_endpoint":"https://auth.server.com/dyn_client_reg_uri",
    "token_endpoint":"https://auth.server.com/token_uri",
    "user_endpoint":"https://auth.server.com/user_uri",
    "resource_set_registration_endpoint":"https://auth.server.com/rs/rsrc_uri",
    "introspection_endpoint":"https://auth.server.com/rs/status_uri",
    "permission_registration_endpoint":"https://auth.server.com/perm_uri",
    "rpt_endpoint":"https://auth.server.com/rpt",
    "authorization_request_endpoint":"https://auth.server.com/authorize"
}
```

Once the resource server is introduced to the authorization server via its configuration data endpoint, the resource server can talk to the dynamic client-registration endpoint (`dynamic_client_endpoint`) to register itself at the authorization server.

■ **Note** The Dynamic Client Registration OAuth 2.0 profile is available at `https://datatracker.ietf.org/doc/draft-ietf-oauth-dyn-reg`.

The dynamic client-registration endpoint exposed by the authorization server can be secured or not. It can be secured with OAuth, HTTP Basic Authentication, Mutual TLS, or any other security protocol as desired by the authorization server. The Dynamic Client Registration profile doesn't enforce any authentication protocols over the registration endpoint, but it must be secured with TLS. If the authorization server decides to allow the endpoint to be public and let anyone be registered, it can do so. To register a client, it has to pass all its metadata to the registration endpoint. Here's a sample JSON message for client registration:

```
POST /register HTTP/1.1
Content-Type: application/json
Accept: application/json
Host: authz.server.com
{
    "redirect_uris":["https://client.org/callback","https://client.org/callback2"],
    "token_endpoint_auth_method":"client_secret_basic",
    "grant_types": ["authorization_code" , "implicit"],
    "response_types": ["code" , "token"],
}
```

A successful client registration results in the following JSON response, which includes the client and the client secret to be used by the resource server:

```
HTTP/1.1 200 OK
Content-Type: application/json
Cache-Control: no-store
Pragma: no-cache
{
            "client_id":"iuyiSgfgfhffgfh",
            "client_secret": "hkjhkiiu89hknhkjhuyjhk",
            "client_id_issued_at":2343276600,
            "client_secret_expires_at":2503286900,
            "redirect_uris":["https://client.org/callback", "https://client.org/callback2"],
            "grant_types": "authorization_code",
            "token_endpoint_auth_method": "client_secret_basic",
}
```

■ **Note**   You aren't required to use the Dynamic Client Registration API. Resource servers can use any method they prefer to register at the authorization server. The registration at the authorization server is a one-time operation, not per resource owner. If a given resource server has already been registered with a given authorization server, then it doesn't need to register again at the authorization server when the same authorization server is introduced by a different resource owner.

Once the initial resource-server registration process is complete, the next step in the first phase is for the resource server to obtain a protection API token (PAT) to access the Protection API exposed by the authorization server. (You learn more on PAT in the section "Protection API," later in the chapter.) PAT is issued per resource server, per resource owner. In other words, each resource owner must authorize a PAT so the resource server can use it to protect resources with the centralized authorization server. The authorization-server configuration file declares the types of PAT tokens it supports. In the previous example, the authorization server supports OAuth 2.0 bearer tokens:

```
pat_profiles_supported":["bearer"]
```

In addition to the PAT token type, the authorization-server configuration file also declares the way to obtain the PAT token. In this case, it should be via the OAuth 2.0 Authorization Code grant type. The resource server must initiate an OAuth flow with the Authorization Code grant type to obtain the PAT token in bearer format:

```
"pat_grant_types_supported":["authorization_code"]
```

■ **Note**   The scope of the PAT token must be http://docs.kantarainitiative.org/uma/scopes/prot.json. This must be included in the scope value of the Authorization Code grant request.

Following is a sample Authorization Code grant request to obtain a PAT token:

```
GET /authorize?response_type=code
                    &client_id=dsdasDdsdsdsdsdas
                    &state=xyz
                    &redirect_uri=https://flickr.com/callback
                    &scope=http://docs.kantarainitiative.org/uma/scopes/prot.json

HTTP/1.1 Host: auth.server.com
```

Once the resource server gets the PAT token, it can be used to access the Resource Set Registration API exposed by the authorization server, to register a set of resources that needs to be protected by the given authorization server. The endpoint of the Resource Set Registration API is defined under the authorization server configuration file (you learn more about the Resource Set Registration API in the section "Protection API"):

```
"resource_set_registration_endpoint":"https://auth.server.com/rs/rsrc_uri",
```

UMA Phase 2: Getting Authorization

According to the UMA specification, phase 2 begins after a failed access attempt by the client. The client tries to access a resource hosted in the resource server and gets an HTTP 401 status code (see Figure 10-7). In addition to the 401 response, the resource server includes the endpoint (as_uri) of the corresponding authorization server where the client can obtain a requesting party token (RPT):

```
HTTP/1.1 401 Unauthorized
WWW-Authenticate: UMA realm="my-realm",
                    host_id="photos.flickr.com",
                    as_uri=https://auth.server.com
```

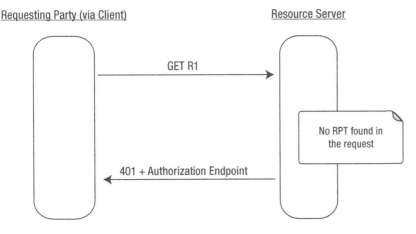

Figure 10-7. *The resource server rejects any request without an RPT*

According to UMA, to access a protected resource, the client must present a valid RPT. (You learn more about RPT in the section "Authorization API.") The RPT endpoint that must be included in the 401 response is declared in the authorization server configuration file:

```
"rpt_endpoint":"https://auth.server.com/rpt"
```

Once rejected by the resource server with a 401, the client has to talk to the RPT endpoint of the authorization server. To do so, the client must have an Authorization API token (AAT). To get an AAT, the client must be registered at the corresponding authorization server. The client can use the OAuth Dynamic Client Registration API or any other way it prefers to register. After it's registered with the authorization server, the client gets a client key and a client secret. The requesting party can be a different entity from the client. For example, the client can be a mobile application or a web application, whereas the requesting party could be a human user who uses either the mobile application or the web application. The ultimate goal is for the requesting party to access an API owned by a resource owner, hosted in a resource server, via a client application. To achieve this, the requesting party should get an RPT from an authorization server trusted by the resource server. To get an RPT, the requesting party should first get an AAT via the client application. To get an AAT, the client must follow the OAuth grant type supported by the authorization server to issue AAT tokens. That is declared in its authorization-server configuration file. In this case, the authorization server supports the Authorization Code grant type to issue AAT tokens:

```
"aat_grant_types_supported":["authorization_code"]
```

Once the client is registered at the authorization server, to get an AAT on behalf of the requesting party, it must initiate the OAuth Authorization Code grant type flow, with the following scope:

```
http://docs.kantarainitiative.org/uma/scopes/authz.json
```

Following is a sample Authorization Code grant request to obtain an AAT token:

```
GET /authorize?response_type=code
                    &client_id=dsdasDdsdsdsdsdas
                    &state=xyz
                    &redirect_uri=https://flickr.com/callback
                    &scope=http://docs.kantarainitiative.org/uma/scopes/authz.json

HTTP/1.1 Host: auth.server.com
```

■ **Note** You aren't required to use the Dynamic Client Registration API. The client can use any method it prefers to register at the authorization server. The registration at the authorization server is a one-time operation and not per resource server or per requesting party. If a given client has already been registered with a given authorization server, then it doesn't need to register again when a different requesting party uses the same authorization server. The AAT is per client per requesting party per authorization server and is independent from the resource server.

Once you have the AAT, upon the 401 response from the resource server, the client can talk to the authorization server's RPT endpoint and get the corresponding RPT (see Figure 10-8). To get an RPT, the client must authenticate with the AAT. In the following example, the AAT is used in the HTTP Authorization header as an OAuth 2.0 bearer token:

```
POST /rpt HTTP/1.1
Host: as.example.com
Authorization: Bearer GghgjhsuyuE8heweds
```

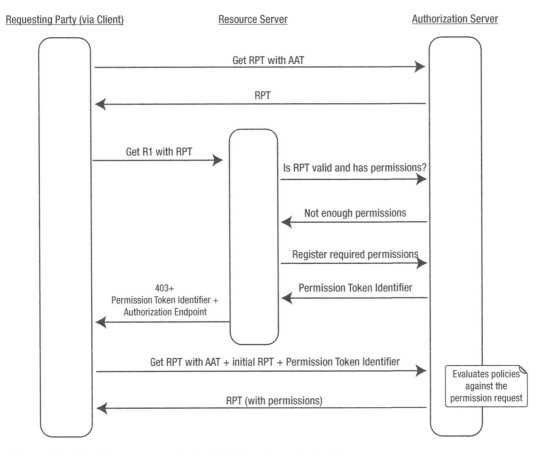

Figure 10-8. *The client gets an authorized RPT from the authorization server*

◼ **Note**   The RPT endpoint is defined under the `rpt_endpoint` attribute of the authorization-server configuration.

The following shows a sample response from the RPT endpoint of the authorization server. If this is the first issuance of the RPT, it doesn't have any authorization rights attached. It can only be used as a temporary token to get the "real" RPT:

```
HTTP/1.1 201 Created
Content-Type: application/json
{
    "rpt": "dsdsJKhkiuiuoiwewjewkej"
}
```

When the client is in possession of the initial RPT, it can once again try to access the resource. In this case, the RPT goes as an OAuth 2.0 bearer token in the HTTP `Authorization` header. Now the resource server extracts the RPT from the resource request and talks to the Introspection API exposed by the authorization server. The Introspection API can tell whether the RPT is valid and, if it is, the permissions associated with it. In this case, because you're still using the initial RPT, there are no permissions associated with it, even though it's a valid token.

■ **Note** The Introspection API exposed by the authorization server is OAuth protected. The resource server must present a valid PAT to access it. The PAT is another bearer token that goes in the HTTP Authorization header.

If the RPT doesn't have enough permissions to access the resource, the resource server talks to the Client Requested Permission Registration API exposed by the authorization server, and registers the required set of permissions to access the desired resource. When permission registration is successfully completed, the authorization server returns a permission-ticket identifier.

■ **Note** The Client Requested Permission Registration endpoint is defined under the permission_registration_end-point attribute in the authorization-server configuration. This endpoint, which is part of the UMA Protection API, is secured with OAuth 2.0. The resource server must present a valid PAT to access the API.

The following is a sample request to the permission registration endpoint of the authorization server. It must include a unique resource_set_id corresponding to the requested resource and the required set of scopes associated with it:

```
POST /perm_uri HTTP/1.1
Content-Type: application/json
Host: auth.server.com
{
    "resource_set_id": "1122wqwq23398100",
    "scopes": [
        "http://photoz.flickr.com/dev/actions/view",
        "http://photoz.flickr.com/dev/actions/all"
        ]
}
```

In response to this request, the authorization server generates a permission token:

```
HTTP/1.1 201 Created
Content-Type: application/json

{ "ticket": "016f88989-f9b9-11e0-bd6f-0cc66c6004de" }
```

When the permission ticket is created at the authorization server, the resource server sends the following response to the client:

```
HTTP/1.1 403 Forbidden
WWW-Authenticate: UMA realm="my-realm",
                  host_id=" photos.flickr.com ",
                  as_uri="https://auth.server.com"
                  error="insufficient_scope"

{ "ticket": "016f88989-f9b9-11e0-bd6f-0cc66c6004de" }
```

Now the client has to get a new RPT with the required set of permissions. Unlike in the previous case, this time the RPT request also includes the `ticket` attribute from the previous 403 response:

```
POST /rpt HTTP/1.1
Host: as.example.com
Authorization: Bearer GghgjhsuyuE8heweds

{
     "rpt": "dsdsJKhkiuiuoiwewjewkej",
     "ticket": "016f88989-f9b9-11e0-bd6f-0cc66c6004de "
}
```

■ **Note**   The RPT endpoint of the authorization server is secured with OAuth 2.0. To access the RPT endpoint, the client must use an AAT in the HTTP `Authorization` header as the OAuth bearer token.

At this point, prior to issuing the new RPT to satisfy the requested set of permissions, the authorization server evaluates the authorization policies set by the resource owner against the client and the requesting party. If the authorization server needs more information regarding the requesting party while evaluating the policies, it can interact directly with the requesting party to gather the required details. Also, if it needs further approval by the resource owner, the authorization server must notify the resource owner and wait for a response. In any of these cases, once the authorization server decides to associate permissions with the RPT, it creates a new RPT and sends it across to the client:

```
HTTP/1.1 201 Created
Content-Type: application/json

{ "rpt": "dsdJhkjhkhk879dshkjhkj877979" }
```

UMA Phase 3: Accessing the Protected Resource

At the end of phase 2, the client got access to a valid RPT with the required set of permissions. Now the client can use it to access the protected resource. The resource server again uses the Introspection API exposed by the authorization server to check the validity of the RPT. If the token is valid and has the required set of permissions, the corresponding resource is returned to the client.

UMA APIs

UMA defines two main APIs: the Protection API and the Authorization API (see Figure 10-9). The Protection API sits between the resource server and the authorization server, and the Authorization API sits between the client and the authorization server. Both APIs are secured with OAuth 2.0. To access the Protection API, the resource server must present a PAT as the bearer token; and to access the Authorization API, the client must present an AAT as the bearer token.

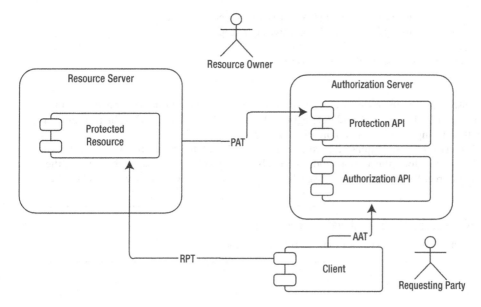

Figure 10-9. *UMA APIs*

Protection API

The Protection API is the interface exposed to the resource server by the authorization server. It consists of three sub-elements: the OAuth Resource Set Registration endpoint, the Client Requested Permission Registration endpoint, and the OAuth Token Introspection endpoint.

■ **Note**   The latest draft of the OAuth Resource Set Registration specification is available at

`http://tools.ietf.org/html/draft-hardjono-oauth-resource-reg-01`.

These three APIs that fall under the Protection API address different concerns. The resource server uses the Resource Set Registration API to publish semantics and discovery properties of its resources to the authorization server. The resource server does this in an ongoing manner. Whenever it finds a resource set that needs to be protected by an external authorization server, it talks to the corresponding Resource Set Registration endpoint to register new resources. This action can be initiated by the resource server itself or by the resource owner. The following example shows a JSON request to the Resource Set Registration API of the authorization server. The value of the name attribute should be human-readable text, and the optional `icon_uri` can point to any image that represents this resource set. The `scopes` array should list all the scope values required to access the resource set. The `type` attribute describes the semantics associated with the resource set; the value of this attribute is meaningful only to the resource server and can be used to process the associated resources:

```
{
    "name": "John's Family Photos",
    "icon_uri": "http://www.flickr.com/icons/flower.png",
    "scopes": [
```

```
                            "http://photoz.flickr.com/dev/scopes/view",
                            "http://photoz.flickr.com/dev/scopes/all"
                    ],
        "type": "http://www.flickr.com/rsets/photoalbum"
}
```

This JSON message is also known as the *resource description*. Each UMA authorization server must present a REST API to create (PUT), update (POST), list (GET), and delete (DELETE) resource-set descriptions. The resource server can utilize this endpoint either during phase 1 or in an ongoing manner.

The resource server accesses the Client Requested Permission Registration endpoint during phase 2 of UMA flow. The resource server uses this API to inform the authorization server about the level of permissions required for the client to access the desired resource. The resource server uses the Introspection API to check the validity of the RPT.

■ **Note**   The OAuth 2.0 Token Introspection Internet draft is available at
`https://datatracker.ietf.org/doc/draft-richer-oauth-introspection/`.

Authorization API

The Authorization API is the interface between the client and the authorization server. The main responsibility of this API is to issue RPTs.

The Role of UMA in API Security

At the time of this writing, UMA is an emerging and promising standard with very few implementations. At its core, it presents a wide range of practical use cases. Even though it hasn't being used widely, the role of UMA in API security shouldn't be underestimated. UMA is the right model to control access in a centralized manner to APIs owned by a single entity but distributed across different servers.

■ **Note**   UMA earned the Best Innovation in Information Security Award in 2014 from the European Identity & Cloud Conference (`https://kantarainitiative.org/uma-takes-home-award-from-eic-2014/`).

Summary

This chapter focused on User Managed Access (UMA), which is an emerging standard built on top of the OAuth 2.0 core specification as a profile. UMA has its roots in ProtectServe, which is built on top of OAuth 1.0 and was discussed at the beginning of the chapter. UMA still has very few vendor implementations, but it promises to be a highly recognized standard in the near future. It's highly recommended that you keep an eye on the Kantara foundation and its UMA initiatives.

In the next chapter, we will delve into how to access and secure APIs beyond enterprise borders.

■ ■ ■

CHAPTER 11

Federation

Recent research performed by Quocirca confirms that many businesses now have more external users who interact with enterprise applications than internal ones. In Europe, 58% of businesses transact directly with users from other firms and/or consumers. In the UK alone, the figure is 65%.

If you look at recent history, most enterprises today grow via acquisitions, mergers, and partnerships. In the United States alone, the volume of mergers and acquisitions totaled $865.1 billion in the first nine months of 2013, according to Dealogic. That's a 39 percent increase over the same period of the previous year, and the highest nine-month total since 2008. What does this mean for API security? It indicates that you need to have the ability to deal with multiple heterogeneous security systems across borders.

Enabling Federation

Federation, in the context of API security, is about propagating user identities across distinct identity-management systems or distinct enterprises. Let's start with a simple use case where you have an API exposed to your partners. How would you authenticate users from different partners? These users belong to the external partners and are managed by them. HTTP Basic Authentication won't work. You don't have access to the external users' credentials and, at the same time, you don't dare expose an LDAP or a JDBC connection outside your firewall to external parties. Asking for usernames and passwords simply doesn't work in a federation scenario. Would OAuth 2.0 work? To access an API secured with OAuth, the client must present an access token issued by the owner of the API. Users from external parties have to authenticate first with the OAuth authorization server and then obtain an access token.

Neither the Authorization Code grant type nor the Implicit grant type mandates how to authenticate users at the authorization server. It's up to the authorization server to decide. If the user is local to the authorization server, then it can use a username and password or any other direct authentication protocol. If the user is from an external entity, then you have to use some kind of brokered authentication.

Brokered Authentication

With brokered authentication, at the time of authentication, the authorization server need not trust each and every individual user from external parties. Instead, it can trust a broker from the given domain. Each external party should have a trust broker whose responsibility is to authenticate its own users (possibly through direct authentication) and then pass the authentication decision back to OAuth authorization server in a reliable and trusted manner. The trust relationship between the broker and the OAuth authorization server (or between two federation domains) must be established out of band. In other words, it has to be established with a prior agreement between two parties. In most scenarios, trust between different entities is established through X.509 certificates. Let's walk through a sample brokered-authentication use case.

Going back to OAuth principles, you need to deal with four entities in a federation scenario: the resource owner, the resource server, the authorization server, and the client application. All these entities can reside in the same domain or in different ones.

Let's start with the simplest scenario first. The resource owner, resource server, and authorization server are in a single domain, and the client application is in a different domain. For example, you're an employee of Foo Inc. and want to access a web application hosted by Bar Inc. Once you log in to the web application at Bar Inc., it needs to access an API hosted by Foo Inc. on your behalf. Using OAuth terminology, you're the resource owner, and the API is hosted in the resource server. Both are from the Foo domain. The web application hosted by Bar Inc. is the OAuth client application.

Figure 11-1 illustrates how brokered authentication works for OAuth client applications. The resource owner from Foo Inc. visits the web application at Bar Inc. (step 1). To authenticate the user, the web application redirects the user to the OAuth authorization server at Foo Inc., which is also the home domain of the resource owner (step 2). To use the OAuth Authorization Code grant type, the web application also needs to pass its client ID along with the authorization code grant request during the redirection. At this time, the authorization server won't authenticate the client application and will only validate its existence. In a federation scenario, the authorization server need not trust every individual application (or OAuth client); rather, it trusts the corresponding domain. The authorization server accepts authorization grant requests from any client that comes from a trusted domain. This also avoids the cost of client registration. You don't need to register each client application from Foo Inc.—instead, you can build a trust relationship between the authorization server from Foo Inc. and the trust broker from Bar Inc. During the authorization code grant phase, the authorization server only needs to record the client ID. It doesn't need to validate the client's existence.

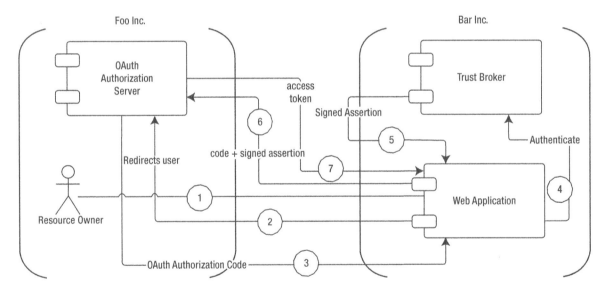

Figure 11-1. *Brokered authentication for OAuth client applications*

■ **Note**   The OAuth client identifier (ID) isn't treated as a secret. It's publicly visible to anyone.

Once the client application gets the authorization code from the authorization server (step 3), the next step is to exchange it for a valid access token. This step requires client authentication. Because the authorization server doesn't trust each individual application, the web application must first authenticate to its own trust broker in its own domain (step 4) and get a signed assertion (step 5). This signed assertion can be used as a token of proof against the authorization server in Foo Inc. The authorization server validates the signature of the assertion and, if it's signed by an entity it trusts, returns the corresponding access token to the client application (steps 6 and 7). The client application can use the access token to access the APIs in Foo Inc. on behalf of the resource owner, or it can talk to a user endpoint at Foo Inc. to get more information about the user.

■ **Note** The definition of *assertion*, according to the Oxford English Dictionary, is: "a confident and forceful statement of fact or belief." The fact or belief here is that the entity that brings this assertion is an authenticated entity at the trust broker. If the assertion isn't signed, anyone in the middle can alter it. Once the trust broker (or the asserting party) signs the assertion with its private key, no one in the middle can alter it. If it's altered, any alterations can be detected at the authorization server during signature validation. The signature is validated using the corresponding public key of the trust broker.

SECURITY ASSERTION MARKUP LANGUAGE (SAML)

Security Assertion Markup Language (SAML) is an OASIS standard for exchanging authentication, authorization, and identity-related data between interested parties in an XML-based data format. SAML 1.0 was adopted as an OASIS standard in 2001, and in 2002 SAML 1.1 was ratified as an OASIS standard. At the same time, the Liberty Alliance donated its Identity Federation Framework to OASIS. SAML 2.0 became an OASIS standard in 2005 by converging SAML 1.1, Liberty Alliance's Identity Federation Framework, and Shibboleth 1.3. SAML 2.0 has four basic elements:

- *Assertions:* Authentication, Authorization, and Attribute assertions.

- *Protocol:* Request and Response elements to package SAML assertions.

- *Bindings:* How to transfer SAML messages between interested parties. HTTP binding and SOAP binding are two examples. If the trust broker uses a SOAP message to transfer a SAML assertion, then it has to use SOAP binding for SAML.

- *Profiles:* How to aggregate the assertions, protocol, and bindings to address a specific use case. A SAML 2.0 Web Single Sign-On (SSO) profile defines a standard way to establish SSO between different service providers via SAML.

■ **Note** The blog post at http://blog.facilelogin.com/2011/11/depth-of-saml-saml-summary.html provides a high-level overview of SAML.

SAML 2.0 Profile for OAuth: Client Authentication

To achieve client authentication with the SAML 2.0 profile for OAuth 2.0, you can use the parameter client_assertion_type with the value urn:ietf:params:oauth:client-assertion-type:saml2-bearer in the access-token request (see step 6 in Figure 11-1). The OAuth flow starts from step 2.

Now let's dig into each step. The following shows a sample authorization code grant request initiated by the web application at Bar Inc.:

```
GET /authorize?response_type=code
                &client_id=wiuo879hkjhkjhk3232
                &state=xyz
                &redirect_uri=https://bar.com/cb
HTTP/1.1
Host: auth.foo.com
```

This results in the following response, which includes the requested authorization code:

```
HTTP/1.1 302 Found
Location: https://bar.com/cb?code=SplwqeZQwqwKJjklje
                            &state=xyz
```

So far it's the normal OAuth authorization code flow. Now the web application has to talk to the trust broker in its own domain to obtain a SAML assertion. This step is outside the scope of OAuth. Because this is machine-to-machine authentication (from the web application to the trust broker), you can use a SOAP-based WS-Trust protocol to obtain the SAML assertion. The web application need not do this each time a user logs in; it can be a one-time operation governed by the lifetime of the SAML assertion. The following is a sample SAML assertion obtained from the trust broker"

```
<?xml version="1.0" encoding="UTF-8"?>
<saml:Assertion xmlns:saml="urn:oasis:names:tc:SAML:2.0:assertion"
            ID="_cd3649b3639560458bc9d9b33dfee8d21378409114655"
                    IssueInstant="2013-09-05T19:25:14.654Z" Version="2.0">
    <saml:Issuer Format="urn:oasis:names:tc:SAML:2.0:nameid-format:entity"
     xmlns:saml="urn:oasis:names:tc:SAML:2.0:assertion">
     bar.com
    </saml:Issuer>
    <ds:Signature xmlns:ds="http://www.w3.org/2000/09/xmldsig#">
      <ds:SignedInfo></ds:SignedInfo>
      <ds:SignatureValue></ds:SignatureValue>
      <ds:KeyInfo></ds:KeyInfo>
    </ds:Signature>
    <saml:Subject xmlns:saml="urn:oasis:names:tc:SAML:2.0:assertion">
        <saml:NameID Format="urn:oasis:names:tc:SAML:1.1:nameid-format:unspecified"
                            xmlns:saml="urn:oasis:names:tc:SAML:2.0:assertion">
            18982198kjk2121
        </saml:NameID>
        <saml:SubjectConfirmation Method="urn:oasis:names:tc:SAML:2.0:cm:bearer"
                xmlns:saml="urn:oasis:names:tc:SAML:2.0:assertion">
        <saml:SubjectConfirmationData NotOnOrAfter="2013-09-05T19:30:14.654Z"
                Recipient="https://foo.com/oauth2/token"/>
        </saml:SubjectConfirmation>
    </saml:Subject>
    <saml:Conditions NotBefore="2013-09-05T19:25:14.654Z" NotOnOrAfter="2013-09-05T19:30:14.654Z"
                        xmlns:saml="urn:oasis:names:tc:SAML:2.0:assertion">
        <saml:AudienceRestriction xmlns:saml="urn:oasis:names:tc:SAML:2.0:assertion">
            <saml:Audience>https://foo.com/oauth2/token</saml:Audience>
```

```
                </saml:AudienceRestriction>
        </saml:Conditions>
        <saml:AuthnStatement AuthnInstant="2013-09-05T19:25:14.655Z"
                                    xmlns:saml="urn:oasis:names:tc:SAML:2.0:assertion">
                    <saml:AuthnContext xmlns:saml="urn:oasis:names:tc:SAML:2.0:assertion">
                        <saml:AuthnContextClassRef>
                                    urn:oasis:names:tc:SAML:2.0:ac:classes:unspecified
                        </saml:AuthnContextClassRef>
                    </saml:AuthnContext>
            </saml:AuthnStatement>
</saml:Assertion>
```

To use this SAML assertion in an OAuth flow to authenticate the client, it must adhere to following rules:

- The assertion must have a unique identifier for the Issuer element, which identifies the token-issuing entity.

- The assertion must have a NameID element inside the Subject element that uniquely identifies the client application. This is treated as the client ID of the client application at the authorization server.

- The SubjectConfirmation method must be set to urn:oasis:names:tc:SAML:2.0:cm:bearer.

- If the assertion issuer authenticates the client, then the assertion must have a single AuthnStatment.

■ **Note** WS-Trust is an OASIS standard for SOAP message security. WS-Trust, which is built on top of the WS-Security standard, defines a protocol to exchange identity information, and it's wrapped in a token (SAML), between two trust domains. The blog post at http://blog.facilelogin.com/2010/05/ws-trust-with-fresh-banana-service.html explains WS-Trust at a high level. The latest WS-Trust specification is available at http://docs.oasis-open.org/ws-sx/ws-trust/v1.4/errata01/ws-trust-1.4-errata01-complete.html.

Once the client web application gets the SAML assertion from the trust broker, it has to base64url-encode the assertion and send it to the authorization server along with the access token request. In the following sample HTTP POST message, client_assertion_type is set to urn:ietf:params:oauth:client-assertion-type:saml2-bearer, and the base64url-encoded SAML assertion is set to the client_assertion parameter:

■ **Note** Base64url encoding is defined in RFC 4648, http://tools.ietf.org/html/rfc4648.

```
POST /token HTTP/1.1
Host: auth.foo.com
Content-Type: application/x-www-form-urlencoded
grant_type=authorization_code&code=SplwqeZQwqwKJjklje
&client_assertion_type=urn:ietf:params:oauth:client-assertion-type:saml2-bearer
&client_assertion=HdsjkkbKLew...[omitted for brevity]...OT
```

■ **Note**   The SAML 2.0 Profile for OAuth 2.0 Client Authentication and Authorization Grants is available at http://tools.ietf.org/html/draft-ietf-oauth-saml2-bearer-20.

Once the authorization server receives the access-token request, it validates the SAML assertion. If it's valid, an access token is issued, along with a refresh token.

SAML 2.0 Profile for OAuth: Grant Type

The previous section explained how to use a SAML assertion to authenticate a client application. That is one federation use case that falls under the context of OAuth. There the trust broker was running inside Bar Inc., where the client application was running. In the other use case, the end user authenticates to the web application with a SAML assertion. A trust broker in the user's domain must issue this assertion. The client application uses this assertion to obtain an access token to access an API on behalf of the logged-in user.

Figure 11-2 illustrates how brokered authentication with a SAML grant type for OAuth 2.0 works. The first three steps are outside the scope of OAuth. The resource owner first logs in to the web application owned by Bar Inc. via SAML 2.0 Web SSO. The SAML 2.0 Web SSO flow is initiated by the web application by redirecting the user to the SAML identity provider at Foo Inc. (step 2). Once the user authenticates to the SAML identity provider, the SAML identity provider creates a SAML response (which wraps the assertion) and sends it back to the web application (step 3). The web application validates the signature in the SAML assertion and, if a trusted identity provider signs it, allows the user to log in to the web application. Once the user logs in to the web application, the web application has to exchange the SAML assertion for an access token by talking to its own internal authorization server (steps 4 and 5). The way to do this is defined in the SAML 2.0 Profile for OAuth 2.0 Client Authentication and Authorization Grants specification.

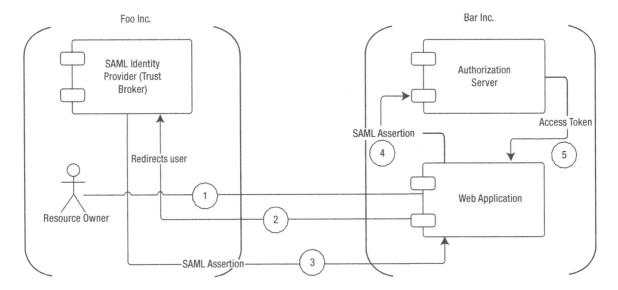

Figure 11-2. *Brokered authentication with the SAML grant type for OAuth 2.0*

The following is a sample POST message from the web application to the authorization server. There the value of grant_type must be urn:ietf:params:oauth:grant-type:saml2-bearer, and the base64url-encoded SAML assertion is set to the assertion parameter:

■ **Note**   No refresh tokens are issued under the SAML Bearer grant type. The lifetime of the access token should not exceed the lifetime of the SAML bearer assertion by a significant amount.

```
POST /token HTTP/1.1
Host: auth.bar.com
Content-Type: application/x-www-form-urlencoded
grant_type=urn:ietf:params:oauth:grant-type:saml2-bearer
&assertion=QBNhbWxwOl...[omitted for brevity]...OT4
```

This request is validated at the authorization server. The SAML assertion is once again validated via its signature; and, if a trusted identity provider signs it, the authorization server issues a valid access token.

■ **Note**   The scope of the access token issued under the SAML Bearer grant type should be set out of band by the resource owner. *Out of band* here indicates that the resource owner makes a pre-agreement with the resource server/authorization server with respect to the scope associated with a given resource when the SAML grant type is being used. The client application can include a scope parameter in the authorization grant request, but the value of the scope parameter must be a subset of the scope defined out of band by the resource owner. If no scope parameter is included in the authorization grant request, then the access token inherits the scope set out of band.

Both federation use cases discussed assume that the resource server and the authorization server are running in the same domain. If that isn't the case, the resource server must invoke an API exposed by the authorization server to validate the access token at the time the client tries to access a resource. If the authorization server supports the OAuth Introspection specification (discussed in Chapter 9), the resource server can talk to the introspection endpoint and finds out whether the token is active or not and also what scopes are associated with the token. The resource server can then check whether the token has the required set of scopes to access the resource.

SAML 2.0 BEARER GRANT TYPE FOR OAUTH WITH WSO2 IDENTITY SERVER

In this exercise, you see how to obtain an OAuth 2.0 access token using the SAML 2.0 Bearer grant type. You run two instances of WSO2 Identity Server: one as the SAML 2.0 identity provider (in domain Foo) and the other as the OAuth authorization server (in domain Bar).

■ **Note**   WSO2 Identity Server is a free-of-charge, open source identity- and entitlement-management server, released under the Apache 2.0 license.

Follow these steps:

1. Download WSO2 Identity Server 5.0.0 from `http://wso2.com/products/identity-server/`, set up the `JAVA_HOME` environment variable, and start the server from `wso2server.sh/wso2server.bat` in WSO2_IS_HOME/bin. If WSO2 Identity Server 5.0.0 isn't available from the main download page, you can find it at `http://wso2.com/more-downloads/identity-server/`.

2. By default, WSO2 Identity Server starts on HTTPS port 9443. You use the default port for the SAML 2.0 identity provider. You also need another identity server running as the OAuth authorization server. For that, unzip the identity server zip file you downloaded before to a different location, and change its port to start on 9445. To change the ports, open `WSO2_IS_HOME/repository/conf/carbon.xml`, search for the element `<Offset>`, and change its value to 2. Now you have two identity server instances running: one on port 9443, and one on port 9445.

3. Let's configure the SAML 2.0 identity provider first. Log in to `https://localhost:9443` with the default username and password: `admin/admin`.

4. First you need to add the web application running in the Bar domain as a trusted service provider. Choose Main ➤ Service Providers ➤ Add. Provide a name, say, `bar-web-app`, and click Register.

5. Choose Inbound Authentication Configuration ➤ SAML2 Web SSO Configuration ➤ Configure.

6. Provide a name for Issuer and `https://localhost:9445/oauth2/token/` for the Assertion Consumer URL. The value of Assertion Consumer URL must be equal to the OAuth token endpoint of the OAuth authorization server running in the Bar domain.

7. Check Enable Assertion Signing, and check Enable Response Signing.

8. Check Enable Audience Restriction, type `https://localhost:9445/oauth2/token/` in the text box, and click Add Audience. This should be the value of the token endpoint of the OAuth authorization server running in the Bar domain.

9. Click Update.

10. Click Update on the service provider page to complete the service provider registration.

11. Now you can start configuring the OAuth authorization server running in the Bar domain. Log in to `https://localhost:9445` with the default username and password: `admin/admin`.

12. The OAuth authorization server in the Bar domain must trust the Foo domain identity provider. Choose Home ➤ Identity Providers ➤ Add. Provide a value for the identity provider name, say `foo.com`.

13. Make sure the value of Alias is set to `https://localhost:9445/oauth2/token/`. This should match the Audience value you set while configuring the SAML 2.0 identity provider.

14. Upload the public certificate of the SAML 2.0 identity provider running on port 9443 in the field Identity Provider Public Certificate. You can download the public certificate of the WSO2 Identity Server by visiting `https://localhost:9443` in Firefox: right-click the page, and choose View Page Info ➤ Security ➤ View Certificate ➤ Details ➤ Export. Select DER as the file format. Similar options are available in other browsers as well.

15. Click Federated Authenticators ➤ SAML2 Web SSO Configuration. Check Enable SAML2 Web SSO, and set localhost as the Identity Provider Entity ID. This is the default entity ID of the SAML 2.0 identity provider running on port 9443. Enter bar.com as the Service Provider Entity ID.

16. Click Register to complete the identity provider registration.

17. In this use case, the web application running on the Foo domain also acts as an OAuth client to its own OAuth authorization server. To talk to the authorization server via the SAML 2.0 bearer grant type, the web application must have a client ID and a client secret.

18. To get an OAuth client ID and a client secret to the web application, you need to register it as a service provider at the OAuth authorization server.

19. Choose Main ➤ Service Providers ➤ Add. Enter a name, say, bar-oauth-app, and click Register.

20. Choose Inbound Authentication Configuration ➤ OAuth and OpenID Connect Configuration ➤ Configure.

21. Uncheck all grant types except SAML. Make sure the OAuth version is set to 2.0.

22. Copy the values of OAuth Client Key and OAuth Client Secret.

23. You're all set. Now comes testing time. First you need to generate the SAML assertion. To do that, log in to the SAML 2.0 identity provider running on port 9443, and choose Tools ➤ SAML ➤ SAML Response Builder. Pick the Service Provider which you registered by the issuer name, type admin in the User Name text box, and click Generate.

24. This generates the complete SAML response in the way that it will be sent to the web application running in the Bar domain. You only need the Assertion part of it. Copy from <saml2:Assertion> to </saml2:Assertion>.

25. You need to base64url-encode the copied assertion. Go to http://kjur.github.io/jsjws/tool_b64uenc.html, paste the copied Assertion value, and click Encode It. Copy the base64url-encoded string from there.

26. Try the following cURL command. Replace the values in bold appropriately:

```
curl -k -X POST -u "oauth client key:oauth client secret"
        -H "Content-Type:application/x-www-form-urlencoded;
                        charset=UTF-8"
        -d "grant_type=urn:ietf:params:oauth:grant-type:saml2-bearer&
            assertion=base64url encoded assertion"
            https://localhost:9445/oauth2/token
```

JWT Profile for OAuth 2.0 Client Authentication and Authorization Grants

JSON Web Token (JWT) is a well-structured JSON message. What the SAML profile does in the XML world, the JWT profile does in the JSON world. Both profiles address the same use cases. The following example shows how to use a JWT assertion for OAuth client authentication. There the `client_assertion_type` parameter is set to `urn:ietf:params:oauth:client-assertion-type:jwt-bearer`, and the `client_assertion` parameter is set to the signed JWT assertion (Chapter 13 discusses JWT further):

```
POST /token HTTP/1.1
Host: auth.foo.com
Content-Type: application/x-www-form-urlencoded
grant_type=authorization_code
&code=vAZEIHjQTHuGgaSvyW9hOORpusLzkvTOww3trZBxZpo
&client_assertion_type=urn:ietf:params:oauth:client-assertion-type:jwt-bearer
&client_assertion=eyJhwsas87NiJ9.eyJpc3Mi[...omitted for brevity...].
                cCwqPo[...omitted for brevity...]
```

The following example shows how to use a JWT assertion with the JWT grant type. Here the value of the grant_type parameter should be set to `urn:ietf:params:oauth:grant-type:jwt-bearer`:

```
POST /token HTTP/1.1
Host: auth.bar.com
Content-Type: application/x-www-form-urlencoded

grant_type=urn:ietf:params:oauth:grant-type:jwt-bearer
&assertion=eewewbGciOiJFUzewqew.eewew3Mi[...omitted for brevity...].
        ewe-ZhwP[...omitted for brevity...]
```

▓ **Note**   The JSON Web Token (JWT) Profile for OAuth 2.0 Client Authentication and Authorization Grants is available at http://tools.ietf.org/html/draft-ietf-oauth-jwt-bearer-09.

Summary

Identity federation is about propagating user identities across boundaries. These boundaries can be between distinct enterprises, or even distinct identity-management systems within the same enterprise. This chapter highlighted two OAuth 2.0 profiles—SAML 2.0 grant type and JWT grant type—to build federation scenarios for API security.

The next chapter takes a closer look at the identity layer built on top of OAuth 2.0: that is, OpenID Connect.

■ ■ ■

CHAPTER 12

OpenID Connect

OpenID Connect was ratified as a standard by its membership on February 26, 2014. OpenID Connect provides a lightweight framework for identity interactions in a RESTful manner. It was developed under the OpenID Foundation and has its roots in OpenID, but it was greatly affected by OAuth 2.0.

■ **Note** The announcement by the OpenID Foundation regarding the launch of the OpenID Connect standard is available at: http://openid.net/2014/02/26/the-openid-foundation-launches-the-openid-connect-standard/.

A Brief History of OpenID Connect

OpenID, which followed in the footsteps of SAML in 2005, revolutionized web authentication. Brad Fitzpatrick, the founder of LiveJournal, initiated it. The basic principle behind both OpenID and SAML, discussed in Chapter 11, is the same. Both can be used to facilitate web single sign-on (SSO) and cross-domain identity federation. OpenID is more community friendly, user centric, and decentralized. Yahoo! added OpenID support in January 2008, MySpace announced its support for OpenID in July of that same year, and Google joined the party in October. By December 2009, there were more than 1 billion OpenID-enabled accounts. It was a huge success as a web SSO protocol.

OPENID QUICK START

How many profiles do you maintain today at different web sites? Perhaps you have one on Yahoo!, one on Facebook, one on Google, and so on. Each time you update your mobile number or home address, either you have to update all your profiles or you risk outdating most of your profiles. OpenID solves the problem of scattered profiles on different web sites. With OpenID, you maintain your profile only at your OpenID provider, and all the other sites become OpenID relying parties. These "talk" with your OpenID provider to obtain your information.

Each time you try to log in to a relying party web site; you're redirected to your OpenID provider. At the OpenID provider, you have to authenticate and approve the request of the relying party for your attributes. Upon approval, you're redirected back to the relying party with the requested attributes. This goes beyond simple attribute sharing to facilitate decentralized SSO.

With SSO, you only log in once at the OpenID provider. That is, a relying party redirects you the first time. After that, your OpenID provider doesn't ask for credentials but uses the authenticated session you created before at the OpenID provider. This authenticated session is maintained either by a cookie until the browser is closed, or with persistent cookies. Figure 12-1 illustrates how OpenID works.

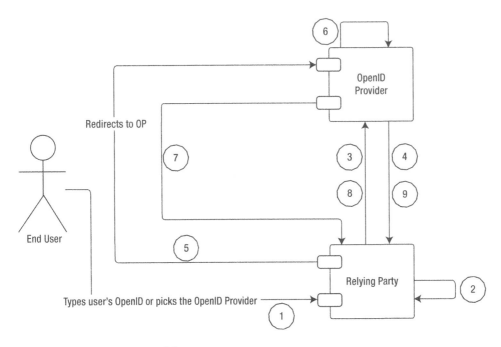

Figure 12-1. *OpenID protocol flow*

The end user initiates the OpenID flow by typing his or her OpenID on the relying party web site (step 1). An OpenID is a unique URL (or an XRI). For example, `http://prabath.myopenid.com` is an OpenID. Once the user types his or her OpenID, the relying party has to do a discovery based on it to find out the corresponding OpenID provider (step 2). The relying party performs an HTTP GET on the OpenID to get back the HTML text behind it. For example, if you view the source that is behind `http://prabath.myopenid.com`, you'll see the following tag. This is exactly what the relying party sees during the discovery phase. This tag indicates what the OpenID provider is behind the provided OpenID:

```
<link rel="openid2.provider" href="http://www.myopenid.com/server" />
```

OpenID has another way of identifying the OpenID provider, other than asking for an OpenID from the end user. This is known as *directed identity*, and Yahoo!, Google, and many other OpenID providers use it. If a relying party uses directed identity, it already knows who the OpenID provider is, so a discovery phase isn't needed. The relying party lists the set of OpenID providers it supports, and the user has to pick which one it wants to authenticate against.

Once the OpenID provider is discovered, the next step depends on the type of the relying party. If it's a smart relying party, then it executes step 3 in Figure 12-1 to create an association with the OpenID provider. During the association, a shared secret key is established between the OpenID provider and the relying party. If a key is already established between the two parties, this step is skipped, even for a smart relying party. A dumb relying party always ignores step 3.

In step 5, the user is redirected to the discovered OpenID provider. In step 6, the user has to authenticate and approve the attribute request from the relying party. Upon approval, the user is redirected back to the relying party. A key known only to the OpenID provider and the corresponding relying party signs this response. Once the relying party receives the response, if it's a smart relying party, it validates the signature itself. The key shared during the association phase should sign the message. If it's a dumb relying party, it directly talks to the OpenID provider in step 8 (not a browser redirect) and asks to validate the signature. The decision is passed back to the relying party in step 9, and that concludes the OpenID protocol flow.

OpenID and OAuth 1.0 address two different concerns. OpenID is about authentication, whereas OAuth 1.0 is about delegated authorization. As both of these standards were gaining popularity in their respective domains, there was interest in combining them so that it would be possible to authenticate a user and also get a token to access their resources on their behalf in a single step.

The Google Step 2 project is the first serious effort in this direction. It introduced an OpenID extension for OAuth, which basically takes OAuth-related parameters in the OpenID request/response. The same people who initiated the Google Step 2 project later brought it into the OpenID Foundation.

■ **Note**   The Google Step 2 OpenID extension for OAuth specification is available at
`http://step2.googlecode.com/svn/spec/openid_oauth_extension/latest/openid_oauth_extension.html`.

OpenID has gone through three generations to date. OpenID 1.0/1.1/2.0 was the first generation, and the OpenID extension for OAuth is the second. OpenID Connect is the third generation of OpenID.

■ **Note**   Yahoo!, Google, and many other OpenID providers will discontinue their support for OpenID 2.0 by mid-2015 and migrate into OpenID Connect.

AMAZON USES OPENID!

Few have noticed that Amazon still uses (at the time of this writing) OpenID for user authentication. Check it out yourself: go to `www.amazon.com`, and click the Sign In button. Then observe the browser address bar. You see something similar to the following, which is an OpenID authentication request:

```
https://www.amazon.com/ap/signin?_encoding=UTF8
    &openid.assoc_handle=usflex
    &openid.claimed_id=
            http://specs.openid.net/auth/2.0/identifier_select
    &openid.identity=
            http://specs.openid.net/auth/2.0/identifier_select
    &openid.mode=checkid_setup
    &openid.ns=http://specs.openid.net/auth/2.0
    &openid.ns.pape=
            http://specs.openid.net/extensions/pape/1.0
    &openid.pape.max_auth_age=0
    &openid.return_to=
            https://www.amazon.com/gp/yourstore/home
```

Understanding OpenID Connect

Unlike the OpenID extension for OAuth, OpenID Connect was built on top of OAuth. It simply introduces an identity layer on top of OAuth 2.0. This identity layer is abstracted into an ID token. An OAuth authorization server that supports OpenID Connect returns an ID token along with the access token.

■ **Note**   See the blog entry "OpenID Connect vs. OAuth 2.0" at
`http://blog.facilelogin.com/2013/11/oauth-20-vs-openid-connect.html`

Anatomy of the ID Token

The ID token is the primary add-on to OAuth 2.0 to support OpenID Connect. It's a JSON web token (JWT) that transports authenticated user information from the authorization server to the client application. Chapter 13 delves deeper into JWT. The structure of the ID token is defined by the OpenID Connect specification. The following shows a sample ID token:

```
{
  "iss":"https://auth.server.com",
  "sub":"prabath@apache.org",
  "aud":"67jjuyuy7JHk12",
  "nonce":"88797jgjg32332",
  "exp":1416283970,
  "iat":1416281970,
  "auth_time":1311280969,
  "acr":"urn:mace:incommon:iap:silver",
  "amr":"password",
  "azp":"67jjuyuy7JHk12"
}
```

Let's examine the definition of each attribute.

iss: The token issuer (authorization server)'s identifier in the format of an HTTPS URL with no query parameters or URL fragments.

sub: The local identifier of the authenticated user.

aud: The audience of the token. This can be an array of identifiers, but it must have the OAuth client ID in it; otherwise the client ID should be added to the azp parameter.

nonce: A new parameter introduced by the OpenID Connect specification to the initial authorization grant request. In addition to the parameters defined in OAuth 2.0, the client application can optionally include the nonce parameter. This parameter was introduced to mitigate replay attacks. The authorization server must reject any request if it finds two requests with the same nonce value. If a nonce is present in the authorization grant request, then the authorization server must include the same value in the ID token. The client application must validate the value of the nonce once it receives the ID token from the authorization server.

exp: The token-expiration time in seconds from 1970-01-01T0:0:0Z (UTC).

iat: The token-issued time in seconds from 1970-01-01T0:0:0Z (UTC).

auth_time: The time at which the end user authenticates with the authorization server. If the user is already authenticated, then the authorization server won't ask user to authenticate back. How a given authorization server authenticates the user, and how it manages the authenticated session, is outside the scope of OpenID Connect. A user can create an authenticated session with the authorization server in its first login attempt from a different application, other than the OpenID client application. In such cases, the authorization server must maintain the authenticated time. This is the value that must be included in the parameter auth_time.

acr: Stands for *authentication context reference*. The value of this parameter must be understood by both the authorization server and the client application. It gives an indication of the level of authentication.

amr: Stands for *authentication method references*. It indicates how the authorization server authenticates the user. It may consist of an array of values. Both the authorization server and the client application must understand the value of this parameter.

azp: Stands for *authorized party*. It's needed when there is one audience (aud) and its value is different from the OAuth client ID. The value of azp must be set to the OAuth client ID.

■ **Note**   The authorization server must sign the ID token, as defined in JSON Web Signature (JWS) specification. Optionally, it can also be encrypted. Token encryption should follow the rules defined in the JSON Web Encryption (JWE) specification. If the ID token is encrypted, it must be signed first and then encrypted. This is because signing the encrypted text is questionable in many legal entities. Chapter 13 talks about JWT, JWS, JWD, and JWE.

OPENID CONNECT WITH WSO2 IDENTITY SERVER

In this exercise, you see how to obtain an OpenID Connect ID token along with an OAuth 2.0 access token. You run WSO2 Identity Server as the OAuth authorization server.

■ **Note**   WSO2 Identity Server is a free, open source identity- and entitlement-management server, released under the Apache 2.0 license.

Follow these steps:

1. Download WSO2 Identity Server 5.0.0 from http://wso2.com/products/identity-server/, set up the JAVA_HOME environment variable, and start the server from the wso2server.sh/wso2server.bat file in WSO2_IS_HOME/bin. If the WSO2 Identity Server 5.0.0 isn't available from the main download page, you can find it at http://wso2.com/more-downloads/identity-server/.

2. By default, the WSO2 Identity Server starts on HTTPS port 9443.

3. Log in to the identity server running at https://localhost:9443 with its default username and password (admin/admin).

4. To get an OAuth client ID and a client secret for the client application, you need to register it as a service provider on the OAuth authorization server. Choose Main ➤ Service Providers ➤ Add. Enter a name, say, `oidc-app`, and click Register.

5. Choose Inbound Authentication Configuration ➤ OAuth and OpenID Connect Configuration ➤ Configure.

6. Uncheck all the grant types except Code. Make sure the OAuth version is set to 2.0.

7. Provide a value for the Callback Url text box—say, `https://localhost/callback`—and click Add.

8. Copy the values of OAuth Client Key and the OAuth Client Secret.

9. You use cURL here instead of a full-blown web application. First you need to get an authorization code. Copy the following URL, and paste it into a browser. Replace the values of `client_id` and `redirect_uri` appropriately. You're directed to a login page where you can authenticate with `admin/admin` and then approve the request by the client:

```
https://localhost:9443/oauth2/authorize?
        response_type=code&scope=openid&
        client_id=NJOLXcfdOW2OEvD6DUOlOpO1u_Ya&
        redirect_uri=https://localhost/callback
```

▦ **Note** In OpenID Connect, the authorization grant request must have openid as the scope.

---

10. Once approved, you're redirected back to `redirect_uri` with the authorization code, as shown here. Copy the value of the authorization code:

```
https://localhost/callback?code=577fc84a51c2aceac2a9e2f723f0f47f
```

11. Now you can exchange the authorization code for an ID token and an access token. Replace the value of `client_id`, `client_secret`, `code`, and `redirect_uri` appropriately. The value of `-u` is constructed as `client_id:client_secret`:

```
curl -v -X POST --basic
            -u NJOLXcfdOW2OEvD6DUOlOpO1u_Ya:EsSP5GfYliU96MQ6BMrUdJ7cZoEa
            -H "Content-Type:application/x-www-form-urlencoded;
                        charset=UTF-8" -k
            -d "client_id=NJOLXcfdOW2OEvD6DUOlOpO1u_Ya&
                grant_type=authorization_code&
                code=577fc84a51c2aceac2a9e2f723f0f47f&
                redirect_uri=https://localhost/callback"
                https://localhost:9443/oauth2/token
```

This results in the following JSON response:

```
{
    "scope":"openid",
    "token_type":"bearer",
```

```
"expires_in":3299,
"refresh_token":"1caf88a1351d2d74093f6b84b8751bb",
"id_token":"eyJhbGciOiJub25lIiwidHlwIjoiSldUInO=\r\n.eyJleHAiO
            jE2NjI3MTYyMzAsImF6cCI6Ik5KMExYY2ZkT1cyMEV2RD
            ZEVTBsMHAwMXVfWWEiLCJz\r\ndWIiOiJhZG1pbkBjYX
            Jib24uc3VwZXIiLCJhdWQiOiJOSjBMWGNmZE9XMjBFdk
            Q2RFUwbDBwMDF1\r\nX1lhIiwiaXNzIjoiaHROcHM6XC9c
            L2xvY2FsaG9zdDo5NDQzXC9vYXV0aDJlbmRwb2ludHNc
            L3Rv\r\na2VuIiwiaWF0IjoxNjU5MTE2MjMwfQ==\r\n.",
"access_token":"6cc611211a941cc95c0c5caf1385295"
}
```

12. The value of id_token is base64-encoded. Once it's base64-decoded, it looks like following:

```
{
    "alg":"none",
    "typ":"JWT"
}.
{
    "exp":1667236118,
    "azp":"NJOLXcfdOW2OEvD6DUOlOpO1u_Ya",
    "sub":"admin@carbon.super",
    "aud":"NJOLXcfdOW2OEvD6DUOlOpO1u_Ya",
    "iss":"https://localhost:9443/oauth2endpoints/token",
    "iat":1663636118
}
```

■ **Note**   At the time of this writing, WSO2 Identity Server doesn't support JWS and JWE. A set of open source libraries that support JWS and JWE is available at `http://openid.net/developers/libraries/`.

OpenID Connect Request

The ID token is the heart of OpenID Connect, but that isn't the only place where it deviates from OAuth 2.0. OpenID Connect introduced some optional parameters to the OAuth 2.0 authorization grant request. The previous exercise didn't use any of those parameters. Let's examine a sample authorization grant request with all the optional parameters:

```
https://localhost:9443/oauth2/authorize?response_type=code
                            scope=openid&
                            client_id=NJOLXcfdOW2OEvD6DUOlOpO1u_Ya&
                            redirect_uri=https://localhost/callback&
                            response_mode=.....&
                            nonce=.....&
                            display=....&
                            prompt=....&
```

```
max_age=.....&
ui_locales=.....&
id_token_hint=.....&
login_hint=.....&
acr_value=.....
```

Let's review the definition of each attribute.

response_mode: Determines how the authorization server sends back the parameters in the response. This is different from the response_type parameter, defined in the OAuth 2.0 core specification. With the response_type parameter in the request, the client indicates whether it expects a code or a token. In the case of an Authorization Code grant type, the value of response_type is set to code, whereas with an Implicit grant type, the value of response_type is set to token.

The response_mode parameter addresses a different concern. If the value of response_mode is set to query, the response parameters are sent back to the client as query parameters appended to the redirect_uri; and if the value is set to fragment, then the response parameters are appended to the redirect_uri as a URI fragment.

nonce: Mitigates replay attacks. The authorization server must reject any request if it finds two requests with the same nonce value. If a nonce is present in the authorization grant request, then the authorization server must include the same value in the ID token. The client application must validate the value of the nonce once it receives the ID token from the authorization server.

display: Indicates how the client application expects the authorization server to display the login page and the user consent page. Possible values are page, popup, touch, and wap.

prompt: Indicates whether to display the login or the user consent page at the authorization server. If the value is none, then neither the login page nor the user consent page should be presented to the user. In other words, it expects the user to have an authenticated session at the authorization server and a preconfigured user consent. If the value is login, the authorization server must reauthenticate the user. If the value is consent, the authorization server must display the user consent page to the end user. The select_account option can be used if the user has multiple accounts on the authorization server. The authorization server must then give the user an option to select from which account he or she requires attributes.

max_age: In the ID token is a parameter that indicates the time of user authentication. The max_age parameter asks the authorization server to compare that value with max_age. If it's less than (current time - max_age), the authorization server must reauthenticate the user. When the client includes the max_age parameter in the request, the authorization server must include the auth_time parameter in the ID token.

ui_locales: Expresses the end user's preferred language for the user interface.

id_token_hint: An ID token itself. This could be an ID token previously obtained by the client application. If the token is encrypted, it has to be decrypted first and then encrypted back by the public key of the authorization server and then placed into the authentication request. If the value of the parameter prompt is set to none, then the id_token_hint should be present in the request, but it isn't a requirement.

login_hint: This is an indication of the login identifier that the end user may use at the authorization server. For example, if the client application already knows the e-mail address or phone number of the end user, this could be set as the value of the login_hint. This helps provide a better user experience.

acr_values: Stands for *authentication context reference values*. It includes a space-separated set of values that indicates the level of authentication required at the authorization server. The authorization server may or may not respect these values.

■ **Note**   All OpenID Connect authentication requests must have a scope parameter with the value openid.

Requesting User Attributes

OpenID Connect defines two ways to request user attributes. The client application can either use the initial OpenID Connect authentication request to request attributes or else later talk to a UserInfo endpoint hosted by the authorization server. If it uses the initial authentication request, then the client application must include the requested claims in the claims parameter as a JSON message. The following authorization grant request asks to include the user's e-mail address and the given name in the ID token:

```
https://localhost:9443/oauth2/authorize?
        response_type=code&
        scope=openid&
        client_id=NJOLXcfdOW20EvD6DUolopO1u_Ya&
        redirect_uri=https://localhost/callback&
        claims={ "id_token":
                     {
                         "email": {"essential": true},
                         "given_name": {"essential": true},
                     }
             }
```

■ **Note**   The core OpenID Connect specification defines 20 standard user claims. These identifiers should be understood by all of the authorization servers and client applications that support OpenID Connect. The complete set of OpenID Connect standard claims is defined in section 5.1 of the OpenID Connect core specification, available at http://openid.net/specs/openid-connect-core-1_0.html.

The other approach to request user attributes is via the UserInfo endpoint. The UserInfo endpoint is an OAuth 2.0-protected resource on the authorization server. Any request to this endpoint must carry a valid OAuth 2.0 token. Once again, there are two ways to get user attributes from the UserInfo endpoint. The first approach is to use the OAuth access token. With this approach, the client must specify the corresponding attribute scope in the authorization grant request. The OpenID Connect specification defines four scope values to request attributes: profile, email, address, and phone. If the scope value is set to profile, that implies that the client requests access to a set of attributes, which includes name, family_name, given_name, middle_name, nickname, preferred_username, profile, picture, website, gender, birthdate, zoneinfo, locale, and updated_at.

The following authorization grant request asks permission to access a user's e-mail address and phone number:

```
https://localhost:9443/oauth2/authorize?
        response_type=code&
        scope=openid phone email&
        client_id=NJOLXcfdOW2OEvD6DUOlOp01u_Ya&
        redirect_uri=https://localhost/callback
```

This results in an authorization code response. Once the client application has exchanged the authorization code for an access token, by talking to the token endpoint of the authorization server, it can use the access token it received to talk to the UserInfo endpoint and get the user attributes corresponding to the access token:

```
GET /userinfo HTTP/1.1
Host: auth.server.com
Authorization: Bearer SJHkhew87Ohooi90
```

The above request to the UserInfo endpoint results in the following JSON message, which includes the user's e-mail address and phone number:

```
HTTP/1.1 200 OK
Content-Type: application/json

  {
   "phone": "94712841302",
   "email": "joe@authserver.com",
  }
```

The other way to retrieve user attributes from the UserInfo endpoint is through the claims parameter. The following example shows how to retrieve the e-mail address of the user by talking to the OAuth-protected UserInfo endpoint:

```
POST /userinfo HTTP/1.1
Host: auth.server.com
Authorization: Bearer SJHkhew87Ohooi90

claims={ "userinfo":
                   {
                       "email": {"essential": true}
                   }
         }
```

Grant Types for OpenID Connect

All the examples in this chapter so far have used an Authorization Code grant type to request an ID token—but it isn't a requirement. It can be Authorization Code grant type, Implicit grant type, or hybrid flow. The type of authorization grant flow is decided by the value of response_type. For an Authorization Code grant type, the value of response_type must be set to code, and both the ID token and access token are returned from the token endpoint of the authorization server.

For implicit flow under the context of OpenID Connect, the value of response_type can be either id_token or id_token token (separated by a space). If it's just id_token, then the authorization endpoint returns an ID token; if it includes both, then both the ID token and the access token are included in the response.

The hybrid flow can use different combinations. If the value of response_type is set to code id_token (separated by a space), then the response from the authorization endpoint includes the authorization code as well as the id_token. If it's code token (separated by a space), then it returns the authorization code along with an access token (for the UserInfo endpoint). If response_type includes all three (code token id_token), then the response includes an ID token, an access token, and the authorization code.

Table 12-1 summarizes this discussion.

Table 12-1. *Grant Types for OpenID Connect*

Type of Flow	response_type	Tokens Returned
Authorization Code	code	Authorization code
Implicit	id_token	ID token
Implicit	id_token token	ID token and access token
Hybrid	code id_token	ID token and authorization code
Hybrid	code id_token token	ID token, authorization code, and access token
Hybrid	code token	Access token and authorization code

■ **Note** When id_token is being used as the response_type in an authorization grant flow, the client application never has access to an access token. In such a scenario, the client application can use the scope parameter to request attributes, and those are added to the ID token.

Requesting Custom User Attributes

As discussed, OpenID Connect defines 20 standard claims. These claims can be requested via the scope parameter or through the claims parameter. The only way to request custom-defined claims is through the claims parameter. The following is a sample authorization grant request that asks for custom-defined claims:

```
https://localhost:9443/oauth2/authorize?
        response_type=code&
        scope=openid&
        client_id=NJoLXcfdOW2OEvD6DUOlOpO1u_Ya&
        redirect_uri=https://localhost/callback&
        claims={ "id_token":
                        {
                            "http://apress.com/claims/email": {"essential": true},
                            "http://apress.com/claims/phone": {"essential": true},
                        }
        }
```

OPENID CONNECT WITH GOOGLE

In this exercise, you register an OpenID Connect client application with Google and get user information via an ID token:

1. Go to `https://console.developers.google.com`, and click Create Project. Provide an appropriate name, and complete the registration.

2. Go to `https://console.developers.google.com`. You see the project you just created listed. Click the project name.

3. Click APIs And Auth.

4. Click the Off button on the Calendar API to switch it to On.

5. Click APIs And Auth, and click Credentials.

6. Choose OAuth ➤ Create New Client ID, and select Web Application as the Application Type. Provide a valid redirect URI, say, `https://mycallback.com` , and click Create Client ID.

7. Copy the value of the Client ID and Client Secret.

8. Copy the following URL; replacing the values of `client_id` and `redirect_uri` appropriately, and paste it into the browser:

```
https://accounts.google.com/o/oauth2/auth?
        scope=openid email&
        state=mystate&
        redirect_uri=https://mycallback.com&
        response_type=code&
        client_id=825249835659te8qgl701kgonnomnp4sqv7erhu1211s.
                apps.googleusercontent.com&
        approval_prompt=force
```

This returns the access token to the `redirect_uri` with the provided state value:

```
https://mycallback.com/?
        state=mystate&
        code=4/dlfuPEHWG8QU9MaJN8vCSEpTzuYo.YlcCVmKswV4SXE-sT2ZLcbQrzK7PiQI
```

9. Once you have the authorization code, you need to exchange it for an access token. Run the following cURL command with the appropriate values for `code`, `redirect_uri`, `client_id`, and `client_secret`. The value of `redirect_uri` should match the value used in the previous step:

```
curl -v -X POST
    -d "grant_type=authorization_code&
        code=4/dlfuPEHWG8QU9MaJN8vCSEpTzuYo.YlcCVmKswV4SXE-sT2ZLcbQrzK7PiQI&
        client_id=825249835659-te8qgl701kgonnomnp4sqv7erhu1211s.
                apps.googleusercontent.com&
        client_secret=jNjXEOD922mmcFopsjJJXNJc&
        redirect_uri=https://mycallback.com"
        https://accounts.google.com/o/oauth2/token
```

This returns the access token in the following JSON response:

```
{
  "access_token":"ya29.1.AADtN_WY1SHPAYomlwrc",
  "token_type":"Bearer",
  "expires_in":3600,
  "id_token":""
}
```

The value of the id_token parameter isn't displayed in the sample code due to its length. It's basically a base64-encoded JWT in three parts. Each part is separated by a dot (.). The first part up to the first dot is the JWT header. The second part is the JWT body. The third part is the signature. Chapter 13 talks more about JWT signatures.

The following is the base64-decoded value of the JWT header from the ID token:

```
{
  "alg":"RS256",
  "kid":"78b4cf23656dc395364f1b6c02907691f2cdffe1"
}
```

The following is the base64-decoded value of the JWT body from the ID token:

```
{
  "iss":"accounts.google.com",
  "id":"110502251158920147732",
  "sub":"110502251158920147732",
  "azp":"825249835659-te8qgl701kgonnomnp4sqv7erhu1211s.apps.googleusercontent.com",
  "email":"prabath@wso2.com",
  "at_hash":"UYIWTcOOQ8mUv1rnOXfdZw",
  "email_verified":true,
  "aud":"825249835659-te8qgl701kgonnomnp4sqv7erhu1211s.apps.googleusercontent.com",
  "hd":"wso2.com",
  "token_hash":"UYIWTcOOQ8mUv1rnOXfdZw",
  "verified_email":true,
  "cid":"825249835659-te8qgl701kgonnomnp4sqv7erhu1211s.apps.googleusercontent.com",
  "iat":1401903279,
  "exp":1401907179
}
```

■ **Note** The value of the at_hash parameter in the ID token is the hash value of the OAuth access token issued along with the ID token. The hash value is calculated using the hashing algorithm (alg) defined in the JWT header.

10. To obtain user information, you need to talk to the Google UserInfo endpoint with the access token obtained in the previous step:

```
curl https://www.googleapis.com/oauth2/v1/userinfo?
          access_token=ya29.1.AADtN_WY1SHPAYomlwrc
```

This returns the following JSON response:

```
{
  "id":"104063262378861625904",
  "email":"siriwardena.prabath@gmail.com",
  "verified_email":true,
  "name":"Prabath Siriwardena",
  "given_name":"Prabath",
  "family_name":"Siriwardena",
  "link":"https://plus.google.com/104063262378861625904",
  "picture":"https://lh3.googleusercontent.com/-nA7Ndz8oYF8/AAAAAAAAAAI/
             AAAAAAAABCO/2vY1M8egglA/photo.jpg",
  "gender":"male",
  "locale":"en"
}
```

OpenID Connect Discovery

The beginning of the chapter discussed how OpenID relying parties discover OpenID providers through the user-provided OpenID (which is a URL). OpenID Connect discovery addresses the same concern, but in a different way (see Figure 12-2). In order to authenticate users via OpenID Connect, the OpenID Connect relying party first needs to figure out what authorization server is behind the end user. OpenID Connect utilizes the WebFinger protocol for this discovery.

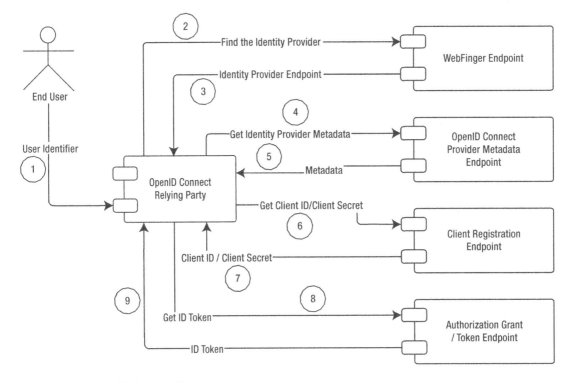

Figure 12-2. *OpenID Connect discovery*

> ■ **Note** The OpenID Connect discovery specification is available at
> `http://openid.net/specs/openid-connect-discovery-1_0.html`. If a given OpenID Connect relying party already knows who the authorization server is, it can simply ignore the discovery phase.

Let's assume a user called Peter visits an OpenID Connect relying party and wants to log in. To authenticate Peter, the OpenID Connect relying party should know the authorization server corresponding to Peter. To discover this, Peter has to provide to the relying party some unique identifier that relates to him. Using this identifier, the relying party should be able to find the WebFinger endpoint corresponding to Peter.

Let's say that the identifier Peter provides is his e-mail address, `peter@apress.com`. The relying party should be able find enough detail about the WebFinger endpoint using Peter's e-mail address. In fact, the relying party should be able derive the WebFinger endpoint from the e-mail address. The relying party can then send a query to the WebFinger endpoint to find out which authorization server (or the identity provider) corresponds to Peter. This query is made according to the WebFinger specification. The following shows a sample WebFinger request for `peter@apress.com`:

> ■ **Note** The WebFinger specification is available at `http://tools.ietf.org/html/rfc7033`.

```
GET /.well-known/webfinger?resource=acct:peter@apress.com&
                        rel=http://openid.net/specs/connect/1.0/issuer
HTTP/1.1
Host: apress.com
```

The WebFinger request has two key parameters: `resource` and `rel`. The `resource` parameter should uniquely identify the end user, whereas the value of `rel` is fixed for OpenID Connect and must be equal to `http://openid.net/specs/connect/1.0/issuer`. The `rel` (relation-type) parameter acts as a filter to determine the OpenID Connect issuer corresponding to the given resource.

A WebFinger endpoint can accept many other discovery requests for different services. If it finds a matching entry, the following response is returned to the OpenID Connect relying party. The value of the OpenID identity provider or the authorization server endpoint is included in the response:

```
HTTP/1.1 200 OK
Access-Control-Allow-Origin: *
Content-Type: application/jrd+json
{
    "subject":"acct:peter@apress.com",
    "links":[
            {
                "rel":"http://openid.net/specs/connect/1.0/issuer",
                "href":"https://auth.apress.com"
            }
        ]
}
```

The `acct` URI scheme is defined in `http://tools.ietf.org/html/draft-ietf-appsawg-acct-uri-07`. When the `acct` URI scheme is being used, everything after the @ sign is treated as the hostname. The WebFinger hostname is derived from an e-mail address as per the `acct` URI scheme, which is the part after the @ sign.

If a URL is being used as the resource identifier, the host name (and port number) of the URL is treated as the WebFinger hostname. If the resource identifier is `https://auth.server.com:9443/prabath`, then the WebFinger hostname is `auth.server.com:9443`.

Once the endpoint of the identity provider is discovered, that concludes the role of WebFinger. Yet you don't have enough data to initiate an OpenID Connect authentication request with the corresponding identity provider. More information about the identity provider is found by talking to its metadata endpoint, which must be a well-known endpoint.

The WebFinger specification has the well-known endpoint `/.well-known/webfinger`. The OpenID Connect Discovery specification has the well-known endpoint for OpenID provider configuration metadata, `/.well-known/openid-configuration`.

OpenID Connect Identity Provider Metadata

An OpenID Connect identity provider, which supports metadata discovery, should host its configuration at the endpoint `/.well-known/openid-configuration`. In most cases, this is a non-secured endpoint, which can be accessed by anyone. An OpenID Connect relying party can send an HTTP GET to the metadata endpoint to retrieve the OpenID provider configuration details as follows:

```
GET /.well-known/openid-configuration HTTP/1.1
Host: auth.server.com
```

This results in the following JSON response, which includes everything an OpenID Connect relying party needs to know to talk to the OpenID provider or the OAuth authorization server:

```
HTTP/1.1 200 OK
  Content-Type: application/json

  {
   "issuer":"https://auth.server.com",
   "authorization_endpoint":"https://auth.server.com/connect/authorize",
```

```
    "token_endpoint":"https://auth.server.com/connect/token",
    "token_endpoint_auth_methods_supported":["client_secret_basic", "private_key_jwt"],
    "token_endpoint_auth_signing_alg_values_supported":["RS256", "ES256"],
    "userinfo_endpoint":"https://auth.sever.com/connect/userinfo",
    "check_session_iframe":"https://auth.server.com/connect/check_session",
    "end_session_endpoint":"https://auth.server.com/connect/end_session",
    "jwks_uri":"https://auth.server.com/jwks.json",
    "registration_endpoint":"https://auth.server.com/connect/register",
    "scopes_supported":["openid", "profile", "email", "address", "phone", "offline_access"],
    "response_types_supported":["code", "code id_token", "id_token", "token id_token"],
    "acr_values_supported":["urn:mace:incommon:iap:silver", urn:mace:incommon:iap:bronze"],
    "subject_types_supported":["public", "pairwise"],
    "userinfo_signing_alg_values_supported":["RS256", "ES256", "HS256"],
    "userinfo_encryption_alg_values_supported":["RSA1_5", "A128KW"],
    "userinfo_encryption_enc_values_supported":["A128CBC-HS256", "A128GCM"],
    "id_token_signing_alg_values_supported":["RS256", "ES256", "HS256"],
    "id_token_encryption_alg_values_supported":["RSA1_5", "A128KW"],
    "id_token_encryption_enc_values_supported":["A128CBC-HS256", "A128GCM"],
    "request_object_signing_alg_values_supported":["none", "RS256", "ES256"],
    "display_values_supported":["page", "popup"],
    "claim_types_supported":["normal", "distributed"],
    "claims_supported":["sub", "iss", "auth_time", "acr",
                        "name", "given_name", "family_name", "nickname",
                        "profile", "picture", "website","email", "email_verified",
                        "locale", "zoneinfo",
                        "http://example.info/claims/groups"],
    "claims_parameter_supported":true,
    "service_documentation":"http://auth.server.com/connect/service_documentation.html",
    "ui_locales_supported":["en-US", "fr-CA"]
    }
```

■ **Note** If the endpoint of the discovered identity provider is `https://auth.server.com`, then the OpenID provider metadata should be available at `https://auth.server.com/.well-known/openid-configuration`. If the endpoint is `https://auth.server.com/openid`, then the metadata endpoint is `https://auth.server.com/openid/.well-known/openid-configuration`.

OpenID Connect Dynamic Client Registration

Once the OpenID provider endpoint is discovered via WebFinger (and all the metadata related to it through OpenID Connect discovery), the OpenID Connect relying party still needs to have a client ID and a client secret (not under the Implicit grant type) registered at the OpenID provider to initiate the authorization grant request or the OpenID Connect authentication request. The OpenID Connect Dynamic Client Registration specification facilitates a mechanism to register dynamically OpenID Connect relying parties at the OpenID provider.

■ **Note** The OpenID Connect Dynamic Client Registration specification is available at `http://openid.net/specs/openid-connect-registration-1_0.html`.

The response from the OpenID provider metadata endpoint includes the endpoint for client registration under the parameter registration_endpoint. To support dynamic client registrations, this endpoint should accept open registration requests, with no authentication requirements.

To fight against denial of service (DoS) attacks, the endpoint can be protected with rate limits, accepting only 10 registration requests from a given IP address within a 60-second timeframe. To initiate client registration, the OpenID relying party sends an HTTP POST message to the registration endpoint with its own metadata.

The following is a sample client registration request:

```
POST /connect/register HTTP/1.1
Content-Type: application/json
Accept: application/json
Host: auth.server.com

{
    "application_type":"web",
    "redirect_uris":["https://app.client.org/callback","https://app.client.org/callback2"],
    "client_name":"Foo",
    "logo_uri":"https://app.client.org/logo.png",
    "subject_type":"pairwise",
    "sector_identifier_uri":"https://other.client.org/file_of_redirect_uris.json",
    "token_endpoint_auth_method":"client_secret_basic",
    "jwks_uri":"https://app.client.org/public_keys.jwks",
    "userinfo_encrypted_response_alg":"RSA1_5",
    "userinfo_encrypted_response_enc":"A128CBC-HS256",
    "contacts":["prabath@wso2.com", "prabath@apache.org"],
    "request_uris":["https://app.client.org/rf.txt#qpXaRLh_n93TTR9F252ValdatUQvQiJi5BDub2BeznA"]
 }
```

In response, the OpenID Connect provider or the authorization server sends back the following response. This response includes client_id and client_secret:

```
HTTP/1.1 201 Created
Content-Type: application/json
Cache-Control: no-store
Pragma: no-cache

  {
    "client_id":"Gjjhj678jhkh89789ew",
    "client_secret":"IUi989jkjo_989klkjuk89080kjkuoikjkUIl",
    "client_secret_expires_at":2590858900,
    "registration_access_token":"this.is.an.access.token.value.ffx83",
    "registration_client_uri":"https://auth.server.com/connect/register?client_id=Gjjhj678jhkh89789ew ",
    "token_endpoint_auth_method":"client_secret_basic",
    "application_type":"web",
    "redirect_uris":["https://app.client.org/callback", "https://app.client.org/callback2"],
    "client_name":"Foo",
    "logo_uri":"https://client.example.org/logo.png",
    "subject_type":"pairwise",
    "sector_identifier_uri":"https://other.client.org/file_of_redirect_uris.json",
    "jwks_uri":"https://app.client.org/public_keys.jwks",
    "userinfo_encrypted_response_alg":"RSA1_5",
```

```
    "userinfo_encrypted_response_enc":"A128CBC-HS256",
    "contacts":["prabath@wso2.com", "prabath@apache.org"],
    "request_uris":["https://app.client.org/rf.txt#qpXaRLh_n93TTR9F252ValdatUQvQiJi5BDub2BeznA"]
}
```

Once the OpenID Connect relying party obtains a client ID and a client secret, it concludes the OpenID Connect discovery phase. The relying party can now initiate the OpenID Connect authentication request.

■ **Note**   Section 2.0 of the OpenID Connect Dynamic Client Registration specification lists all the attributes that can be included in an OpenID Connect client registration request:

`http://openid.net/specs/openid-connect-registration-1_0.html`.

OpenID Connect for Securing APIs

So far, you have seen a detailed discussion about OpenID Connect. But in reality, how will it help you in securing APIs? OpenID Connect can be used to authenticate into web applications, mobile applications, and much more. Nonetheless, why would you need OpenID Connect to secure a headless API? At the end of the day, all the APIs are secured with OAuth 2.0, and you need to present an access token to talk to the API. The API (or the policy-enforcement component) validates the access token by talking to the authorization server. Why would you need to pass an ID token to an API?

OAuth is about delegated authorization, whereas OpenID Connect is about authentication. An ID token is an assertion about your identity: that is, a proof of your identity. It can be used to authenticate into an API. As of this writing, no HTTP binding is defined for JWT.

The following example suggests passing the JWT assertion (or the ID token) to a protected API as an access token in the HTTP Authorization header. The ID token, or the signed JWT, is base64-encoded in three parts. Each part is separated by a dot (.). The first part up to the first dot is the JWT header. The second part is the JWT body. The third part is the signature. Once the JWT is obtained by the client application, it can place it in the HTTP Authorization header in the manner shown here:

```
POST /employee HTTP/1.1
Content-Type: application/json
Accept: application/json
Host: resource.server.com
Authorization: Bearer eyJhbGciOiIjiuo98kljlk2KJl.IUojlkoiaos298jkkdksdosiduIUiopo.oioYJ21sajds
{
    "empl_no":"109082",
    "emp_name":"Peter John",
    "emp_address":"Mountain View, CA, USA"
}
```

To validate the JWT, the API (or the policy-enforcement component) has to extract the JWT assertion from the HTTP Authorization header, base64-decode it, and validate the signature to see whether it's signed by a trusted issuer. In addition, the claims in the JWT can be used for authentication and authorization.

▪ **Note**   When an OpenID Connect identity provider issues an ID token, it adds the aud parameter to the token to indicate the audience of the token. This can be an array of identifiers.

When using ID tokens for authenticating APIs, a URI known to the API should also be added to the aud parameter. Currently this can't be done in the OpenID Connect authentication request, so it must be set out of band at the OpenID Connect identity provider.

Summary

OpenID Connect, which was developed under the OpenID Foundation, adds the identity layer to OAuth 2.0. This chapter discussed the evolution of OpenID Connect from OpenID and its applications as an OAuth 2.0 profile. It also discussed how OpenID Connect utilizes the WebFinger protocol in its discovery process along with OpenID Connect dynamic client registration and identity provider metadata configuration.

The next chapter takes a deeper look at JSON Web Signature (JWS) and JSON Web Encryption (JWE).

CHAPTER 13

■ ■ ■

JWT, JWS, and JWE

JavaScript Object Notation (JSON) provides a way of exchanging data in a language-neutral, text-based, and lightweight manner. It was originally derived from the ECMAScript programming language. JSON data interchange format is defined in RFC 7159: http://tools.ietf.org/html/rfc7159. JSON and XML are the most commonly used data exchange formats for APIs. Looking at the trend over the last five years, it's more than obvious that JSON is replacing XML. Most of the APIs out there have support for JSON, and some support both JSON and XML. It's now very difficult even to find an XML-only API.

JSON Web Token

JSON Web Token (JWT) defines a container to transport data between interested parties in JSON. The ongoing work of the JWT specification group under IETF is available at https://datatracker.ietf.org/doc/draft-ietf-oauth-json-web-token/. The OpenID Connect specification, discussed in Chapter 12, uses a JWT to represent the ID token. Let's examine the OpenID Connect ID token returned from the Google API:

eyJhbGciOiJSUzI1NiIsImtpZCI6Ijc4YjRjZjIzNjU2ZGMzOTUzNjRmMWI2YzAyOTA3
NjkxZjJjZGZmZTEifQ.eyJpc3MiOiJhY2NvdW50cy5nb29nbGUuY29tIiwic3ViIjoiMT
EwNTAyMjUxMTU4OTIwMTQ3NzMyIiwiYXpwIjoiODI1MjQ5ODM1NjU5LXRlOHF
nbDcwMWtnb25ub21ucDRzcXY3ZXJodTEyMTFzLmFwcHMuZ29vZ2xldXNlcmNvb
nRlbnQuY29tIiwiZW1haWwiOiJwcmFiYXRoQHdzbzIuY29tIiwiYXRfaGFzaCI6InpmO
DZ2TnVsc0xCOGdGYXFSd2R6R6WWciLCJlbWFpbF92ZXJpZmllZCI6dHJ1ZSwiYXVkI
joiODI1MjQ5ODM1NjU5LXRlOHFnbDcwMWtnb25ub21ucDRzcXY3ZXJodTEyMTFz
LmFwcHMuZ29vZ2xldXNlcmNvbnRlbnQuY29tIiwiaGQiOiJ3c28yLmNvbSIsImlhdCI6
MTQwMTkwODI3MswiZXhwIjoxNDAxOTEyMTcxfQ.TVKv-pdyvk2gW8sGsCbsnkq
srSOT-H0OxnY6ETkIfgIxfotvFn5IwKm3xyBMpyOFFeORb5Ht8AEJV6PdWyxz8rMgX
2HROWqSo_RfEfUpBb4iOsq4W28KftW5HOIA44VmNZ6zU4YTqPSt4TPhyFC9fP2D
_Hg7JQozpQRUfbWTJI

    This entire JWT is base64url-encoded. It's divided into three sections. Each section is separated by a period (.).

    Let's identify each separate section. The first part is called the *JavaScript Object Signing and Encryption (JOSE)* header. The *JOSE* header describes the cryptographic operations applied on the JWT claim set.

eyJhbGciOiJSUzI1NiIsImtpZCI6Ijc4YjRjZjIzNjU2ZGMzOTUzNjRmMWI2YzAyOTA3
NjkxZjJjZGZmZTEifQ

    The following shows the base64url-decoded JOSE header:

```
{"alg":"RS256","kid":"78b4cf23656dc395364f1b6c02907691f2cdffe1"}
```

The second part is known as either the *JWT payload* or the *JWT claim set*. It carries the real business data. In the following example, it includes information about the authenticated user:

eyJpc3MiOiJhY2NvdW50cy5nb29nbGUuY29tIiwic3ViIjoiMTEwNTAyMjUxMTU4OT
IwMTQ3NzMyIiwiYXpwIjoiODI1MjQ5ODM1NjU5LXRlOHFnbDcwMWtnb25ub21uc
DRzcXY3ZXJodTEyMTFzLmFwcHMuZ29vZ2xldXNlcmNvbnRlbnQuY29tIiwiZW1haa
WwiOiJwcmFiYXRoQHdzbzIuY29tIiwiYXRfaGFzaCI6InpmODZ2TnVsc0xCOGdGYX
FSd2R6WWciLCJlbWFpbF92ZXJpZmllZCI6dHJ1ZSwiYXVkIjoiODI1MjQ5ODM1NjU
5LXRlOHFnbDcwMWtnb25ub21ucDRzcXY3ZXJodTEyMTFzLmFwcHMuZ29vZ2xld
XNlcmNvbnRlbnQuY29tIiwiaGQiOiJ3c28yLmNvbSIsImlhdCI6MTQwMTkwODI3MS
wiZXhwIjoxNDAxOTEyMTcxfQ

The following shows the base64url-decoded JWT claim set

```
{
    "iss":"accounts.google.com",
    "sub":"110502251158920147732",
    "azp":"825249835659-te8qgl701kgonnomnp4sqv7erhu1211s.apps.googleusercontent.com",
    "email":"prabath@wso2.com",
    "at_hash":"zf86vNulsLB8gFaqRwdzYg",
    "email_verified":true,
    "aud":"825249835659-te8qgl701kgonnomnp4sqv7erhu1211s.apps.googleusercontent.com",
    "hd":"wso2.com",
    "iat":1401908271,
    "exp":1401912171
}
```

■ **Note** Whitespaces can be explicitly retained while building the JWT claim set—no canonicalization is required before base64url-encoding. *Canonicalization* is the process of converting different forms of a message into a single standard form. This is used mostly before signing XML messages.

In XML, the same message can be represented in different forms but carries the same meaning. For example, <vehicles><car></car></vehicles> and <vehicles><car/></vehicles> are equivalent in meaning, but have two different canonical forms. Before signing an XML message, you should follow a canonicalization algorithm to build a standard form.

The JWT specification defines three classes of claims: registered claims, public claims, and private claims. *Registered claims* are registered in the Internet Assigned Numbers Authority (IANA) JSON Web Token Claims registry, as follows:

- iss: Issuer of the JWT.
- sub (subject): The issued token is about this entity.
- aud (audience): The intended recipient list of the token.
- exp: The token will be expired after the specified time.
- nbf (not before): The token isn't valid before the specified time.

- iat (issued at): The time at which the token was issued.

- jti (JWT ID): A unique token identifier.

Even though these claims are treated as registered claims, the JWT specification doesn't mandate their usage. It's totally up to the corresponding application to decide which are mandatory and which aren't. For example, in OpenID Connect, iss is a mandatory claim.

Public claims are defined by the applications that use JWT. In these cases, to avoid any collisions, names should either be registered in the IANA JSON Web Token Claims registry or defined in a collision-resistant manner with a proper namespace. For example, the OpenID Connect specification defines its own set of claims to be included in an ID token, and those claims are registered in the IANA JSON Web Token Claims registry.

Private claims should indeed be private and shared between a given identity provider and a selected set of client applications. These claims should be used with caution, because there is a chance for collision.

The third part of the JWT is the signature, which is also base64url-encoded. The cryptographic parameters related to the signature are defined in the JOSE header. In this scenario, Google uses RSASSA-PKCS1-V1_5 with the SHA-256 hashing algorithm, which is denoted by RS256.

■ **Note** Plaintext JWT doesn't have a signature. It has only two parts. The value of the alg parameter in the JOSE header must be set to none.

The following shows the signature element of the JWT returned back from Google:

```
TVKv-pdyvk2gW8sGsCbsnkqsrSOTHOOxnY6ETkIfgIxfotvFn5IwKm3xyBMpyO
FFeORb5Ht8AEJV6PdWyxz8rMgX2HROWqSo_RfEfUpBb4iOsq4W28KftW5
HOIA44VmNZ6zU4YTqPSt4TPhyFC-9fP2D_Hg7JQozpQRUfbWTJI
```

■ **Note** RSASSA-PKCS1-V1_5 is defined in RFC 3447: www.ietf.org/rfc/rfc3447.txt. It uses the signer's RSA private key to sign the message in the way defined by PKCS#1.

GENERATING A PLAINTEXT JWT

The following Java code generates a plaintext JWT. You need to add references to nimbus-jose-jwt-2.26.jar, json-smart-1.1.1.jar, jcip-annotations-1.0.jar, and bcprov-jdk15on-1.50.jar. You can download all of these jars from https://svn.wso2.org/repos/wso2/people/prabath/api-security/jose/lib:

```java
import java.text.ParseException;
import java.util.ArrayList;
import java.util.Date;
import java.util.List;
import java.util.UUID;

import com.nimbusds.jose.*;
import com.nimbusds.jwt.*;
```

```java
public static String buildPlainJWT() {

        // create a claim set.
        JWTClaimsSet jwtClaims = new JWTClaimsSet();

        // set the value of the issuer.
        jwtClaims.setIssuer("https://apress.com");

        // set the subject value - JWT belongs to this subject.
        jwtClaims.setSubject("john");

        // set values for audience restriction.
        List<String> aud = new ArrayList<String>();
        aud.add("https://app1.foo.com");
        aud.add("https://app2.foo.com");
        jwtClaims.setAudience(aud);

        // expiration time set to 10 minutes.
        jwtClaims.setExpirationTime(new Date(new Date().getTime() + 1000 * 60 * 10));

        Date currentTime = new Date();

        // set the valid from time to current time.
        jwtClaims.setNotBeforeTime(currentTime);

        // set issued time to current time.
        jwtClaims.setIssueTime(currentTime);

        // set a generated UUID as the JWT identifier.
        jwtClaims.setJWTID(UUID.randomUUID().toString());

        // create plaintext JWT with the JWT claims.
        PlainJWT plainJwt = new PlainJWT(jwtClaims);

        // serialize into string.
        String jwtInText = plainJwt.serialize();

        // print the value of the JWT.
        System.out.println(jwtInText);

        return jwtInText;
}
```

This code produces the following output, which is the JWT:

eyJhbGciOiJub25lIn0.eyJleHAiOjEOMDIwMzcxNDEsInN1YiI6ImpvaG4iLCJuYm
YiOjEOMDIwMzY1NDEsImF1ZCI6WyJodHRwczpcL1wvYXBwMS5mb28uY29tIi
wiaHROcHM6XC9cL2FwcDIuZm9vLmNvbSJdLCJpc3MiOiJodHRwczpcL1wvYX
ByZXNzLmNvbSIsImpOaSI6IjVmMmQzM2RmLTEyYNDktNGIwMSO4MmYxLWJl
MjliM2NhOTY4OSIsImlhdCI6MTQwMjAzNjU0OMX0.

The following Java code shows how to parse a base64-encoded JWT:

```java
public static PlainJWT parsePlainJWT() throws ParseException {

        // get JWT in base64-encoded text.
        String jwtInText = buildPlainJWT();

        // build a plain JWT from the bade64 encoded text.
        PlainJWT plainJwt  = PlainJWT.parse(jwtInText);

        // print the JOSE header in JSON.
        System.out.println(plainJwt.getHeader().toString());

        // print JWT body in JSON.
        System.out.println(plainJwt.getPayload().toString());

        return plainJwt;
}
```

This code produces the following output, which includes the parsed JOSE header and the payload:

```
{"alg":"none"}
{
    "exp":1402038339,
    "sub":"john",
    "nbf":1402037739,
    "aud":["https:\/\/app1.foo.com","https:\/\/app2.foo.com"],
    "iss":"https:\/\/apress.com",
    "jti":"1e41881f-7472-4030-8132-856ccf4cbb25",
    "iat":1402037739
}
```

■ **Note** Way back in 2009, Microsoft introduced Simple Web Token (SWT). It is neither JSON nor XML. It simply defines a token format to carry out a set of HTML form-encoded name/value pairs. Even though this was developed as a proposed standard for IETF, it never got that far. More information about Microsoft SWT is available at: http://msdn.microsoft.com/en-us/library/hh781551.aspx.

JOSE Working Group

Many working groups within the IETF work directly with JSON, including the OAuth working group and the System for Cross-domain Identity Management (SCIM) working group. The SCIM working group is building a provisioning standard based on JSON. Outside the IETF, the OASIS XACML working group is working on building a JSON profile for XACML 3.0.

The OpenID Connect specification, which is developed under the OpenID Foundation, is also heavily based on JSON. Due to the rise of standards built around JSON and the heavy usage of JSON for data exchange in APIs, it has become absolutely necessary to define how to secure JSON messages at the message level. Use of Transport Layer

Security (TLS) only provides confidentiality and integrity at the transport layer. The JOSE working group, formed under the IETF, has the goal of coming up with a set of standards for protecting JSON messages with integrity and confidentiality. JSON Web Signature, JSON Web Encryption, JSON Web Key, and JSON Web Algorithms standards are currently being developed under the JOSE working group.

■ **Note** To follow the rest of the chapter, you're expected to have a basic knowledge of cryptography.

JSON Web Signature

The *JSON Web Signature (JWS)* specification, developed under the IETF JOSE working group, defines how JSON messages can be digitally signed or MACed. It introduces ten attributes to be included in the JWS header of a signed JSON payload; the signed JSON payload is known as a JWS. The following shows a sample JWS header, which carries attributes related to the message signature:

■ **Note** The JSON Web Signature specification is available at `http://tools.ietf.org/html/draft-ietf-jose-json-web-signature-26`.

```
{
    "alg": "",
    "jku": "",
    "jwk": "",
    "kid": "",
    "x5u": "",
    "x5c": "",
    "x5t": "",
    "typ": "",
    "cty": "",
    "crti": ""
}
```

Let's review the definition of each attribute:

alg: The name of the algorithm, which is used to sign the JSON payload.

jku: JSON Web Key Set URL. This points to a set of JSON-encoded public keys, where one of the keys is used to sign the JSON payload.

jwk: JSON Web Key. This is the public key corresponding to the key that is used to sign the JSON payload. The key is represented as defined in the JSON Web Key specification.

kid: Key identifier of the key that is used to sign the JSON payload.

x5u: X.509 URL. This URL points to the X.509 certificate (or the certificate chain) that corresponds to the private key used to sign the JSON payload.

x5c: The X.509 certificate (or the certificate chain), which corresponds to the private key, is used to sign the JSON payload. The certificate or the certificate chain has to be represented in a JSON array of certificate value strings. The certificate corresponding to the key used to sign the message should be in the first element of the array, and each element in the array should be a base64-encoded DER PKIX certificate value.

x5t: The thumbprint of the X.509 certificate corresponding to the key used to sign the JSON payload.

typ: The media type of the JWS. For JWSs using JWS compact serialization and JWEs using JWE compact serialization, the value JOSE can be used. For JWSs using JWS JSON serialization and JWEs using JWE JSON serialization, the value JOSE+JSON can be used. (JWS/JWE serialization is discussed later in this chapter.)

cty: The content type of the JWS.

crit: Indicates that custom header parameters are being used in the JWS header, and those should be well understood and processed by the recipient. The value of this attribute is an array of names of custom attributes.

Signature Algorithms

Table 13-1 lists acceptable JWS signature algorithms.

Table 13-1. JWS Signature Algorithms

Identifier (alg)	Signature or MAC algorithm
HS256	HMAC using SHA256
HS384	HMAC using SHA384
HS512	HMAC using SHA512
RS256	RSASSA-PKCS-V1_5 using SHA256
RS384	RSASSA-PKCS-V1_5 using SHA384
RS512	RSASSA-PKCS-V1_5 using SHA512
ES256	ECDSA using P-256 and SHA256
ES384	ECDSA using P-384 and SHA384
ES512	ECDSA using P-512 and SHA512
PS256	RSASSA-PSS using SHA256 and MGF1 with SHA256
PS384	RSASSA-PSS using SHA384and MGF1 with SHA384
PS512	RSASSA-PSS using SHA512 and MGF1 with SHA512
None	No signature or MAC

■ **Note** Further details of JWS algorithms are explained in the JSON Web Algorithms specification at http://tools.ietf.org/html/draft-ietf-jose-json-web-algorithms-26.

Serialization

The JWS (a signed JSON payload) can be serialized in two ways. One is known as *JWS compact serialization* and the other is known as *JWS JSON serialization*. The Google OpenID Connect example discussed earlier uses JWS compact serialization. In fact, the OpenID Connect specification mandates the use of JWS compact serialization and JWE compact serialization whenever necessary.

JWS/JWE JSON serialization isn't used in OpenID Connect. JWS compact serialization represents a signed JSON payload as a compact URL-safe string. As discussed earlier, this compact string has three sections separated by periods (.). The last section is the signature. If you use compact serialization against a JSON payload, then you can have only a single signature, and that signature is over the complete JWS header and JWS body.

JWS JSON serialization can produce multiple signatures. The following code shows a signed JSON payload with JSON serialization. It introduces five new attributes that should be present in a JWS, which are described after the listing:

```
{
"payload":"eyJpc3MiOiJqb2UiLA0KICJleHAiOjEzMDA4MTkzOD",
"signatures":[
                {
                    "protected":"eyJhbGciOiJSUzI1NiJ9",
                    "header":{"kid":"2014-06-29"},
                    "signature":"cC4hiUPoj9Eetdgtv3hF80EGrhuB"
                },
                {
                    "protected":"eyJhbGciOiJFUzI1NiJ9",
                    "header":{"kid":"e909097a-ce81-4036-9562-d21d2992db0d"},
                    "signature":"DtEhU3ljbEg8L38VWAfUAqOyKAM"
                }
            ]
}
```

Let's review the definition of each attribute:

> payload: Contains the base64url-encoded value of the complete JWS body.

> signatures: Contains an array of JSON objects, where each element contains a signature and the associated metadata.

> protected: Includes the base64url-encoded JWS header elements, which should be signed along with the JWS body. If you base64url-decode the value of the first protected element in the previous example, you see {"alg":"RS256"}.

> header: Contains other header elements corresponding to this signature, but these elements should not be signed. The final JWS header corresponding to this signature is calculated by combining both the protected headers and unprotected headers. In the previous example, the complete JWS header would be {"alg":"RS256", "kid":"2010-12-29"}.

> signature: The value of the signature calculated against the protected header elements and the body.

■ **Note** JWT must use JWS compact serialization.

GENERATING A SIGNED JWT WITH HMAC-SHA256

The following Java code generates a signed JWT with HMAC-SHA256. You need to add references to nimbus-jose-jwt-2.26.jar, json-smart-1.1.1.jar, jcip-annotations-1.0.jar, and bcprov-jdk15on-1.50.jar. You can download all of these jars from https://svn.wso2.org/repos/wso2/people/prabath/api-security/jose/lib. The method buildHmacSha256SignedJWT() should be invoked by passing a secret value that is used as the shared key to sign:

```java
import java.text.ParseException;
import java.util.ArrayList;
import java.util.Date;
import java.util.List;
import java.util.UUID;

import com.nimbusds.jose.*;
import com.nimbusds.jwt.*;
import com.nimbusds.jose.crypto.*;

public static String buildHmacSha256SignedJWT(String sharedSecretString)
                                                    throws JOSEException {
        // create a claim set.
        JWTClaimsSet jwtClaims = new JWTClaimsSet();

        // set the value of the issuer.
        jwtClaims.setIssuer("https://apress.com");

        // set the subject value - JWT belongs to this subject.
        jwtClaims.setSubject("john");

        // set values for audience restriction.
        List<String> aud = new ArrayList<String>();
        aud.add("https://app1.foo.com");
        aud.add("https://app2.foo.com");
        jwtClaims.setAudience(aud);

        // expiration time set to 10 minutes.
        jwtClaims.setExpirationTime(new Date(new Date().getTime() + 1000 * 60 * 10));

        Date currentTime = new Date();

        // set the valid from time to current time.
        jwtClaims.setNotBeforeTime(currentTime);

        // set issued time to current time.
        jwtClaims.setIssueTime(currentTime);
```

```
        // set a generated UUID as the JWT identifier.
        jwtClaims.setJWTID(UUID.randomUUID().toString());

        // create JWS header with HMAC-SHA256 algorithm.
        JWSHeader jswHeader = new JWSHeader(JWSAlgorithm.HS256);

        // create signer with the provider shared secret.
        JWSSigner signer = new MACSigner(sharedSecretString);

        // create the signed JWT with the JWS header and the JWT body.
        SignedJWT signedJWT = new SignedJWT(jswHeader, jwtClaims);

        // sign the JWT with HMAC-SHA256.
        signedJWT.sign(signer);

        // serialize into base64-encoded text.
        String jwtInText = signedJWT.serialize();

        // print the value of the JWT.
        System.out.println(jwtInText);

        return jwtInText;
}
```

This code produces the following output, which is the signed JSON payload (a JWS):

eyJhbGciOiJIUzI1NiJ9.eyJleHAiOjEOMDIwMzky0TIsInN1YiI6ImpvaG4iLCJuYm
YiOjEOMDIwMzg2OTIsImF1ZCI6WyJodHRwczpcL1wvYXBwMS5mb28uY29tIiw
iaHR0cHM6XC9cL2FwcDIuZm9vLmNvbSJdLCJpc3MiOiJodHRwczpcL1wvYXBy
ZXNzLmNvbSIsImp0aSI6ImVkNjkwN2YwLWR1OGEtNDMyNi1hZDU2LWE5ZmE
5NjA2YTVhOCIsImlhdCI6MTQwMjAzODY5Mn0.3v_pa-QFCRwoKUORaP7pLOox
T57okVuZMe_AOUcqQ8

The following Java code shows how to validate the signature of a signed JSON message with HMAC-SHA1. To do that, you need to know the shared secret used to sign the JSON payload:

```
public static boolean isValidHmacSha256Signature()
                                    throws JOSEException, ParseException {

        String sharedSecretString = "mysecretkey";

        // get signed JWT in base64-encoded text.
        String jwtInText = buildHmacSha256SignedJWT(sharedSecretString);

        // create verifier with the provider shared secret.
        JWSVerifier verifier = new MACVerifier(sharedSecretString);

        // create the signed JWT with the base64-encoded text.
        SignedJWT signedJWT = SignedJWT.parse(jwtInText);
```

```
    // verify the signature of the JWT.
    boolean isValid = signedJWT.verify(verifier);

    if (isValid) {
        System.out.println("valid JWT signature");
    } else {
        System.out.println("invalid JWT signature");
    }

    return isValid;
}
```

GENERATING A SIGNED JWT WITH RSA-SHA256

The following Java code generates a signed JWT with RSA-SHA256. You need to add references to nimbus-jose-jwt-2.26.jar, json-smart-1.1.1.jar, jcip-annotations-1.0.jar, and bcprov-jdk15on-1.50.jar. You can download all of these jars from https://svn.wso2.org/repos/wso2/people/prabath/api-security/jose/lib. First you need to invoke the method generateKeyPair() and pass the PrivateKey (generateKeyPair().getPrivateKey()) into the method buildRsaSha256SignedJWT():

```
import java.text.ParseException;
import java.util.ArrayList;
import java.util.Date;
import java.util.List;
import java.util.UUID;
import java.security.*;
import java.security.interfaces.*;

import com.nimbusds.jose.*;
import com.nimbusds.jwt.*;
import com.nimbusds.jose.crypto.*;

public static KeyPair generateKeyPair()
                            throws NoSuchAlgorithmException {

    // instantiate KeyPairGenerate with RSA algorithm.
    KeyPairGenerator keyGenerator = KeyPairGenerator.getInstance("RSA");

    // set the key size to 1024 bits.
    keyGenerator.initialize(1024);

    // generate and return private/public key pair.
    return keyGenerator.genKeyPair();
}
```

```java
public static String buildRsaSha256SignedJWT(PrivateKey privateKey)
                                        throws JOSEException {

    // create a claim set.
    JWTClaimsSet jwtClaims = new JWTClaimsSet();

    // set the value of the issuer.
    jwtClaims.setIssuer("https://apress.com");

    // set the subject value - JWT belongs to this subject.
    jwtClaims.setSubject("john");

    // set values for audience restriction.
    List<String> aud = new ArrayList<String>();
    aud.add("https://app1.foo.com");
    aud.add("https://app2.foo.com");
    jwtClaims.setAudience(aud);

    // expiration time set to 10 minutes.
    jwtClaims.setExpirationTime(new Date(new Date().getTime() + 1000 * 60 * 10));

    Date currentTime = new Date();

    // set the valid from time to current time.
    jwtClaims.setNotBeforeTime(currentTime);

    // set issued time to current time.
    jwtClaims.setIssueTime(currentTime);

    // set a generated UUID as the JWT identifier.
    jwtClaims.setJWTID(UUID.randomUUID().toString());

    // create JWS header with RSA-SHA256 algorithm.
    JWSHeader jswHeader = new JWSHeader(JWSAlgorithm.RS256);

    // create signer with the RSA private key..
    JWSSigner signer = new RSASSASigner((RSAPrivateKey)privateKey);

    // create the signed JWT with the JWS header and the JWT body.
    SignedJWT signedJWT = new SignedJWT(jswHeader, jwtClaims);

    // sign the JWT with HMAC-SHA256.
    signedJWT.sign(signer);

    // serialize into base64-encoded text.
    String jwtInText = signedJWT.serialize();

    // print the value of the JWT.
    System.out.println(jwtInText);

    return jwtInText;
}
```

The following Java code shows how to invoke the previous two methods:

```
KeyPair keyPair = generateKeyPair();
buildRsaSha256SignedJWT(keyPair.getPrivate());
```

Let's examine how to validate a JWT signed by RSA-SHA256. You need to know the PublicKey corresponding to the PrivateKey used to sign the message:

```
public static boolean isValidRsaSha256Signature()
                                    throws NoSuchAlgorithmException,
                                        JOSEException, ParseException {

        // generate private/public key pair.
        KeyPair keyPair = generateKeyPair();

        // get the private key - used to sign the message.
        PrivateKey privateKey = keyPair.getPrivate();

        // get public key - used to verify the message signature.
        PublicKey publicKey = keyPair.getPublic();

        // get signed JWT in base64-encoded text.
        String jwtInText = buildRsaSha256SignedJWT(privateKey);

        // create verifier with the provider shared secret.
        JWSVerifier verifier = new RSASSAVerifier((RSAPublicKey) publicKey);

        // create the signed JWT with the base64-encoded text.
        SignedJWT signedJWT = SignedJWT.parse(jwtInText);

        // verify the signature of the JWT.
        boolean isValid = signedJWT.verify(verifier);

        if (isValid) {
            System.out.println("valid JWT signature");
        } else {
            System.out.println("invalid JWT signature");
        }
        return isValid;
}
```

JSON Web Encryption

The *JSON Web Encryption (JWE)* specification, developed under the IETF JOSE working group, defines how JSON messages can be encrypted. It introduces two new attributes (enc and zip) to be included in the JWE header of an encrypted JSON payload, in addition to those discussed in the section "JSON Web Signature." An encrypted JSON payload is known as a *JWE*.

The following shows a sample JWE header, which carries attributes related to message encryption:

```
{
    "alg": "",
    "enc": "",
    "zip": "",
    "jku": "",
    "jwk": "",
    "kid": "",
    "x5u": "",
    "x5c": "",
    "x5t": "",
    "typ": "",
    "cty": "",
    "crti": ""
}
```

Let's review the definition of each attribute:

alg: Represents the name of the algorithm that is used to encrypt the content-encryption key. The content-encryption key is used to encrypt the actual content, and this key is encrypted using the algorithm specified by the alg attribute. In most cases, symmetric encryption is used to encrypt the content, whereas an asymmetric encryption algorithm is used to encrypt the content-encryption key.

enc: Represents the name of the algorithm that is used to encrypt the content.

zip: Specifies the compression algorithm. The plaintext content can be compressed before encryption.

jku: JSON Web Key Set URL. This points to a set of JSON-encoded public keys, where one is used to encrypt the JSON payload.

jwk: JSON Web Key. This is the public key that is used to encrypt the JSON payload. The key is represented as defined in the JSON Web Key specification.

kid: Key identifier of the key. It's used to encrypt the JSON payload.

x5u: X.509 URL. This points to the X.509 certificate (or the certificate chain), which is used to encrypt the JSON payload.

x5c: X.509 certificate (or the certificate chain), which is used to encrypt the JSON payload. The certificate or the certificate chain has to be represented in a JSON array of certificate value strings. The certificate corresponding to the key used to encrypt the message should be in the first element of the array, and each element in the array should be a base64-encoded DER PKIX certificate value.

x5t: Represents the thumbprint of the X.509 certificate used to encrypt the JSON payload.

typ: Indicates the media type of the JWE. For JWSs using JWS compact serialization and JWEs using JWE compact serialization, the value JOSE can be used. For JWSs using JWS JSON serialization and JWEs using JWE JSON serialization, the value JOSE+JSON can be used. (JWE serialization is discussed later in this chapter.)

cty: Indicates the content type of the JWE.

crit: Indicates that custom header parameters are being used in the JWE header, and those should be well understood and processed by the recipient. The value of this attribute is an array of names of custom attributes.

■ **Note** The JSON Web Encryption specification is available at http://tools.ietf.org/html/draft-ietf-jose-json-web-encryption-26.

Content Encryption vs. Key Wrapping

The JWE header uses the enc parameter to indicate the content encryption algorithm, and it uses the alg parameter to specify the key wrapping or the key encryption algorithm. Let's look at the following JWE header:

{"alg":"RSA-OAEP","enc":"A256GCM"}

■ **Note** Authenticated Encryption simultaneously provides a confidentiality, integrity, and authenticity guarantee for data. ISO/IEC 19772:2009 has standardized six different authenticated encryption modes: GCM, OCB 2.0, CCM, Key Wrap, EAX, and Encrypt-then-MAC. *Authenticated Encryption with Associated Data (AEAD)* extends this model to add the ability to preserve the integrity and authenticity of additional authenticated data that isn't encrypted. AEAD algorithms take two inputs: plaintext to be encrypted and the associated authentication data, and result in two outputs: the ciphertext and the authentication tag. The authentication tag ensures the integrity of the ciphertext and the associated authenticated data. RFC 5116 defines an interface and algorithms for Authenticated Encryption: http://tools.ietf.org/html/rfc5116.

For content encryption, this uses A256GCM; and for key wrapping, it uses RSA-OAEP. A256GCM uses AES GCM with a 256-bit key, and it's a symmetric key algorithm used for AEAD. Symmetric keys are mostly used for content encryption. Symmetric-key encryption is much faster than asymmetric-key encryption. At the same time, asymmetric encryption can't be used to encrypt large messages.

In this scenario, the entity that encrypts the message generates a random key and encrypts the message using the key following the AES GCM algorithm. Next, the key used to encrypt the message is encrypted using RSA-OAEP, which is an asymmetric encryption scheme. The encrypted symmetric key is placed in the JWE.

Serialization

Similar to JWS, a JWE can be serialized in two ways: JWE compact serialization and JWE JSON serialization. JWE compact serialization produces five parts separated by periods (.). With compact serialization, you can't encrypt the content encryption key with different keys. JWE JSON serialization lets you encrypt the content encryption key for distinct recipients using different keys, using the following data structure:

```
{
    "protected":"eyJlbmMiOiJBMTI4Q0JDLUhTMjU2In0",
    "unprotected":{
                "jku":"https://server.example.com/keys.jwks"
            },
```

```
    "recipients":[
                  {
                    "header":{"alg":"RSA1_5","kid":"2011-04-29"},
                    "encrypted_key":"UGhIOguC7IuEvf_NPVaXsGMoLOmwvc1GyqlI
                                     KOK1nN94nHPoltGRhWhw7ZxO-kFm1NJn8LE
                                     9XShH59_i8JOPH5ZZyNfGy2xGd"
                  },
                  {
                    "header":{"alg":"A128KW","kid":"7"},
                    "encrypted_key":"6KB707dM9YTIgHtLvtgWQ8mKwboJW3of9locizkDTHzBC2IlrT1oOQ"
                  }
                 ],
    "iv":"AxY8DCtDaGlsbGljb3RoZQ",
    "ciphertext":"KDlTtXchhZTGufMYmOYGS4HffxPSUrfmqCHXaI9wOGY",
    "tag":"Mz-VPPyU4RlcuYv1IwIvzw"
}
```

Let's look at the definition of each attribute used in this code snippet:

protected: Contains the base64url-encoded value of the JWE header elements protected for integrity by authenticated encryption. There is one protected element in a JWE.

unprotected: Contains the value of the JWE header elements that aren't protected for integrity by authenticated encryption. There is one unprotected element in a JWE, at the root level.

recipients: An array of recipient elements. Each member consists of a header element and an encrypted key element, which expresses the cryptographic properties of each recipient.

header: Contains the value of the JWE header elements that aren't protected for integrity by authenticated encryption for each recipient.

encrytedkey: Base64url-encoded value of the encrypted key. This is the key used to encrypt the message payload. The key is encrypted in different ways for each recipient.

iv: The value of the initial vector used for encryption.

ciphertext: Base64url-encoded value of the resultant ciphertext.

tag: Base64url-encoded value of the authenticated tag, which resulted in AEAD.

◼ **Note** As mentioned earlier, unlike a JWS, a JWE has five parts (with JWE compact serialization), separated by periods (.). Each part must be base64url-encoded before being placed into the JWE. The first part is the JWE header. The second part is the encrypted key; this is the key used to encrypt the content. The third part is the *initialization vector*: a random value generated by the entity that encrypts the message. Some encryption algorithms require an initialization vector. To decrypt the message successfully, the value of the initialization vector must be passed to the entity that decrypts the message. The fourth part is the encrypted text, and the fifth part is the JWE authentication tag.

GENERATING AN ENCRYPTED JWT WITH RSA-OAEP AND AES

The following Java code generates an encrypted JWT with RSA-OAEP and AES. You need to add references to nimbus-jose-jwt-2.26.jar, json-smart-1.1.1.jar, jcip-annotations-1.0.jar, and bcprov-jdk15on-1.50.jar. You can download all of these jars from https://svn.wso2.org/repos/wso2/people/prabath/api-security/jose/lib. First you need to invoke the method generateKeyPair() and pass the PublicKey (generateKeyPair().getPublicKey()) into the method buildEncryptedJWT():

```java
import java.text.ParseException;
import java.util.ArrayList;
import java.util.Date;
import java.util.List;
import java.util.UUID;
import java.security.*;
import java.security.interfaces.*;

import com.nimbusds.jose.*;
import com.nimbusds.jwt.*;
import com.nimbusds.jose.crypto.*;

public static KeyPair generateKeyPair() throws NoSuchAlgorithmException {

        // instantiate KeyPairGenerate with RSA algorithm.
        KeyPairGenerator keyGenerator = KeyPairGenerator.getInstance("RSA");

        // set the key size to 1024 bits.
        keyGenerator.initialize(1024);

        // generate and return private/public key pair.
        return keyGenerator.genKeyPair();
}

public static String buildEncryptedJWT(PublicKey publicKey) throws JOSEException {

        // create a claim set.
        JWTClaimsSet jwtClaims = new JWTClaimsSet();

        // set the value of the issuer.
        jwtClaims.setIssuer("https://apress.com");

        // set the subject value - JWT belongs to this subject.
        jwtClaims.setSubject("john");

        // set values for audience restriction.
        List<String> aud = new ArrayList<String>();
        aud.add("https://app1.foo.com");
        aud.add("https://app2.foo.com");
        jwtClaims.setAudience(aud);
```

```
        // expiration time set to 10 minutes.
        jwtClaims.setExpirationTime(new Date(new Date().getTime() + 1000 * 60 * 10));

        Date currentTime = new Date();

        // set the valid from time to current time.
        jwtClaims.setNotBeforeTime(currentTime);

        // set issued time to current time.
        jwtClaims.setIssueTime(currentTime);

        // set a generated UUID as the JWT identifier.
        jwtClaims.setJWTID(UUID.randomUUID().toString());

        // create JWE header with RSA-OAEP and AES/GCM.
        JWEHeader jweHeader = new JWEHeader(JWEAlgorithm.RSA_OAEP,
                        EncryptionMethod.A128GCM);

        // create encrypter with the RSA public key.
        JWEEncrypter encrypter = new RSAEncrypter((RSAPublicKey) publicKey);

        // create the encrypted JWT with the JWE header and the JWT payload.
        EncryptedJWT encryptedJWT = new EncryptedJWT(jweHeader, jwtClaims);

        // encrypt the JWT.
        encryptedJWT.encrypt(encrypter);

        // serialize into base64-encoded text.
        String jwtInText = encryptedJWT.serialize();

        // print the value of the JWT.
        System.out.println(jwtInText);

        return jwtInText;
}
```

The following Java code shows how to invoke the previous two methods:

```
KeyPair keyPair = generateKeyPair();
buildEncryptedJWT(keyPair.getPublic());
```

Let's see how to decrypt a JWT encrypted by RSA-OAEP. You need to know the PrivateKey corresponding to the PublicKey used to encrypt the message:

```
public static void decryptJWT() throws NoSuchAlgorithmException,
                                        JOSEException, ParseException {

        // generate private/public key pair.
        KeyPair keyPair = generateKeyPair();
```

```
    // get the private key - used to decrypt the message.
    PrivateKey privateKey = keyPair.getPrivate();

    // get the public key - used to encrypt the message.
    PublicKey publicKey = keyPair.getPublic();

    // get encrypted JWT in base64-encoded text.
    String jwtInText = buildEncryptedJWT(publicKey);

    // create a decrypter.
    JWEDecrypter decrypter = new RSADecrypter((RSAPrivateKey) privateKey);

    // create the encrypted JWT with the base64-encoded text.
    EncryptedJWT encryptedJWT = EncryptedJWT.parse(jwtInText);

    // decrypt the JWT.
    encryptedJWT.decrypt(decrypter);

    // print the value of JOSE header.

    System.out.println("JWE Header:" + encryptedJWT.getHeader());

    // JWE content encryption key.
    System.out.println("JWE Content Encryption Key: " + encryptedJWT.getEncryptedKey());

    // initialization vector.
    System.out.println("Initialization Vector: " + encryptedJWT.getInitializationVector());

    // ciphertext.
    System.out.println("Ciphertext : " + encryptedJWT.getCipherText());

    // authentication tag.
    System.out.println("Authentication Tag: " + encryptedJWT.getAuthenticationTag());

    // print the value of JWT body
    System.out.println("Decrypted Payload: " + encryptedJWT.getPayload());

}
```

This code produces the following output:

```
JWE Header:{
            "alg":"RSA-OAEP",
            "enc":"A128GCM"
        }

JWE Content Encryption Key: NbIuAjnNBwmwlbKiIpEzffU1duaQfxJpJaodkxDj
SC2s3tO76ZdUZ6YfPrwSZ6DU8F51pbEw2f2MK_C7kLpgWUl8hMHP7g2_Eh3y
Th5iK6Agx72o8IPwpD4woY7CVvIB_iJqz-cngZgNAikHjHzOC6JF748MwtgSiiyrI
9BsmU
```

```
Initialization Vector: JPPFsk6yimrkohJf

Ciphertext: XF2kAcBrAX_4LSOGejsegoxEfb8kV58yFJSQO_WOONP5wQO7HG
mMLTyR713ufXwannitR6d2eTDMFe1xkTFfF9ZskYj5qJ36rOvhGGhNqNdGEpsB
YK5wmPiRlk3tbUtd_DulQWEUKHqPc_VszWKFOlLQW5UgMeHndVi3JOZgiwN
gy9bvzacWazK8lTpxSQVf-NrD_zu_qPYJRisvbKI8dudv7ayKoE4mnQW_fUY-U1o
AMy-7Bg4WQE4j6dfxMlQGoPOo

Authentication Tag: pZWfYyt2kO-VpHSW7btznA

Decrypted Payload:
{
    "exp":1402116034,
    "sub":"john",
    "nbf":1402115434,
    "aud":["https:\/\/app1.foo.com","https:\/\/app2.foo.com"],
    "iss":"https:\/\/apress.com",
    "jti":"a1b41dd4-ba4a-4584-b06d-8988e8f995bf",
    "iat":1402115434
}
```

Summary

In this chapter, you had a closer look at JSON security. JSON has nearly become the de facto message-exchange format for APIs. Here you saw examples of how to sign a JSON message with JWS and encrypt with JWE.

The next chapter takes a deeper look at common API security patterns used in the industry.

■ ■ ■

CHAPTER 14

Patterns and Practices

Chapter 2 touched on some of the key patterns surrounding API security. This chapter expands on that discussion with more concrete details. Here we present ten API security patterns to address the ten most common enterprise security problems. All of the patterns are derived from the concepts and theories discussed in previous chapters.

Direct Authentication with the Trusted Subsystem Pattern

Suppose a medium-scale enterprise has a limited number of RESTful APIs. Company employees are allowed to access these APIs via a single web application while they're behind the company firewall. All user data is stored in a Microsoft Active Directory, and the web application is connected to it to authenticate users. The web application passes the logged-in user's identifier to the back-end APIs, and it retrieves data related to the user.

The problem is straightforward, and Figure 14-1 illustrates the solution. You need to use some kind of direct-authentication pattern. User authentication happens at the front-end web application, and once the user is authenticated, the web application needs to access the back-end APIs. The catch here is that the web application passes the logged-in user's identifier to the API. That implies that the APIs can be invoked in a user-aware manner by the web application.

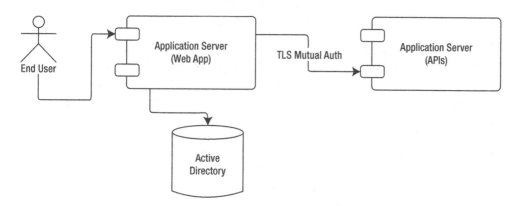

Figure 14-1. *Direct authentication with the Trusted Subsystem pattern*

You need to worry not about authenticating the end user to the back-end API, but about authenticating them to the web application. This is the Trusted Subsystem pattern. The web application acts as the trusted subsystem. In such a scenario, the best way to secure APIs is through Transport Layer Security (TLS) mutual authentication. All requests generated from the web application are secured with TLS mutual authentication.

In some scenarios, there is a resistance to using TLS due to the overhead it adds. In such cases, in a controlled environment, security between the application server and the container that hosts APIs can be achieved at the network level. Network-level security must provide the assurance that no component other than the web application server can talk to the container that hosts the APIs.

■ **Note**   The article "Trusted Subsystem Design" by Frederick Chong provides a great deal of information about the Trusted Subsystem pattern. You can find it at http://msdn.microsoft.com/en-us/library/aa905320.aspx.

Single Sign-On with the Delegated Access Control Pattern

Next, suppose a medium-scale enterprise has a limited number of RESTful APIs. Company employees are allowed to access these APIs via web applications while they're behind the company firewall. All user data is stored in a Microsoft Active Directory, and all the web applications are connected to a Security Assertion Markup Language (SAML) 2.0 identity provider to authenticate users. The web applications need to access back-end APIs on behalf of the logged-in user.

The catch here is this last statement: "The web applications need to access back-end APIs on behalf of the logged-in user." This suggests the need for an access-delegation protocol: OAuth. However, users don't present their credentials directly to the web application—they authenticate through a SAML 2.0 identity provider.

In this case, you need to find a way to exchange the SAML token received via the SAML 2.0 Web SSO protocol for an OAuth access token, which is defined in the SAML grant type for the OAuth 2.0 specification. Once the web application receives the SAML token, as shown in step 3 of Figure 14-2, it has to exchange it with an access token by talking to the OAuth authorization server.

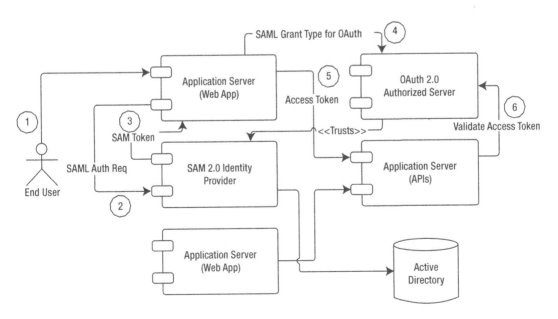

Figure 14-2. *Single sign-on with the Delegated Access Control pattern*

The authorization server must trust the SAML 2.0 identity provider. Once the web application gets the access token, it can use it to access back-end APIs. The SAML grant type for OAuth doesn't provide a refresh token. The lifetime of the access token issued by the OAuth authorization server must match the lifetime of the SAML token used in the authorization grant.

After the user logs in to the web application with a valid SAML token, the web application creates a session for the user from then onward, and it doesn't worry about the lifetime of the SAML token. This can lead to some issues. Say the SAML token expires, but the user still has a valid browser session in the web application. Because the SAML token has expired, you can expect that the corresponding OAuth access token obtained at the time of user login has expired as well. Now, if the web application tries to access a back-end API, the request will be rejected because the access token is expired. In such a scenario, the web application has to redirect the user back to the SAML 2.0 identity provider, get a new SAML token, and exchange that token for a new access token. If the session at the SAML 2.0 identity provider is still live, then this redirection can be made transparent to the end user.

Single Sign-On with the Integrated Windows Authentication Pattern

Now, let's consider a medium-scale enterprise that has a limited number of RESTful APIs. Company employees are allowed to access these APIs via multiple web applications while they're behind the company firewall. All user data is stored in Microsoft Active Directory, and all the web applications are connected to a SAML 2.0 identity provider to authenticate users. The web applications need to access back-end APIs on behalf of the logged-in user. All the users are in a Windows domain, and once they're logged in to their workstations, they shouldn't be asked to provide credentials at any point for any other application.

This use case is very similar to that for SSO with the Delegated Access Control pattern. The catch here is the statement, "All the users are in a Windows domain, and once they're logged in to their workstations, they shouldn't be asked to provide credentials at any point for any other application."

You need to extend the solution provided using SSO with the Delegated Access Control pattern. In that case, the user logs in to the SAML 2.0 identity provider with their Active Directory username and password. Here, this isn't acceptable. Instead, you can use Integrated Windows Authentication (IWA) to secure the SAML 2.0 identity provider. When you configure the SAML 2.0 identity provider to use IWA, then once the user is redirected there for authentication, the user is automatically authenticated; as in the case of SSO with the Delegated Access Control Pattern, a SAML response is passed to the web application. The rest of the flow remains unchanged.

Identity Proxy with the Delegated Access Control Pattern

Suppose a medium-scale enterprise has a limited number of RESTful APIs. Company employees, as well as employees from trusted partners, are allowed to access these APIs via web applications. All the internal user data is stored in Microsoft Active Directory, and all the web applications are connected to a SAML 2.0 identity provider to authenticate users. The web applications need to access back-end APIs on behalf of the logged-in user.

This use case is an extension of using SSO with the Delegated Access Control pattern. The catch here is the statement, "Company employees, as well as employees from trusted partners, are allowed to access these APIs via web applications." You now have to go beyond the company domain. Everything in Figure 14-2 remains unchanged. The only thing you need to do is to change the authentication mechanism at the SAML 2.0 identity provider.

Regardless of the end user's domain, the client web application only trusts the identity provider in its own domain. Internal as well as external users are first redirected to the internal SAML identity provider. The identity provider should offer the user the option of whether to authenticate with their username and password (for internal users) or to pick their corresponding domain. Then the identity provider can direct the user to the identity provider running in the external user's home domain. Now the external identity provider returns a SAML response to the internal identity provider.

The external identity provider signs this SAML token. If the signature is valid, and if it's from a trusted external identity provider, the internal identity provider issues a new SAML token signed by itself to the calling application. The flow then continues as shown in Figure 14-3.

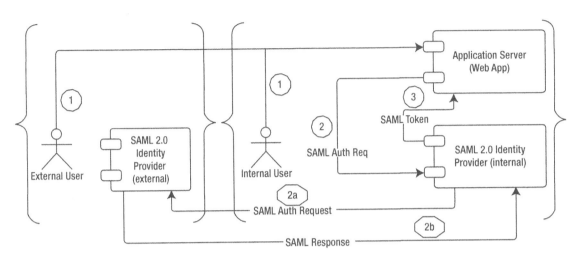

Figure 14-3. Identity proxy with the Delegated Access Control pattern

---

■ **Note**   One benefit of this approach is that the internal applications only need to trust their own identity provider. The identity provider handles the brokering of trust between other identity providers outside its domain. In this scenario, the external identity provider also talks SAML, but that can't be expected all the time. There are also identity providers that support other protocols. In such scenarios, the internal identity provider must be able to transform identity assertions between different protocols.

Delegated Access Control with the JSON Web Token Pattern

Now, consider a medium-scale enterprise that has a limited number of RESTful APIs. Company employees are allowed to access these APIs via web applications while they're behind the company firewall. All user data is stored in Microsoft Active Directory, and all the web applications are connected to an OpenID Connect identity provider to authenticate users. The web applications need to access back-end APIs on behalf of the logged-in user.

This use case is also an extension of SSO with the Delegated Access Control pattern. The catch here is the statement, "all the web applications are connected to an OpenID Connect identity provider to authenticate users." You need to replace the SAML identity provider shown in Figure 14-2 with an OpenID Connect identity provider, as illustrated in Figure 14-4. This also suggests the need for an access-delegation protocol (OAuth).

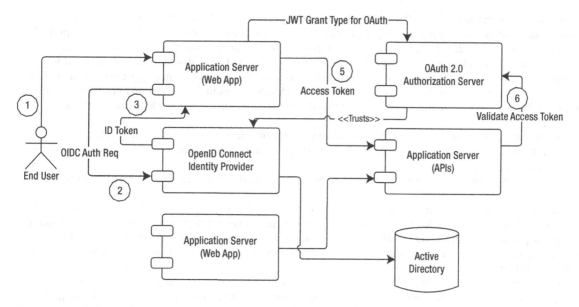

Figure 14-4. *Delegated access control with the JWT pattern*

In this case, however, users don't present their credentials directly to the web application; rather, they authenticate through an OpenID Connect identity provider. Thus you need to find a way to exchange the ID token received in OpenID Connect authentication for an OAuth access token, which is defined in the JWT grant types for the OAuth 2.0 specification. Once the web application receives the ID token in step 3, which is also a JWT, it has to exchange it for an access token by talking to the OAuth authorization server. The authorization server must trust the OpenID Connect identity provider. When the web application gets the access token, it can use it to access back-end APIs.

■ **Note** Why would someone exchange the ID token obtained in OpenID Connect for an access token when it directly gets an access token along with the ID token? This is not required when both the OpenID Connect server and the OAuth authorization server are the same. If they aren't, you have to use the JWT Bearer grant type for OAuth 2.0 and exchange the ID token for an access token. The access token issuer must trust the OpenID Connect identity provider.

Nonrepudiation with the JSON Web Signature Pattern

Next, suppose a medium-scale enterprise in the finance industry needs to expose an API to its customers through a mobile application, as illustrated in Figure 14-5. One major requirement is that all the API calls should support nonrepudiation.

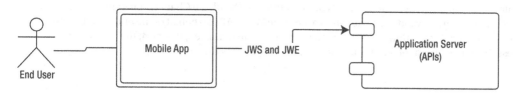

Figure 14-5. *Nonrepudiation with the JSON Web Signature pattern*

The catch here is the statement, "all the API calls should support nonrepudiation." When you do a business transaction via an API by proving your identity, you shouldn't be able to reject it later or repudiate it. The property that ensures the inability to repudiate is known as *nonrepudiation*. Basically, you do it once, and you own it forever.

Nonrepudiation should provide proof of the origin and the integrity of data in an unforgeable manner, which a third party can verify at any time. Once a transaction is initiated, none of its content, including the user identity, date, time, and transaction details, should be altered while in transit, in order to maintain transaction integrity and to allow for future verifications. Nonrepudiation has to ensure that the transaction is unaltered and logged after it's committed and confirmed.

Logs must be archived and properly secured to prevent unauthorized modifications. Whenever there is a repudiation dispute, transaction logs, along with other logs or data, can be retrieved to verify the initiator, date, time, transaction history, and so on.

The way to achieve nonrepudiation is via signature. Each message should be signed by a key known only to the end user.

In this case, the financial institution must issue a key pair to each of its customers, signed by a certificate authority under its control. It should only store the corresponding public certificate, not the private key. The customer can install the private key in his or her mobile device and make it available to the mobile application. All API calls generated from the mobile application must be signed by the private key of the user and encrypted by the public key of the financial institution.

To sign the message, the mobile application can use JSON Web Signature (JWS); and for encryption, it can use JSON Web Encryption (JWE). When using both the signature and encryption on the same payload, the message must be signed first, and then the signed payload must be encrypted for legal acceptance.

Chained Access Delegation Pattern

Suppose a medium-scale enterprise that sells bottled water has a RESTful API (Water API) that can be used to update the amount of water consumed by a registered user. Any registered user can access the API via any client application. It could be an Android app, an iOS app, or even a web application.

The company only provides the API—anyone can develop client applications to consume it. All the user data is stored in Microsoft Active Directory. Client applications shouldn't be able to access the API directly and query to find out information about users. Only registered users can access the API. These users shouldn't be able to see other users' information. At the same time, for each update made by a user, the Water API must update the user's healthcare record maintained at MyHealth.org. The user also has a personal record at MyHealth.org, and it too exposes an API (MyHealth API). The Water API has to call the MyHealth API to update the user record on the user's behalf.

In summary, a mobile application accesses the Water API on behalf of the end user, and then the Water API has to access the MyHealth API on behalf of the end user. The Water API and the MyHealth API are in two independent domains. This suggests the need for an access-delegation protocol.

Again, the catch here is the statement, "the Water API must also update the user's healthcare record maintained at MyHealth.org." This has two solutions. In the first solution, the end user must get an access token from MyHealth.org for the Water API (the Water API acts as the OAuth client), and then the Water API must store the token internally against the user's name. Whenever the user sends an update through a mobile application to the Water API, the Water API first updates its own record and then finds the MyHealth access token corresponding to the end user and uses it to access the MyHealth API. With this approach, the Water API has the overhead of storing the MyHealth API access token, and it should refresh the access token whenever needed.

The second solution is explained in Figure 14-6. It's built around the OAuth 2.0 Chain Grant Type profile. The mobile application must carry a valid access token to access the Water API on behalf of the end user. In step 3, the Water API talks to its own authorization server to validate the access token. Then, in step 4, the Water API exchanges the access token it got from the mobile application for a JWT access token.

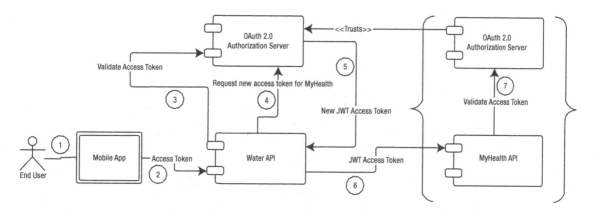

Figure 14-6. *Chained Access Delegation pattern*

The JWT access token is a special access token that carries some meaningful data, and the authorization server in the Water API's domain signs it. The JWT includes the end user's local identifier as well as its mapped identifier in the MyHealth domain. The end user must permit this action at the Water API domain.

In step 6, the Water API accesses the MyHealth API using the JWT access token. The MyHealth API validates the JWT access token by talking to its own authorization server. It verifies the signature; and, if it's signed by a trusted entity, the access token is treated as valid.

Because the JWT includes the mapped username from the MyHealth domain, it can identify the corresponding local user record. However, this raises a security concern. If you let users update their profiles in the Water API domain with the mapped MyHealth identifier, they can map it to any user identifier, and this leads to a security hole. To avoid this, the account-mapping step must be secured with OpenID Connect authentication. When the user wants to add his or her MyHealth account identifier, the Water API domain initiates the OpenID Connect authentication flow and receives the corresponding ID token. Then the account mapping is done with the user identifier in the ID token.

Trusted Master Access Delegation Pattern

Now let's look at a large-scale enterprise that has a set of RESTful APIs. The APIs are hosted in different departments, and each department runs its own OAuth authorization server due to vendor incompatibilities in different deployments. Company employees are allowed to access these APIs via web applications while they're behind the company firewall, regardless of the department to which they belong.

All user data is stored in a centralized Active Directory, and all the web applications are connected to a centralized OAuth authorization server (which also supports OpenID Connect) to authenticate users. The web applications need to access back-end APIs on behalf of the logged-in user. These APIs may come from different departments, each of which has its own authorization server. The company also has a centralized OAuth authorization server, and an employee having an access token from the centralized authorization server must be able to access any API hosted in any department.

Once again, this is an extended version of using SSO with the Delegated Access Control pattern. You have a master OAuth authorization server and a set of secondary authorization servers. An access token issued from the master authorization server should be good enough to access any of the APIs under the control of the secondary authorization servers. In other words, the access token returned to the web application, as shown in step 3 of Figure 14-7, should be good enough to access any of the APIs.

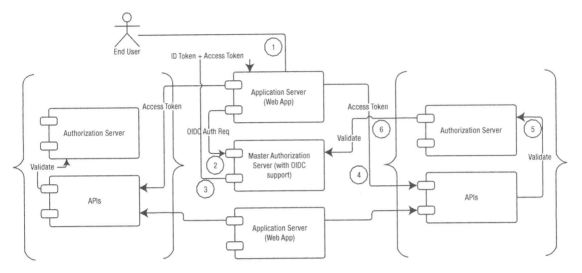

Figure 14-7. *Trusted Master Access Delegation pattern*

To make this possible, you need to make the access token self-explanatory. Ideally, you should make the access token a JWT with the `iss` (issuer) field. In step 4, the web application accesses the API using the access token; and in step 5, the API talks to its own authorization server to validate the token. The authorization server can look at the JWT header and find out whether it issued this token or if a different server issued it. If the master authorization server issued it, then the secondary authorization server can talk to the master authorization server's OAuth introspection endpoint to find out more about the token. The introspection response specifies whether the token is active and identifies the scopes associated with the access token. Using the introspection response, the secondary authorization server can build an eXtensible Access Control Markup Language (XACML) request and call a XACML policy decision point (PDP). If the XACML response is evaluated to Permit, then the web application can access the API.

Resource Security Token Service (STS) with the Delegated Access Control Pattern

Suppose a global organization has APIs and API clients are distributed across different regions. Each region operates independently from the others. Currently, both clients and APIs are non-secured. You need to secure the APIs without making any changes either at the API or the client end.

The solution is based on a simple theory in software engineering: introducing a layer of indirection can solve any problem. You need to introduce two interceptors. One sits in the client region, and all the non-secured messages generated from the client are intercepted. The other interceptor sits in the API region, and all the API requests are intercepted. No other component except this interceptor can access the API in a non-secured manner.

This restriction can be enforced at the network level. Any request generated from outside has no path to the API other than through the API interceptor. You can also call this component a Policy Enforcement Point (PEP). The PEP validates the security of all incoming API requests. The interceptor's responsibility, sitting in the client region, is to add the necessary security parameters to the non-secured message generated from the client and to send it to the API. In this way, you can secure the API without making changes at either the client or the API end.

Still, you have a challenge. How do you secure the API at the PEP? This is a cross-domain scenario, and the obvious choice is to use SAML grant type for OAuth 2.0.

Figure 14-8 explains how the solution is implemented. Non-secured requests from the client application are captured by the interceptor component in step 1. Then it has to talk to its own Security Token Service (STS). In step 2, the interceptor uses a default user account to access the STS through SOAP-based WS-Trust. STS authenticates the request and issues a SAML token having the STS in the API region as the audience of the token.

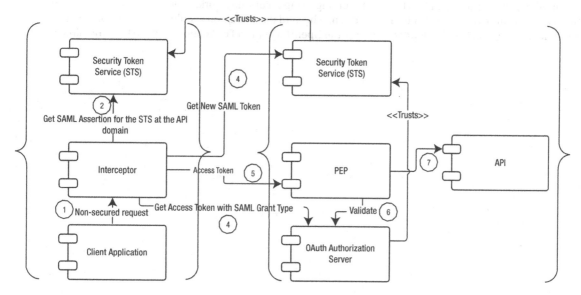

Figure 14-8. *Resource STS with the Delegated Access Control Pattern*

In step 3, the client side interceptor authenticates to the STS at the API region with the SAML token and gets a new SAML token. The audience of the new SAML token is the OAuth authorization server running in the API region. Step 3 also happens through SOAP-based WS-Trust. Before issuing the new SAML token, the STS at the API region must validate its signature and check whether a trusted entity has signed it.

To make this scenario happen, the STS in the API region must trust the STS on the client side. The OAuth authorization server only trusts its own STS. That is why step 4 is required. Step 4 initiates the SAML grant type for OAuth 2.0, and the client interceptor exchanges the SAML token for an access token. Then it uses the access token to access the API in step 5.

The PEP in the API region intercepts the request and calls the authorization server to validate the access token. If the token is valid, the PEP lets the request hit the API (step 7).

Delegated Access Control with the Hidden Credentials Pattern

Finally, suppose a company wants to expose an API to its employees. However, user credentials must never go over the wire.

This is a straightforward problem with an equally straightforward solution. Both OAuth 2.0 bearer tokens and HTTP Basic Authentication take user credentials over the wire. Even though both these approaches use TLS for protection, still some companies worry about passing user credentials over communication channels.

You have two options: use either HTTP Digest authentication or OAuth 2.0 MAC tokens. Using OAuth 2.0 MAC tokens is the better approach because the access token is generated for each API, and the user can also revoke the token if needed without changing the password.

Summary

This chapter highlights the ten most-used solution patterns in API security. Each pattern is built on top of the concepts discussed throughout the book. API security is an ever-evolving subject. More and more standards and specifications are popping up, and most of them are built around the core OAuth 2.0 specification. Security around JSON is another evolving area, and the IETF JOSE working group is currently working on it.

It's highly recommended that if you wish to continue beyond this book, you should keep an eye on the IETF OAuth working group, the IETF JOSE working group, the OpenID Connect Foundation, and the Kantara Initiative.

Index

Get the eBook for only $10!

Now you can take the weightless companion with you anywhere, anytime. Your purchase of this book entitles you to 3 electronic versions for only $10.

This Apress title will prove so indispensible that you'll want to carry it with you everywhere, which is why we are offering the eBook in 3 formats for only $10 if you have already purchased the print book.

Convenient and fully searchable, the PDF version enables you to easily find and copy code—or perform examples by quickly toggling between instructions and applications. The MOBI format is ideal for your Kindle, while the ePUB can be utilized on a variety of mobile devices.

Go to www.apress.com/promo/tendollars to purchase your companion eBook.

Apress®
THE EXPERT'S VOICE™